A GUIDE TO MILITARY ART

—

THE VOLUNTEER, 1859-1908

A GUIDE TO MILITARY ART

—

THE VOLUNTEER, 1859-1908

RAY WESTLAKE

The Naval & Military Press

Published by

The Naval & Military Press Ltd
Unit 5 Riverside
Bellbrook Industrial Estate
Uckfield, East Sussex
TN22 1QQ
England

Tel: +44 (0) 1825 749494

www.naval-military-press.com

ACKNOWLEDGEMENTS

I must, as always, acknowledge the help and encouragement given to me by my wonderful wife Claire. Also to Peter Harrington of the Anne SK Brown Military Collection held at the Brown University Library, Providence Rhode Island, USA. I cannot thank the Collection enough for its generosity in allowing me to used many of the images in this book. Much is always owed by the author to his publisher, in this case Chris and Gary Buckland of the Naval and Military Press.

INTRODUCTION

This 'Guide' is in no way intended to be a history of the many hundreds of volunteer corps raised after the invasion scare of 1859 who would become the predecessors of Britain's Territorial Force in 1908.

It was film producer and pioneer of the American animation industry Walt Disney who said, 'Of all of our inventions for mass communication, pictures still speak the most universally understood language.' And, of course, we must not forget the wider use of, 'A picture is worth a thousand words.' Certainly, if we set out to make a study of uniform, we can learn much from looking at pictures. But, as that superb reference work published by the Army Museums Ogilby Trust in 1972, *Index To British Military Costume Prints 1500-1914*, points out, '...it must not be supposed that a contemporary artist, however celebrated, does not make mistakes in drawing what he thought he had seen.' To this we could add, 'or what he thought might look good'—artistic licence, in fact. Here, as an example, I bring to mind a comment made by none less than Richard Caton Woodville who, after the end of the Great War, was given a commission by the London Scottish to paint a picture recalling that regiment's brave stand at Messines Ridge at the end of October 1914. Up in the Mess went the finished article. Those who were there pointed out recognisable faces and features of the battle and in general were pleased at what they saw. But up stepped one veteran who, with finger pointing, exclaimed, 'They're wearing sporrans. We never had them on the Ridge, they were left behind at our billets.' This point was raised with the artist who remarked without hesitation, 'Yes, I'm quite aware of this. I included them as I thought the men looked quite empty without them.'

At this point the serious student of military dress may well abandon the idea of including prints and pictures in his study of the subject, and instead content him or herself with official publications such as Dress or Clothing Regulations. 'But, before the critic condemns an artist for depicting a uniform that was never approved under the regulations' (*Index to British Military Costume Prints* again) 'let him remember that the British officer has long been noted for his independence from Dress Regulations.'

With all that said, let us now set about enjoying what talented people have placed on paper and canvas for centuries.

INDEX

Plate number	
51	Forfarshire Rifle Volunteers
52	1st Fifeshire Artillery Volunteers
53	Grand Volunteer Field Day at Sefton Park, 5 October 1867
54	George Hamilton Chichester Marquis Of Donegall
55	Lieutenant-Colonel Joseph Walker Pearse, 1st Yorkshire (East Riding) Rifle Volunteer Corps
56	London Scottish Rifle Volunteer Corps
57	The Right Honourable Viscount Ranelagh
58	The Ladies Darling
59	Grand Review in Hyde Park on 23June 1860
60	A Rifle Volunteer
61	2nd Volunteer Battalion Gordon Highlanders
62	1st Volunteer Battalion Cameron Highlanders
63	The Funeral Cortege of Sergeant Monger
64	Step Together, The Volunteer's Song
65	National Rifle Association Competition, Wimbledon 2 July 1860
66	Volunteers at a Firing Point, Wimbledon 1866
67	The Grey Tower Valse
68	1st Middlesex Volunteer Artillery March
69	1st Renfrewshire and Dumbarton Royal Garrison Artillery (Volunteers)
70	5th Volunteer Battalion Scottish Rifles
71	1st Dumbartonshire Volunteer Rifle Corps
72	Officer, Royal Engineers Volunteers, 1901
73	22nd Middlesex Rifle Volunteer Corps
74	Our British Volunteers
75	Tommy Atkins
76	4th Volunteer Battalion Royal Scots
77	1st Middlesex Rifle Volunteer Corps (Victoria Rifles)
78	The Awkward Squad
79	2nd Shropshire Rifle Volunteer Corps
80	13th Middlesex Rifle Volunteer Corps
81	1st Volunteer Battalion Royal Warwickshire Regiment
82	3rd Volunteer Battalion Royal Fusiliers
83	Middlesex Rifle Volunteers
84	20th Middlesex Rifle Volunteer Corps (Artists)
85	The London Scottish
86	5th Volunteer Battalion Gordon Highlanders
87	Volunteer Corps of London
88	4th Volunteer Battalion Gordon Highlanders
89	3rd Volunteer Battalion Gordon Highlanders
90	1st (City of Dundee) Volunteer Battalion Black Watch
91	6th (Fifeshire) Volunteer Battalion Black Watch
92	7th Middlesex (London Scottish) Volunteer Rifle Corps
93	Army Service Corps (Volunteers) and Royal Army Medical Corps (Volunteers)
94	7th (Clackmannan and Kinross) Volunteer Battalion Argyll and Sutherland Highlanders
95	1st Lanarkshire Royal Engineers (Volunteers)
96	Bugler, 4th Roxburghshire Rifle Volunteer Corps
97	The Queen's Rifle Volunteer Brigade
98	1st Argyllshire Artillery Volunteer Corps
99	1st Argyllshire Artillery Volunteer Corps
100	1st Yorkshire (East Riding) Artillery Volunteers
101	The Firing Exercise
102	Our Battalion

1 – OFFICER, HUDDERSFIELD RIFLE VOLUNTEERS, 1859

Print after PW Reynolds facing page 403 of *A History of the Formation and Development of The Volunteer Infantry*, by Robert Potter Berry and published in 1903 by Simpkin, Marshall, Hamilton, Kent & Co, Ltd of 4 Stationers' Hall Court, London, and J Broadbent & Co of High Street and Albion Street in Huddersfield. A single figure against a plain background with the caption, 'Officer, 1859'.

The image features an officer of the 6th Yorkshire (West Riding) Rifle Volunteer Corps, raised at Huddersfield, its offer of service having been accepted on 3 November 1859. It soon comprised four companies with Captain Henry Frederick Beaumont in command. Robert Potter Bury records in his history how the uniform decided upon was based on that of the 1st Middlesex (Victoria Rifles) Rifle Volunteer Corps, its cost £9.11.0.

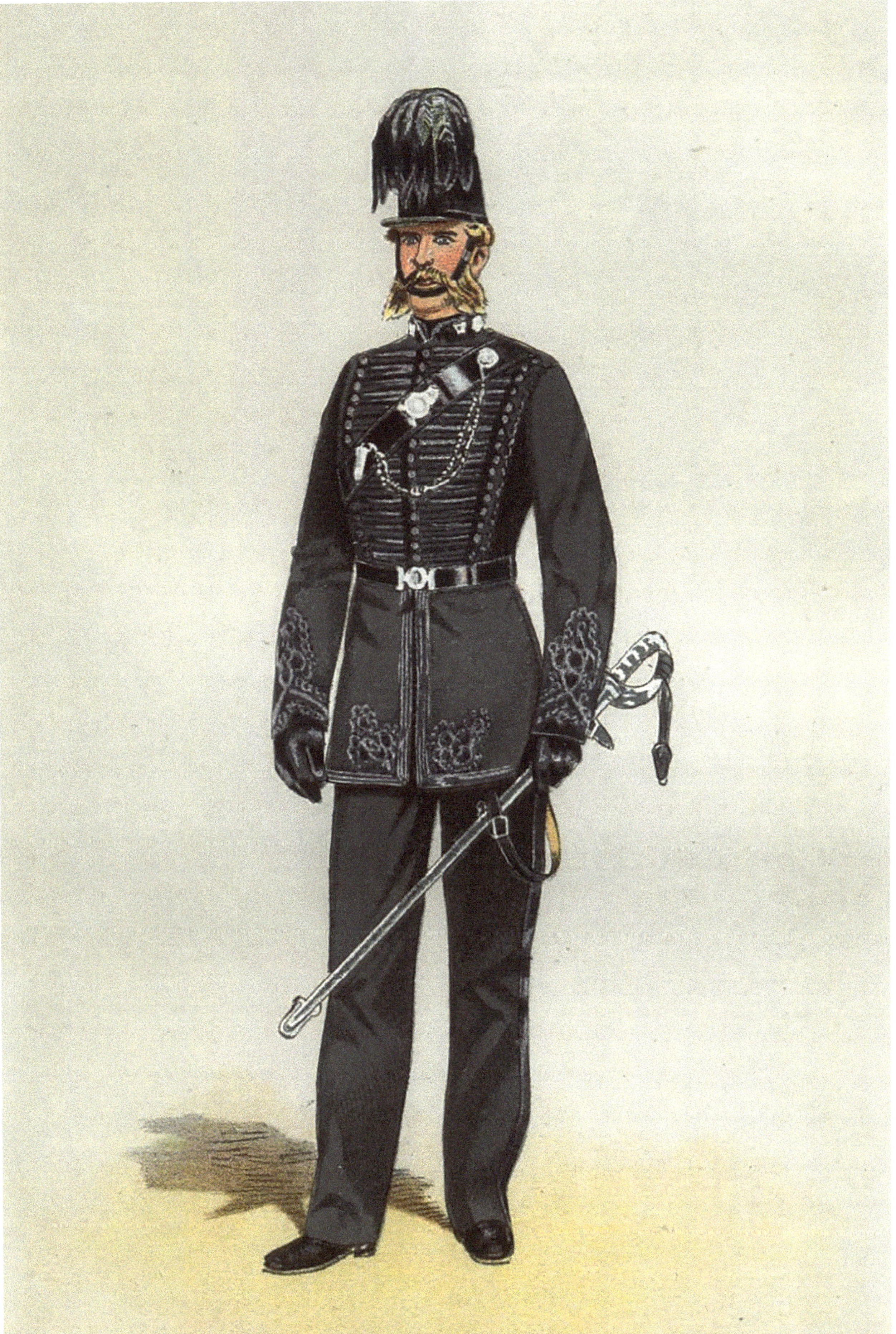

2 – OFFICER, HUDDERSFIELD VOLUNTEERS, 1863

Print after PW Reynolds facing page 454 of *A History of the Formation and Development of The Volunteer Infantry*, by Robert Potter Berry and published in 1903 by Simpkin, Marshall, Hamilton, Kent & Co, Ltd of 4 Stationers' Hall Court, London, and J Broadbent & Co of High Street and Albion Street in Huddersfield. A single figure against a plain background with the caption, 'Officer, 1863'.

The final PW Reynolds plate in Potter Berry's book is dated 1863 and shows an officer wearing the new uniform adopted that year described by the author as follows: 'It seems that many corps, on the opportunity arising for the first renewal of clothing, had adopted a new type of uniform. The Huddersfield corps did not escape the general feeling, and in 1863 their first uniform was discarded, and with the approval of the authorities, a smarter and more useful one adopted.' From Reynolds's colour plate we can see that the new choice was much shorter and decorated with less elaborate braid and with scarlet collar, cuffs and piping.

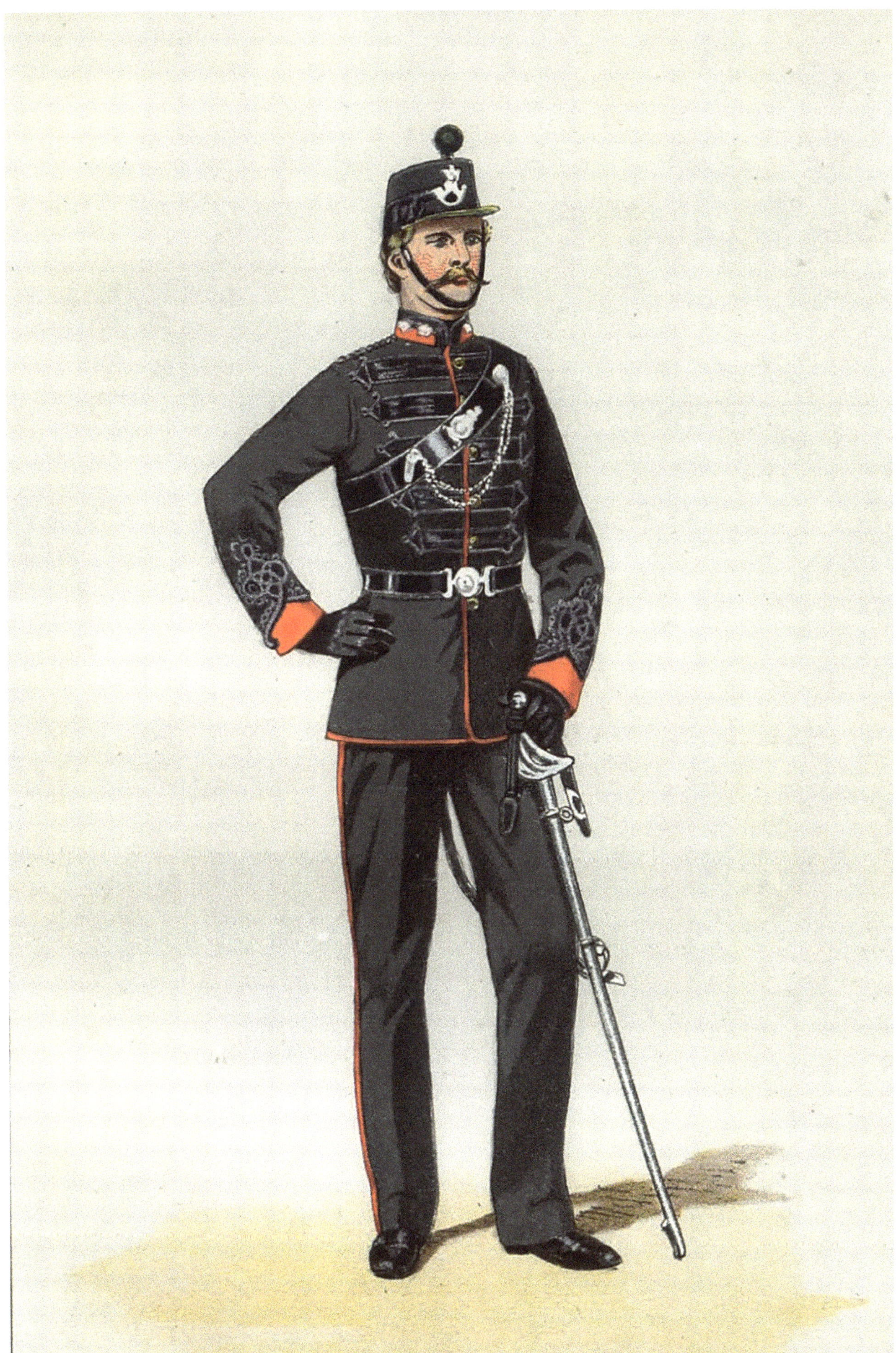

3 – 1st EDINBURGH AND 1st MIDLOTHIAN RGA (VOLS)

Plate 2 from *Records of the Scottish Volunteer Force 1859-1908* by Lieutenant-General Sir James Moncrieff Grierson who also produced the artwork. Four figures, two from each corps, the first pair showing gunners of 1866 and 1907 of the 1st Edinburgh, the second a gunner of 1860 and a sergeant of 1905 belonging to the 1st Midlothian.

The 1st Edinburgh Artillery was formed as a brigade in 1860 from nine batteries all raised within the city. Grierson tells us that the original uniform consisted of a dark blue single-breasted tunic with blue collar and cuffs and flat black braid. Shoulder cords and the Austrian knots on the sleeves were of black round lace. Trousers were also blue with a half-inch red stripe with black braid on both sides. In 1863 the cuffs and collars were made scarlet and we can see this change in Grierson's first figure. The black lace was, at the same time, changed to white. Another change, this time seeing the white cord altered to red (see second figure), occurred in 1878.

The 1st Midlothian Artillery Volunteers were formed with six batteries at Leith in 1859. Grierson's first figure shows the uniform being in use at 1860, with its scarlet collar and five rows of black cord lace on the breast. In the second image, a sergeant wears a blue helmet with white metal Royal Arms plate. Note how the usual spike has been replaced by a ball, this so as to protect the sides of horses when adjusting girth straps.

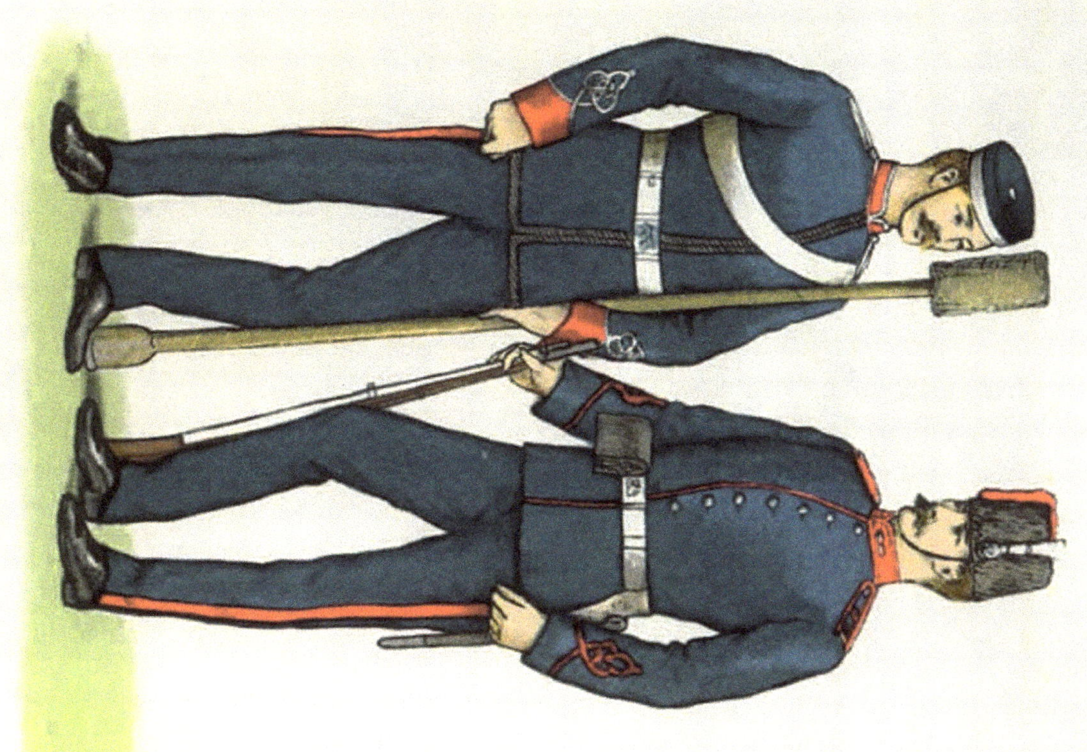

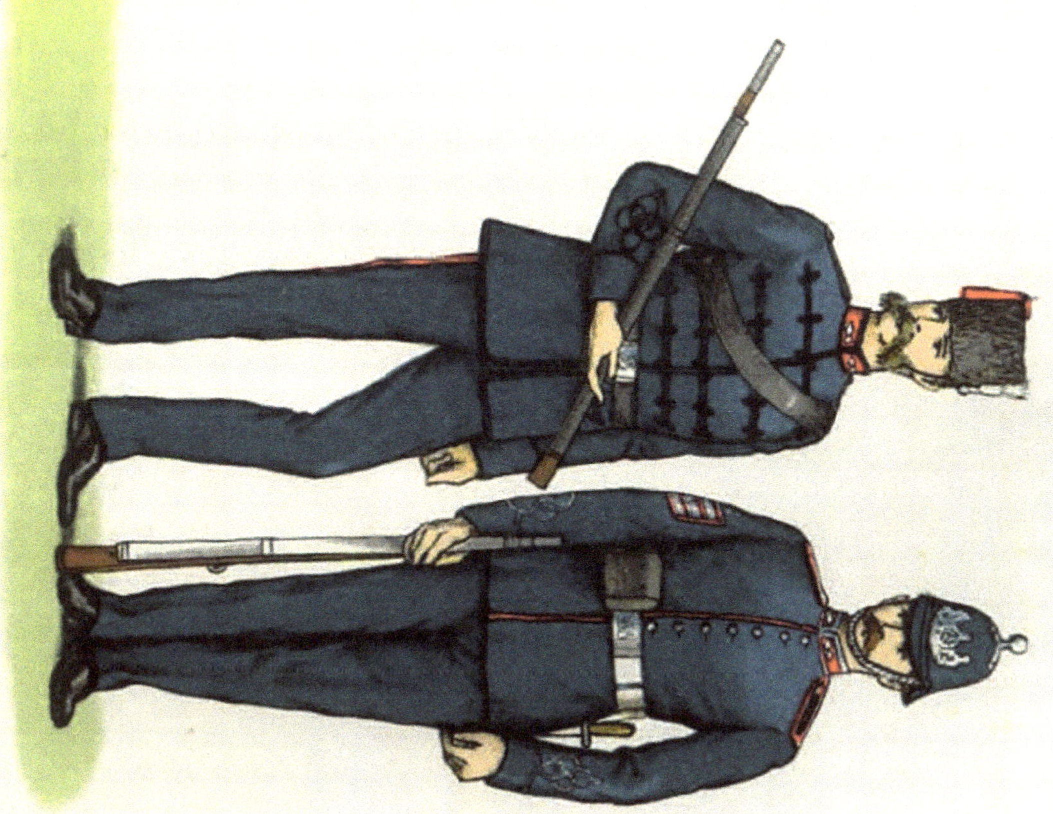

4 – 14TH MIDDLESEX RIFLE VOLUNTEER CORPS, 1860

Lithograph by Henry Joseph Fleuss for Day & Son after Robert Thomas Landells and published by SW Silver & Co of Cornhill, City of London c1860 with the following caption: 14th Middlesex / Highgate Volunteer Rifles. Below this a representation of a target in the centre of a strap inscribed, '14th Middx. V. R. The Captn. To The Best Shot.' The plate features four figures identified from left to right as, 'Private with Great Coat', 'Officer Full Dress', 'Private Full Dress', and 'Officer Undress.' Above the image the badge of the corps, a crowned star with the arms of Essex in the centre.

ET Evans records in his book *Records of the Third Middlesex Rifle Volunteers* that the origins of the 14th Corps lay in a private meeting held to discuss the possibilities of forming a volunteer rifle corps in Highgate and its vicinity at the home of William H Bodkin (afterwards Sir William Bodkin) on 24 May 1859. A subsequent meeting was held at the Swain's Lane cricket field on 21 June 1859. First drills later took place at Swain's Lane. The services of the Highgate Volunteers were accepted in the autumn of 1859, the War Office allotting the title 14th Middlesex RVC and an establishment of one company. The first officers' commissions were dated 2 November 1859, Captain Josiah Wilkinson taking command. Headquarters were established at Southwood Lane, Highgate in a building belonging to the governors of Highgate School. An additional company was authorized on 16 February 1860 and a third in June 1860, although the latter was never formed.

Rifle practice took place at Hornsey Wood House and drills were held not only in Highgate but in Gray's Inn Hall and frequently at Albany Street Barracks. Efforts were made to form companies at Kentish Town and Finchley where many members of the corps resided, but without success. A cadet corps did exist later, however, between 1864 and 1867 at Christ College, Finchley.

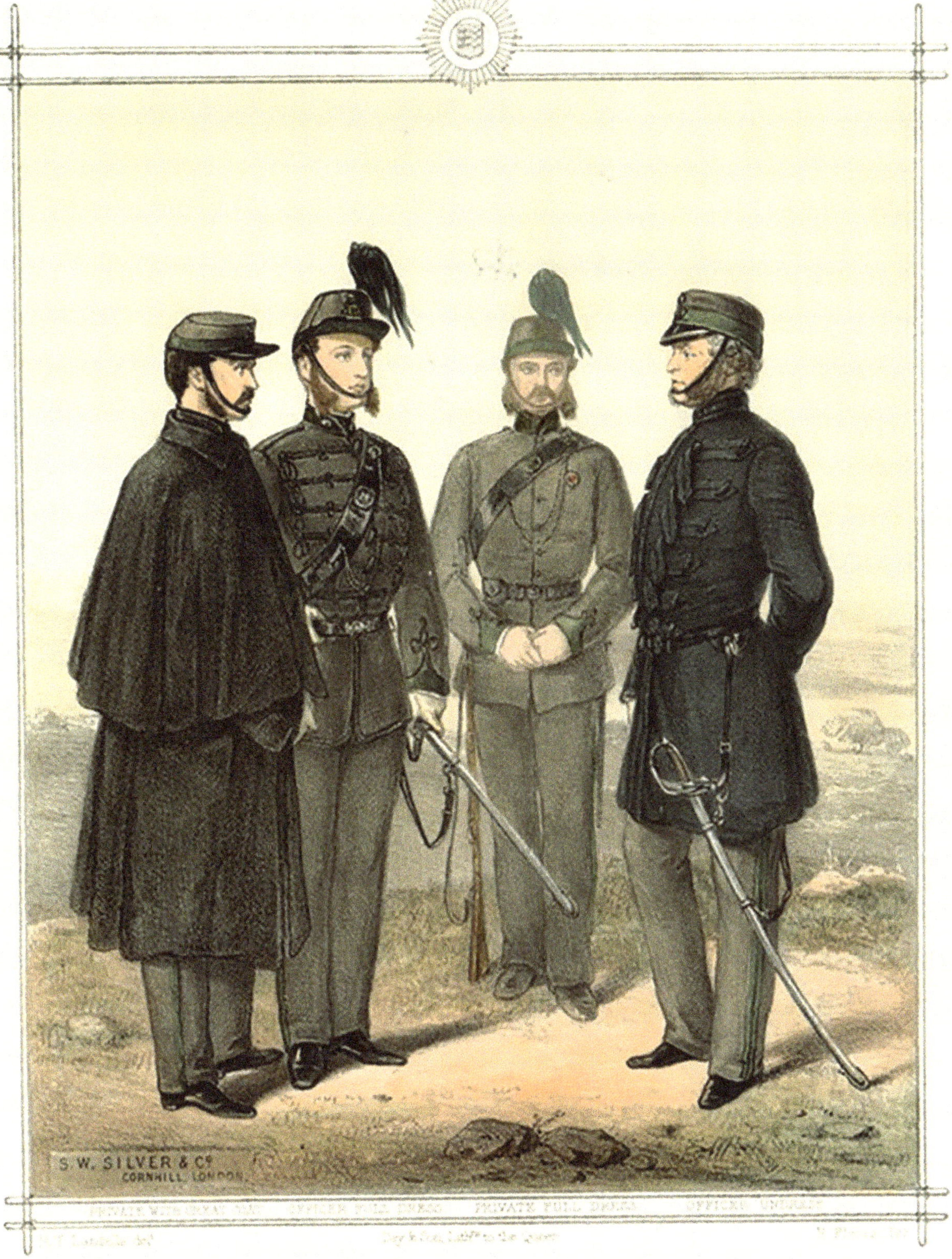

S.W. SILVER & Co.
CORNHILL, LONDON

PRIVATE WITH GREAT COAT | OFFICER FULL DRESS | PRIVATE FULL DRESS | OFFICERS UNDRESS

Day & Son, Lithrs to the Queen

HIGHGATE VOLUNTEER RIFLES.

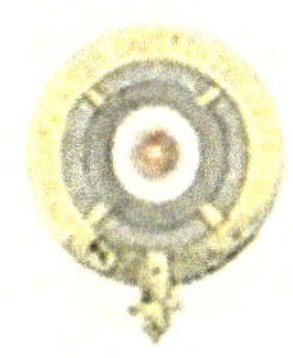

5 – WILLIAM COUTTS, VISCOUNT BURY

Colour lithograph drawn from life on stone by Henry Joseph Fleuss, lithographer Vincent Brooks. One of a set of eight prints published in 1861 with the title page, 'The Volunteer Corps of Great Britain drawn from life by Henry Fleuss.' The image has the following caption printed below, 'William Coutts Viscount Bury, MP / Lieut Col. Commandant of the Civil Service V.R.C.' Colonel Bury is featured with a bugler and several riflemen of the Civil Service Rifles behind.

From the very beginning of the Volunteer Movement in 1859 it had been intended to merge all units raised by government departments into one corps. In the early months there had been formed the 21st, 27th, 31st and 34th Middlesex Rifle Volunteer Corps, all of which were manned by civil servants, and it would be these that in June 1860 were merged as the 21st Middlesex (Civil Service) RVC with former Scots Guards officer Lieutenant Colonel William Coutts Viscount Bury in command. Headquarters were placed at Somerset House and the several companies, eight in all, were organised: 'A' (Audit Office), 'B' (Post Office), 'C' (Post Office), 'D' (Inland Revenue), 'E' (Inland Revenue), 'F' (Whitehall), 'G' (Whitehall) and 'H' (Admiralty).

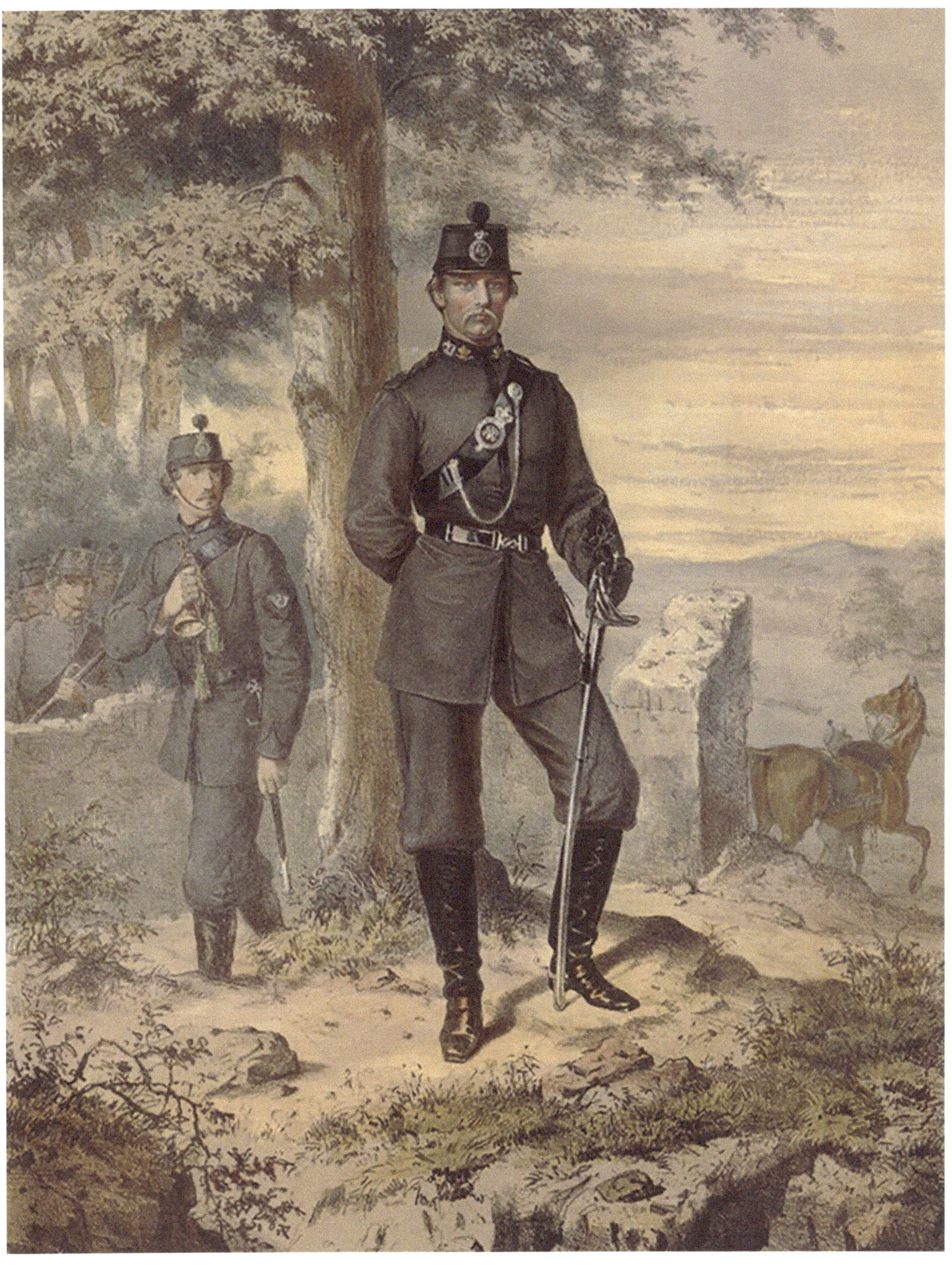

6 – CAPTAIN HENRY H WILLIAMS, 19TH MIDDLESEX RIFLE VOLUNTEER CORPS

From the *Illustrated London News*, a portrait of Captain Henry H Williams of the 19th Middlesex Rifle Volunteer Corps who had won the Earl Dudley shooting prize at Wimbledon in 1862. The uniform is of a blueish-grey with scarlet collar, cuffs, piping and cap band. Clearly seen on the headdress is the corps number within a bugle horn.

Formed at Bloomsbury of three companies on 13 December 1859, personnel of the corps were provided by members of the Working Men's College in Great Ormond Street, Holborn. The commanding officer was Thomas Hughes, author of *Tom Brown's Schooldays*, which led to the corps often being referred to as 'Tom Brown's Corps'. The 19th later comprised ten companies of which three were supplied by the college and others by the St John's Institute in Cleveland Street, the Price Belmont Works at Battersea, the Working Men's College in Paddington Green and the Westminster parishes of St Luke and St. Anne's. Headquarters later moved to 33 Fitzroy Square.

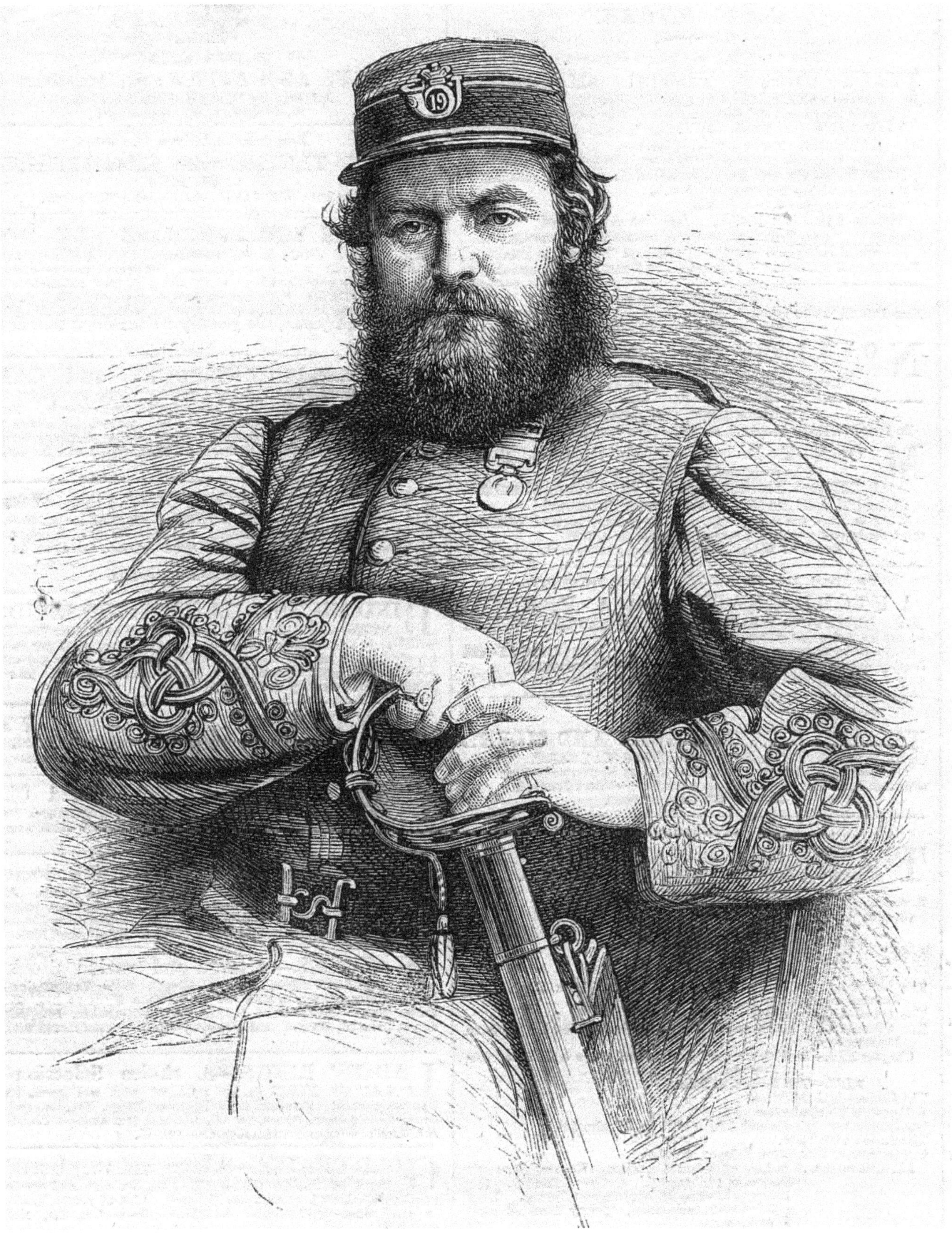

7 – THE CADET CORPS GALOP

Sheet music cover for 'The Cadet Corps Galop' by C W Smith, published in 1861 by Metzler & Co of 37 and 38 Great Marlborough Street, London. Artwork by Robert Jacob Hamerton, printing by Stannard & Dixon.

In a grey uniform piped with red, a young cadet salutes another boy who stands nonchalantly with his hands in his pockets. To the right, another raises his kepi cap to a young lady who wears a pink dress and has her hair held in place by a net. With a drummer in front, the parade looks on, as do the bonneted and top-hatted grownups behind. A pleasant countryside scene with a white mansion nestling behind trees on the slope of a hill. Cadet companies had been formed and attached to volunteer corps from almost the very beginning of the Volunteer Movement in 1859 and were usually made up of thirty boys each.

Metzler & Co were piano manufacturers and published music from the 1820s to the 1920s. *(Image courtesy of the Anne SK Brown Military Collection, Brown University Library)*

Dedicated to Miss Danson.

THE CADET CORPS GALOP,

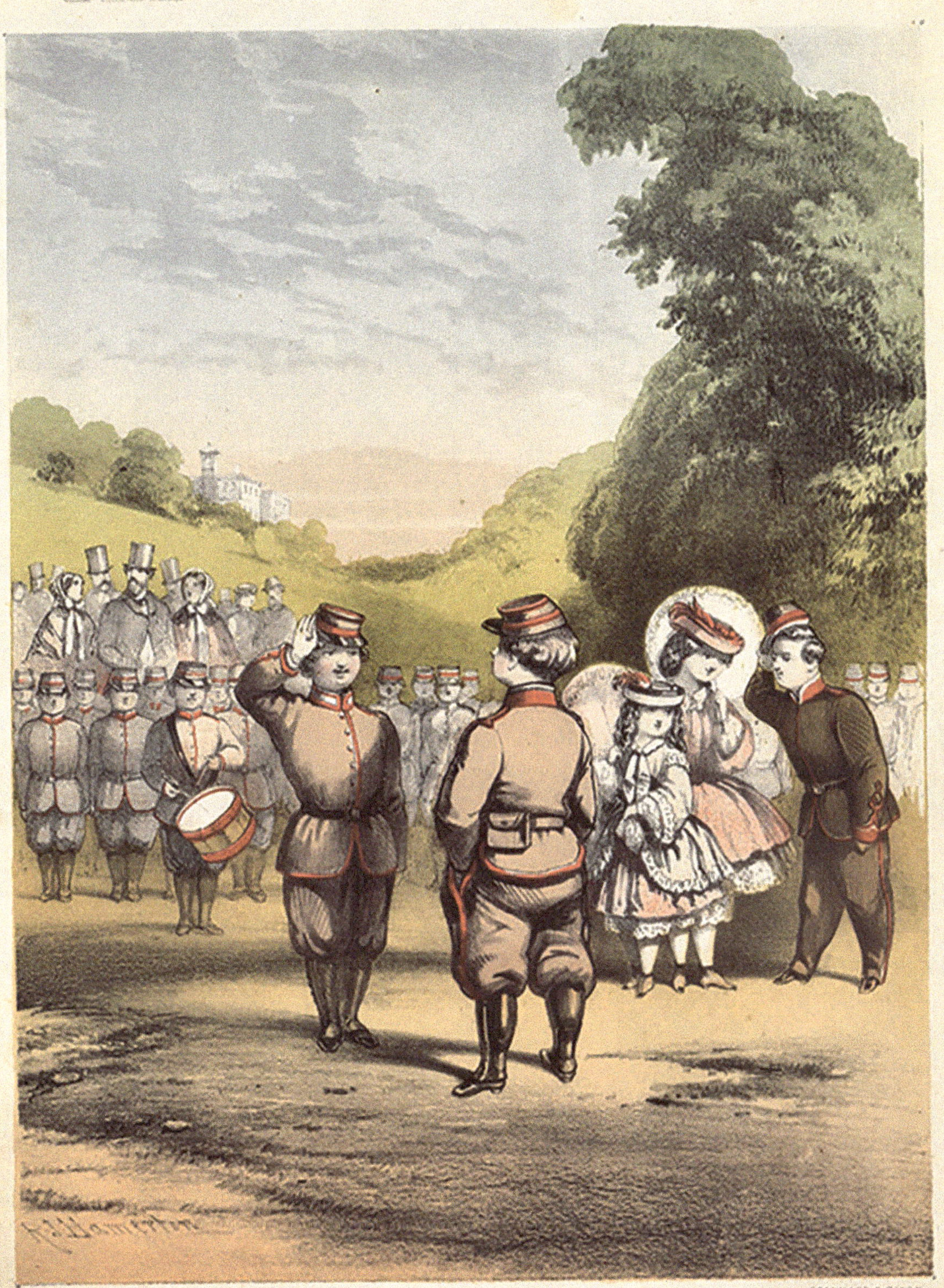

STANNARD & DIXON

BY

C. W. SMITH.

ENT. STA. HALL

c. 1860

c. 1860

Pr. 3/.

LONDON, METZLER & Co. 37 & 38 & 35, Gt. MARLBOROUGH Stt. W.

8 – THE DEVIL'S OWN WALTZ

Sheet music cover for 'The Devil's Own Waltz' composed by Louis John Islip and published by Partridge & Cozens of 1 Chancery Lane, London. Artwork by Thomas W Lee, the song dedicated to Colonel Montague McMurdo, CB and the officers and gentlemen of the 23rd Middlesex (Inns of Court) Rifle Volunteer Corps.

When King George III reviewed a volunteer corps composed of members of the legal profession, it was possibly his less than enjoyable experience with lawyers which caused him to refer to the troops as 'The Devil's Own.' After a lull in volunteer activity in Britain, 1859 once again saw civilians putting on uniform as a precaution against invasion and from the four Inns came the 23rd Middlesex Rifle Volunteer Corps. And here he is, the Devil himself, dressed in the grey and scarlet uniform of the 23rd, tail in hand, flames bursting from a hoofed foot, his pipe being lit by lighting from the sky. In the bottom right corner of the image is the letter D within a circle inscribed 'Painted not so black as he is'. Behind this, a three-pronged fork. *(Image courtesy of the Anne SK Brown Military Collection, Brown University Library)*

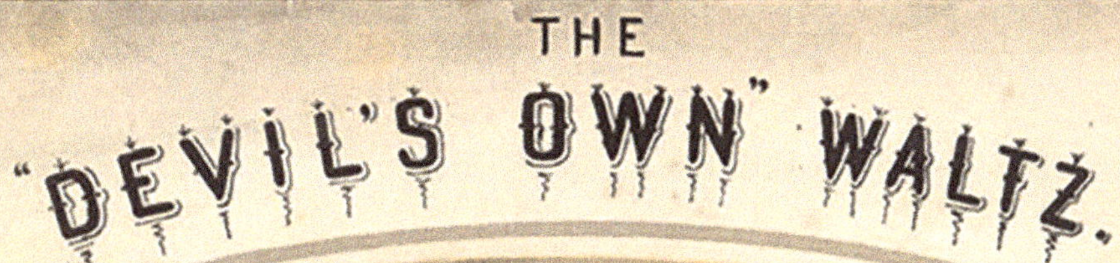

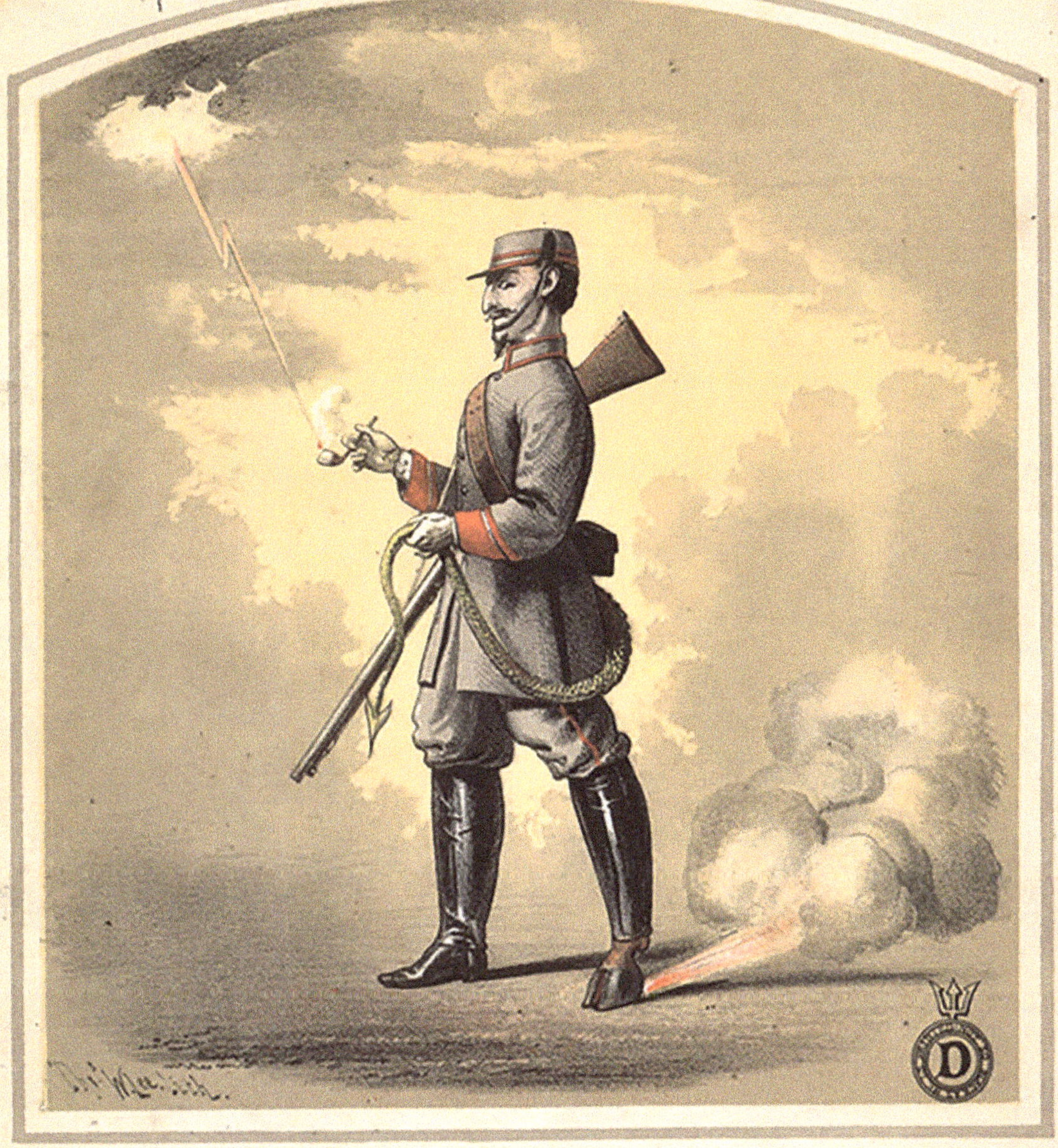

DEDICATED (BY PERMISSION) TO

Colonel M'Murdo, C.B.

AND THE OFFICERS & GENTLEMEN

OF THE

23RD MIDDLESEX (INNS OF COURT) RIFLE VOLUNTEER CORPS.

COMPOSED BY

LOUIS JOHN ISLIP.

COMPOSER OF THE RICHMOND RIFLE QUADRILLE, MAID OF HONOUR VALSE &c &c

ENT STA. HALL.

Copyright

Pr 4/.

LONDON,

PARTRIDGE & COZENS,
1, CHANCERY LANE.

WILLIAM ROBINSON,
368, STRAND.

& TO BE HAD OF THE AUTHOR 4 ROYAL TERRACE RICHMOND S.W.

9 – 3RD MIDDLESEX RIFLE VOLUNTEERS, 1859

Colour plate after Edward Thornton Evans opposite page 48 of his book *Records of The Third Middlesex Rifle Volunteers*, published by Simkin, Marshall & Co, London 1885. The Hampstead Rifle Volunteers of 1859-1908 (later designated as 3rd Middlesex) had originated at the famous 'Spaniards Inn' in 1859 when, in about June of that year, a number of residents met to consider the formation of a volunteer company of riflemen. Sixty men enrolled that day and the company's first officers were commissioned on 6 December 1859, drills soon commencing at the Holly Bush Assembly Rooms. The original uniform is illustrated, which had a loose light blue blouse and trousers with black braiding and a black round hat with red plume. The belts and accoutrements were of brown leather.

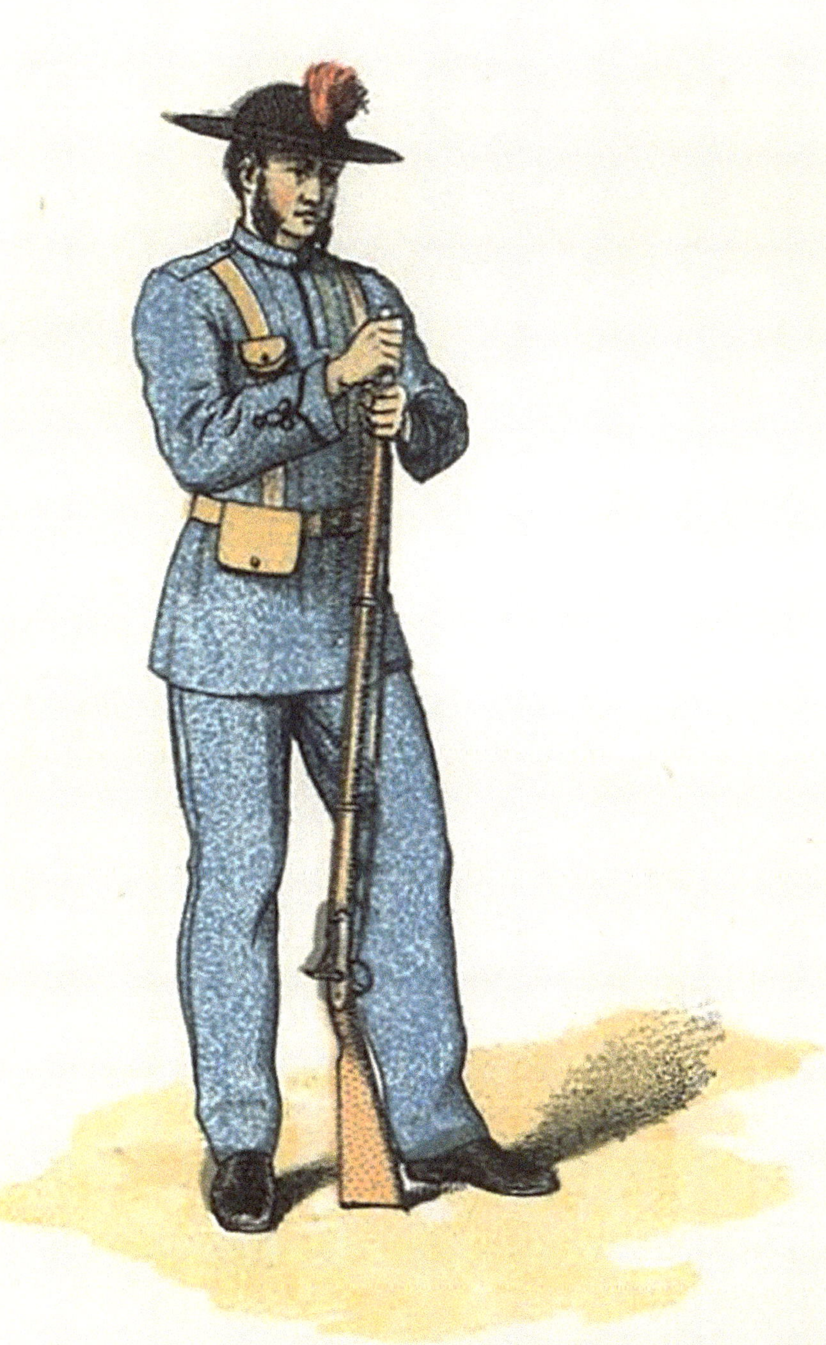

10 – 3RD MIDDLESEX RIFLE VOLUNTEERS, 1860

Colour plate after Edward Thornton Evans opposite page 50 of his book *Records of The Third Middlesex Rifle Volunteers*, published by Simkin, Marshall & Co, London 1885. ET Evans recalls that the original uniform adopted (see plate above) found little favour in Hampstead, so much so that in April 1860 it was discarded for that shown—a light reddish grey tunic and trousers of War Office pattern, with blue piping and grey braid. The shoulder straps and collar are blue and Austrian knots of the same colour were placed as edging to the jacket's pointed cuffs. The grey cap has a blue pompom and band, the belts and ammunition pouch of brown leather.

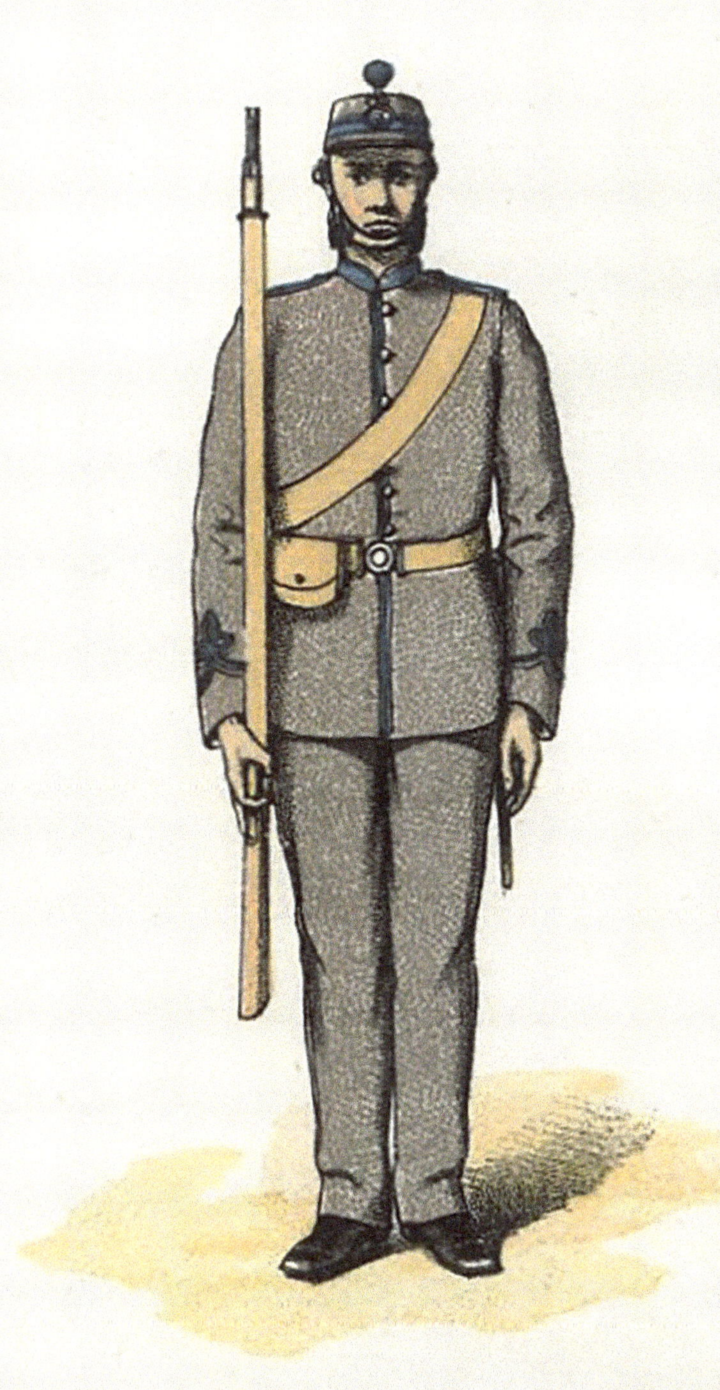

11 – 12th MIDDLESEX RIFLE VOLUNTEERS, 1859

Colour plate after Edward Thornton Evans opposite page 70 of his book *Records of The Third Middlesex Rifle Volunteers*, published by Simkin, Marshall & Co, London 1885. Regarding the 12th Middlesex Rifle Volunteer Corps (a post-1880 component of the 3rd Middlesex RVC) ET Evans writes, 'This corps was brought into existence through the exertions of Mr Wilbraham Taylor of Hadley Hurst, a gentleman-usher to the Queen.' Mr Taylor had organised a public meeting at Barnet Town Hall on 6 July 1859 to consider the question of forming a volunteer corps from residents in the area. All present were in favour of the venture and members were sworn in on the following 11 August. Drills later commenced at the Militia Barracks at Barnet and while at a parade on the following 15 October, news of the Queen's acceptance of the services of the 12th Middlesex Rifle Volunteer Corps was read out. The uniform selected was rifle green with black braiding, black leather gaiters and belts. The headdress (the so-called wide-brimmed 'Garibaldi') was also black and with a plume of black cock feathers.

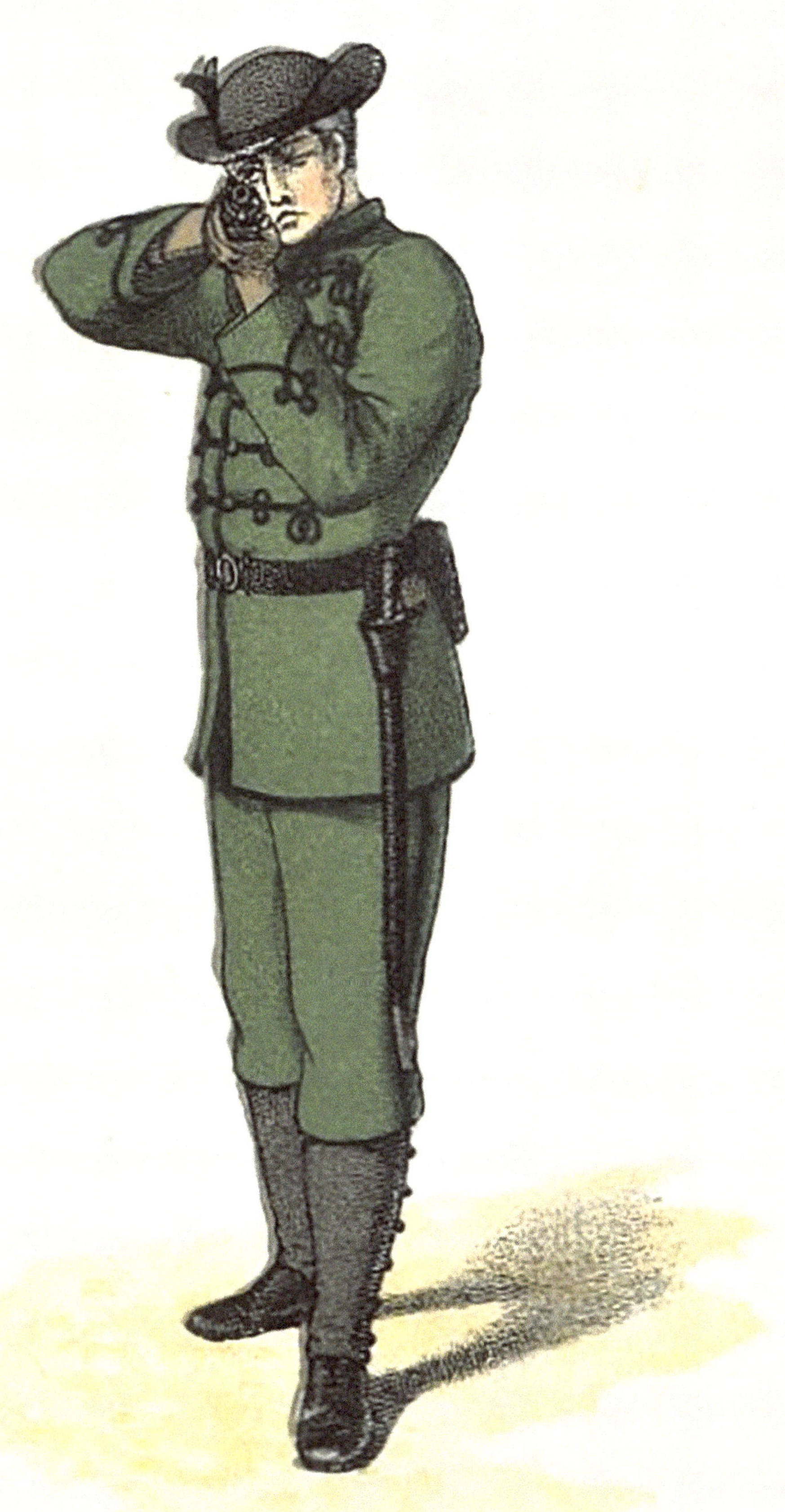

12 – 13TH MIDDLESEX RIFLE VOLUNTEERS, 1860

Colour plate after Edward Thornton Evans opposite page 88 of his book *Records of The Third Middlesex Rifle Volunteers*, published by Simkin, Marshall & Co, London 1885. As mentioned above, the 12th Middlesex Rifle Volunteer Corps became part of the 3rd in 1880. This was as a result of the general consolidation of all existing 'Administrative' battalions into single corps. It followed that the several corps which then made up the 2nd Admin Battalion of Middlesex Rifle Volunteers: the 3rd (Hampstead), 12th (Barnet), 13th (Hornsey), 14th (Highgate), 33rd (Tottenham) and 41st (Enfield Lock), were in 1880 amalgamated as a single battalion with the title of 3rd Middlesex RVC. The subject of this image by ET Evans is a private of the 13th (Horsey) in 1860 wearing the uniform adopted that year: grey tunic and trousers with red piping, the cap grey with red cord around the crown and bottom. Belts and gaiters were brown.

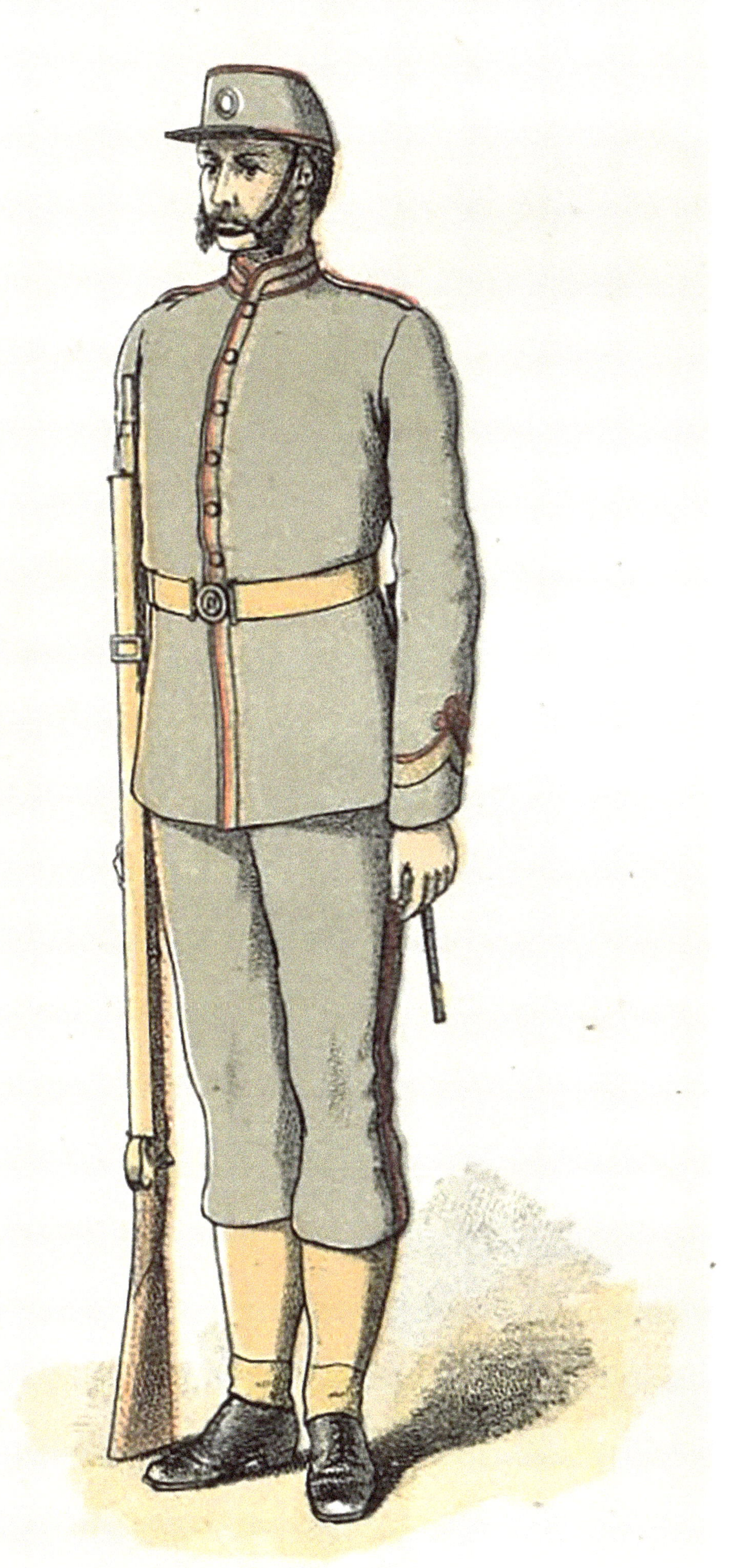

13 – 14TH MIDDLESEX RIFLE VOLUNTEERS, 1856-60

Colour plate after Edward Thornton Evans opposite page 118 of his book *Records of The Third Middlesex Rifle Volunteers*, published by Simkin, Marshall & Co, London 1885. Representing the 14th Middlesex Rifle Volunteer Corps, ET Evans's colour plate shows three figures: a private of 1859, and two officers, one in full dress, the other in undress frock coat, for 1860. The green facing colour agreed upon can be seen in all three volunteers. Belts are of black patent leather, those worn across the left shoulder having a central badge and silver whistle and chain set. Black cord and lace adorns the coats of both officers.

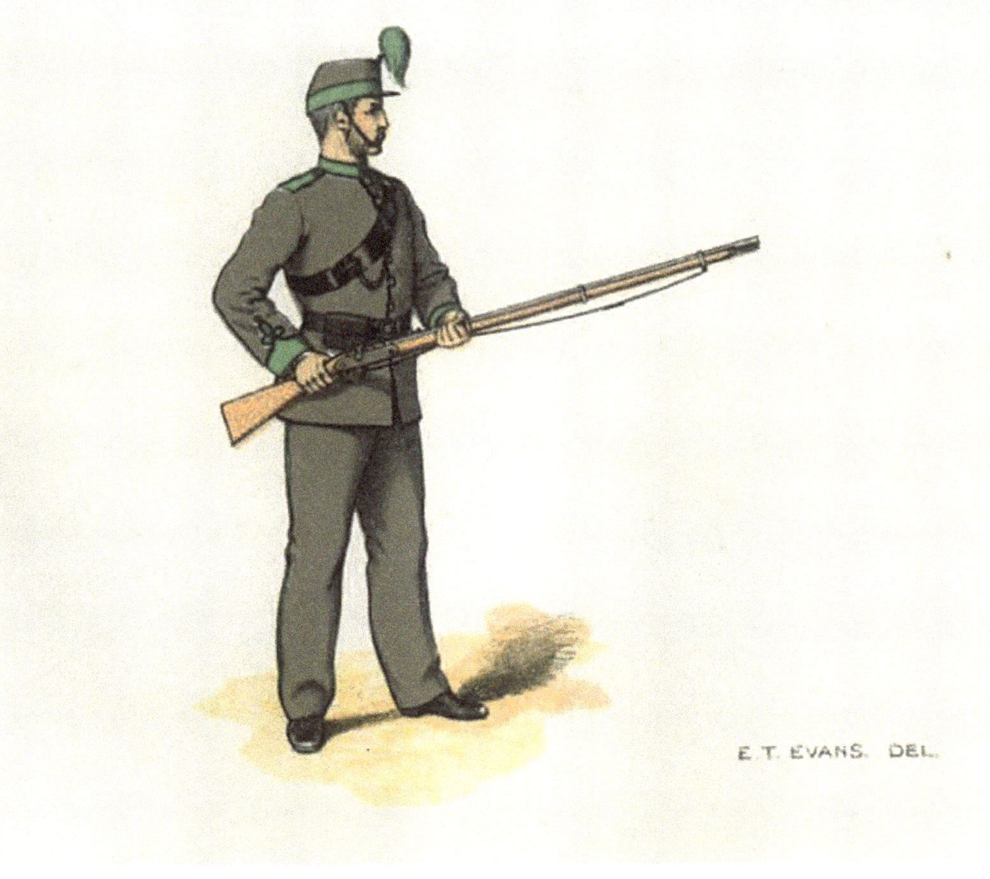
E.T. EVANS. DEL.

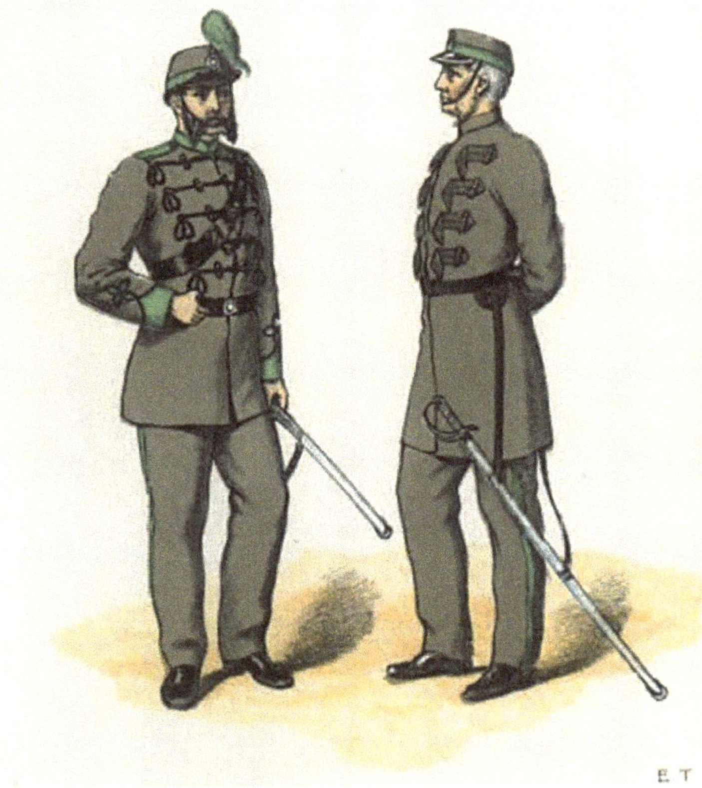
E T EVANS DEL

14 – 2nd ADMIN BATTALION MIDDLESEX RIFLE VOLUNTEERS, 1876

Colour plate after Edward Thornton Evans opposite page 209 of his book *Records of The Third Middlesex Rifle Volunteers*, published by Simkin, Marshall & Co, London 1885. In his notes for the 2nd Administrative Battalion, ET Evans mentions that 'In March of this year [1875] an undress grey Glengarry cap was approved for the rank and file…also a full-dress busby.' The officers' busby was grey Astrakhan fur with 'red and white plume, and grey lines with plated ornaments and chain.' We can see from Evans' illustration of a 2nd Admin Battalion officer for 1876 that the headdress ornament, certainly in the case of the 41st Middlesex, took the form of a crowned star with the corps numeral in the centre. A similar silver badge can also be seen on the light brown pouch-belt, together with whistle and chain. Note the red cloth backing to the collar and chest cord.

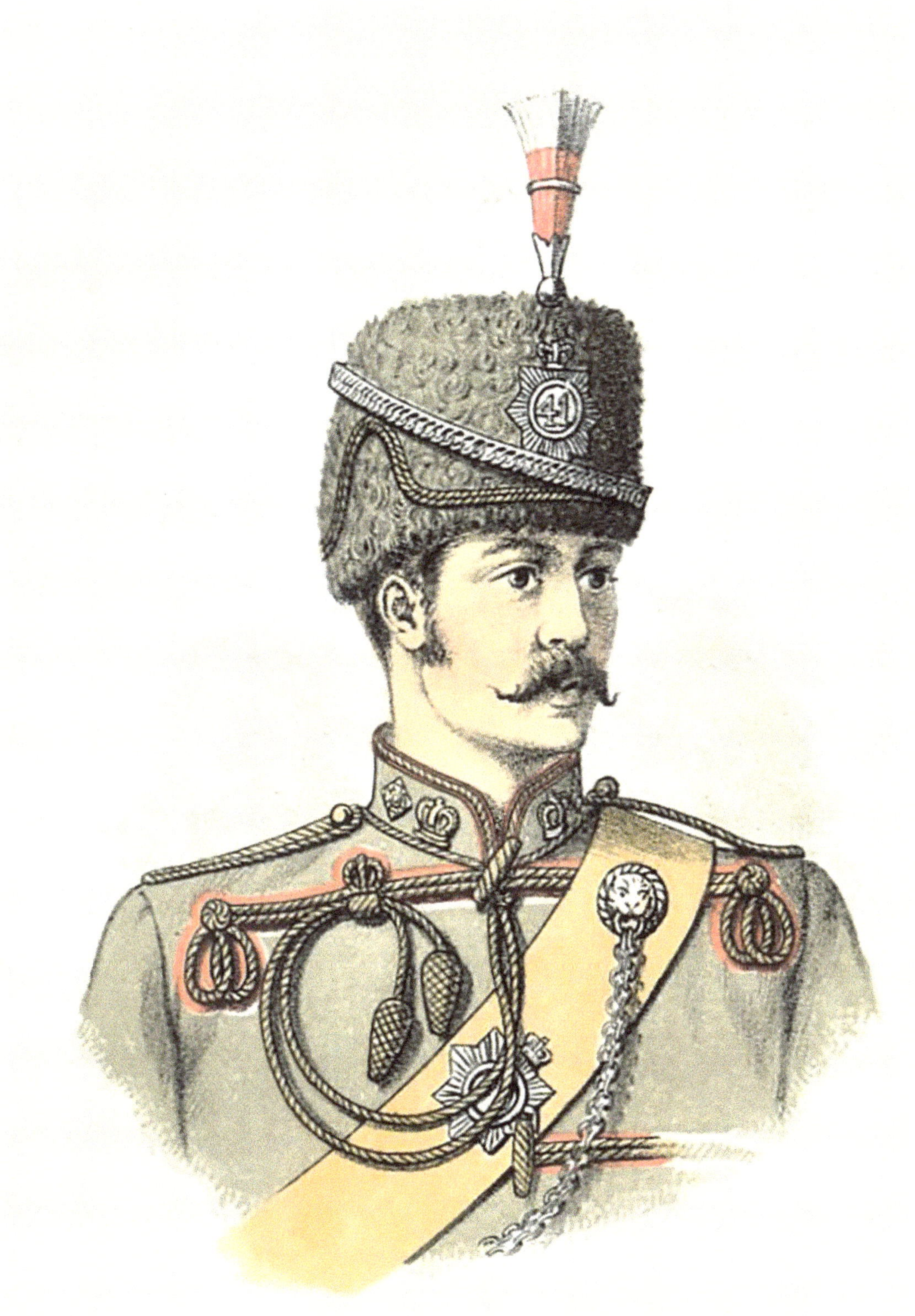
41

15 – 3rd Middlesex Rifle Volunteer Corps

Colour plate after Edward Thornton Evans opposite page 227 of his book *Records of The Third Middlesex Rifle Volunteers*, published by Simkin, Marshall & Co, London 1885. The adopted officers' post-1880 uniforms are illustrated in this fine plate. Of light grey, the jackets were trimmed and edged with grey braid. Red appears around the undress caps and again down the seams of the trousers. On the right we have an officer in mess uniform who wears a red waistcoat. By the end of 1900 the 3rd Middlesex Rifle Volunteer Corps comprised thirteen companies: Hampstead (1), Barnet (1), Hornsey (4), Highgate (2), Tottenham (3) and Enfield (2). Eight years later in 1908, the corps transferred to the Territorial Force as the Middlesex Regiment's 7th Battalion.

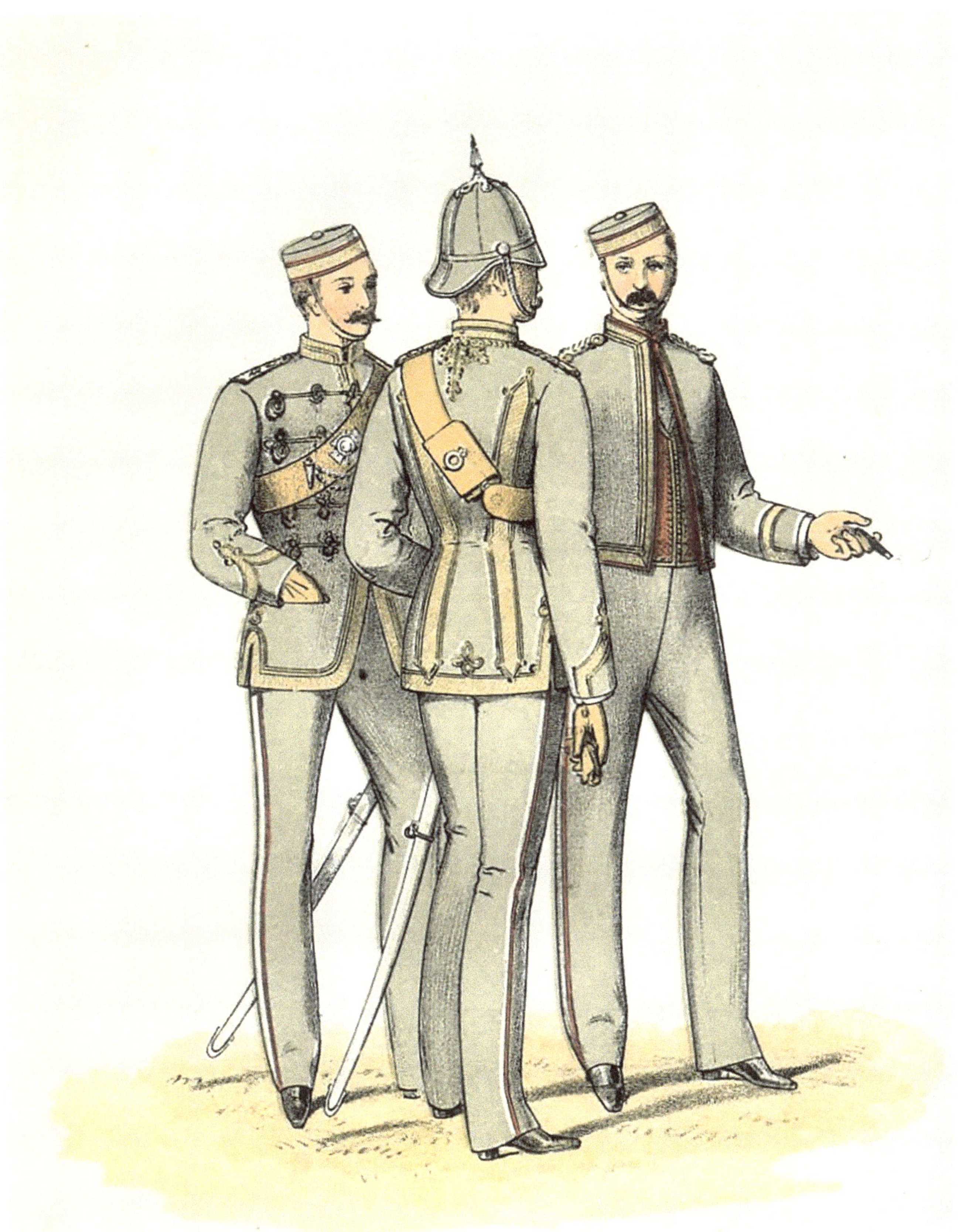
E. T. EVANS, DEL.

16 – MOUNTED RIFLES AND LIGHT HORSE

Plate 1 after Lieutenant-General Sir James Moncrieff Grierson from his book, *Records of the Scottish Volunteer Force*, published in 1909 by William Blackwood & Sons. Not to be confused with the Yeomanry, several regiments of Mounted Rifles and Light Horse were raised throughout the Volunteer Force. General Grierson's plate shows six figures from these two arms. From left to right we have a private of the 1st Fifeshire Mounted Rifles in 1860, followed by a captain wearing the uniform of the 1st Fifeshire Light Horse Volunteers in 1890. The third figure is also a captain, this time wearing the undress uniform of the 1st Forfarshire Light Horse. Next, and wearing a scarlet jacket and brown leather equipment, we have a private of the 1st Dumfrieshire Mounted Rifles for the period 1874-1880. For the remaining two figures, Grierson shows a corporal (1872-1880) and private (1880-1892), from the Border Mounted Rifles.

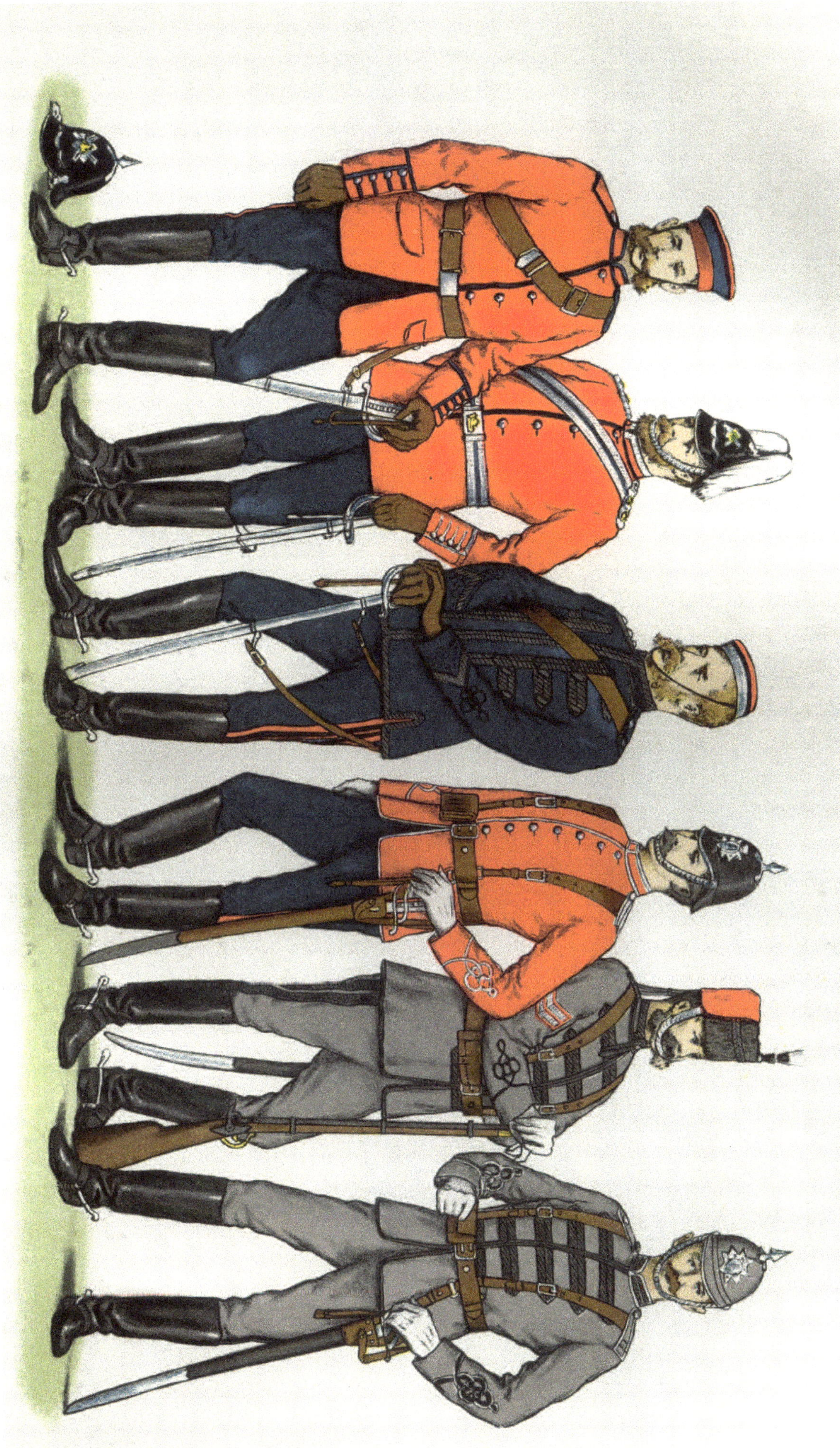

17 – METROPOLITAN VOLUNTEERS IN HYDE PARK

Colour chromolithograph supplement to the *Illustrated London News* issued 27 October 1860. The print recalls the first review by Queen Victoria of volunteers in Hyde Park which took place on 23 June 1860 and involved almost 19,000 volunteers. Printed below the image are the following corps identifications working from left to right: 'Working Men's College, South Middlesex, South Kensington, London Scottish & Kilted Company, St George's, 1st Surrey, Honourable Artillery, City of London, Civil Service, Volunteer Guards, Inns of Court, Victoria Rifles, 1st Middlesex Artillery, Queen's Westminster, London Irish, West Middlesex and 1st Surrey Mounted Rifles'.

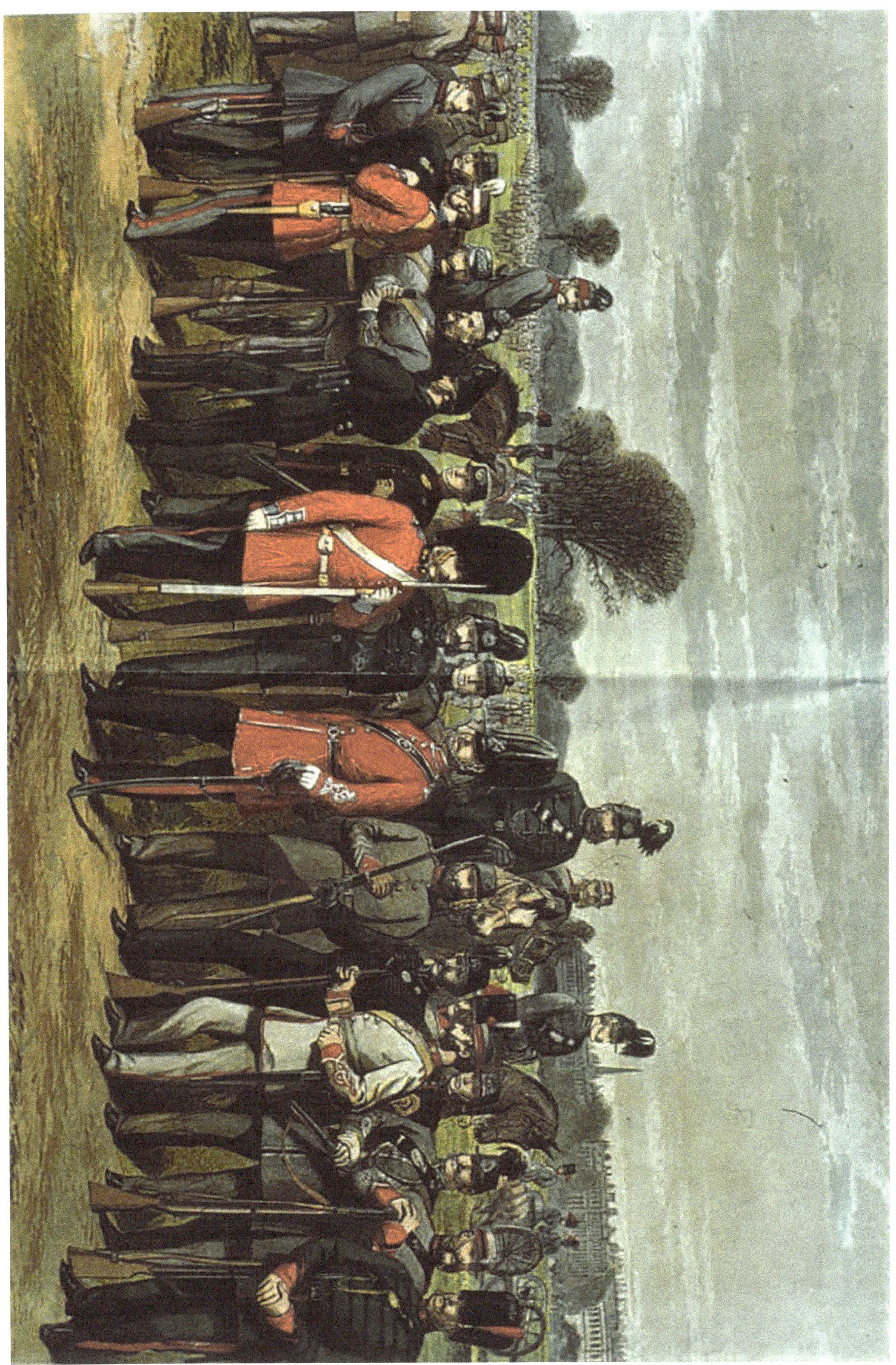

18 – THE VOLUNTEER GUARDS (32ND MIDDLESEX)

Engraving from the *Illustrated London News* featuring members of the 32nd Middlesex Rifle Volunteer Corps with the following captions from left to right: 'Undress Private', 'Undress Officer', 'Full Dress Officer', 'Full Dress Private' and 'Undress Private'.

The 32nd Middlesex RVC was formed of two companies with headquarters in Seymour Place, St Marylebone in February 1860. On 27 October 1860, the *Illustrated London News* published a short item regarding the corps which mentioned, 'The 32nd Middlesex Rifle Corps, known to the public as the Six-foot Volunteer Guards, was established last February, with a view to meet the requirements of men whose stature…rendered their appearance in the ranks of ordinary-sized corps somewhat awkward. More than one hundred and fifty gentlemen of the required standard, including several military officers and six-footers from other corps, have been enrolled.'

The corps carried on their drills at either St George's Barracks or Hungerford Hall. The military artist Lady Butler mentions in her autobiography how 'I stuffed my sketch books with British Volunteers…there was a very short-lived corps called the Six-foot Guards.' The 32nd Middlesex Rifle Volunteer Corps, with its scarlet coats and black belts, was disbanded in 1868.

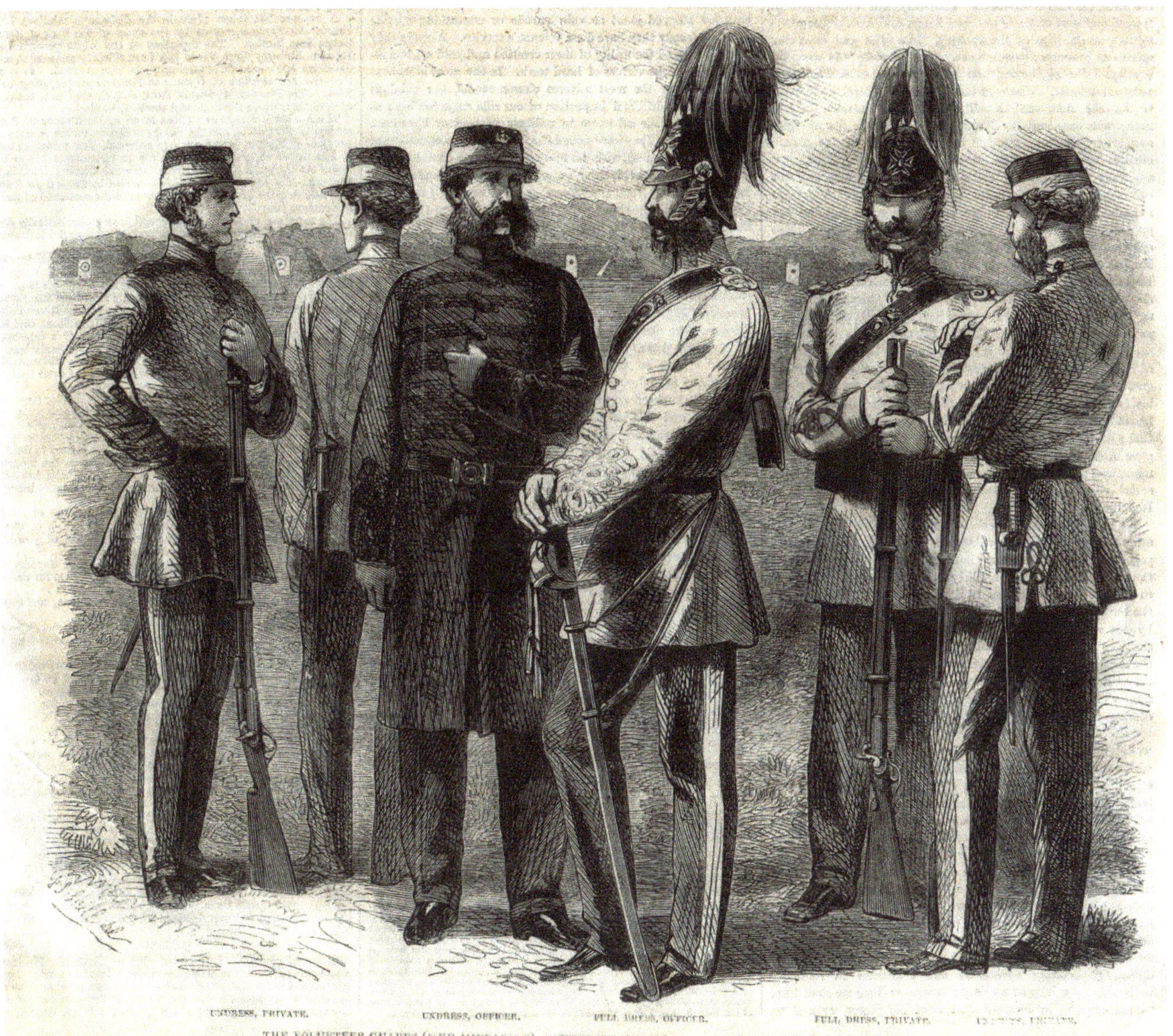

UNDRESS, PRIVATE. UNDRESS, OFFICER. FULL DRESS, OFFICER. FULL DRESS, PRIVATE. UNDRESS, PRIVATE.

THE VOLUNTEER GUARDS (22ND MIDDLESEX), GENERALLY KNOWN AS THE SIX-FOOT CORPS.—SEE PAGE 295.

19 – 1st MIDDLESEX LIGHT HORSE

An original watercolour painting by George Henry Laporte featuring four members of the corps with others formed up in the background. The men are wearing dark green uniforms with red piping, a short light brown busby with red bag and lines and a white plume on the left side.

The corps was formed in January 1861 at Messrs Tattersall's horse sale yard on Hyde Park Corner. Known unofficially as the 1st Metropolitan Light Horse, the corps in July 1861 merged with the 2nd Middlesex Light Horse which had been formed on 14 February at 1 St James's Place. Disbandment was in December 1866. *(Image courtesy of the Anne SK Brown Military Collection, Brown University Library)*

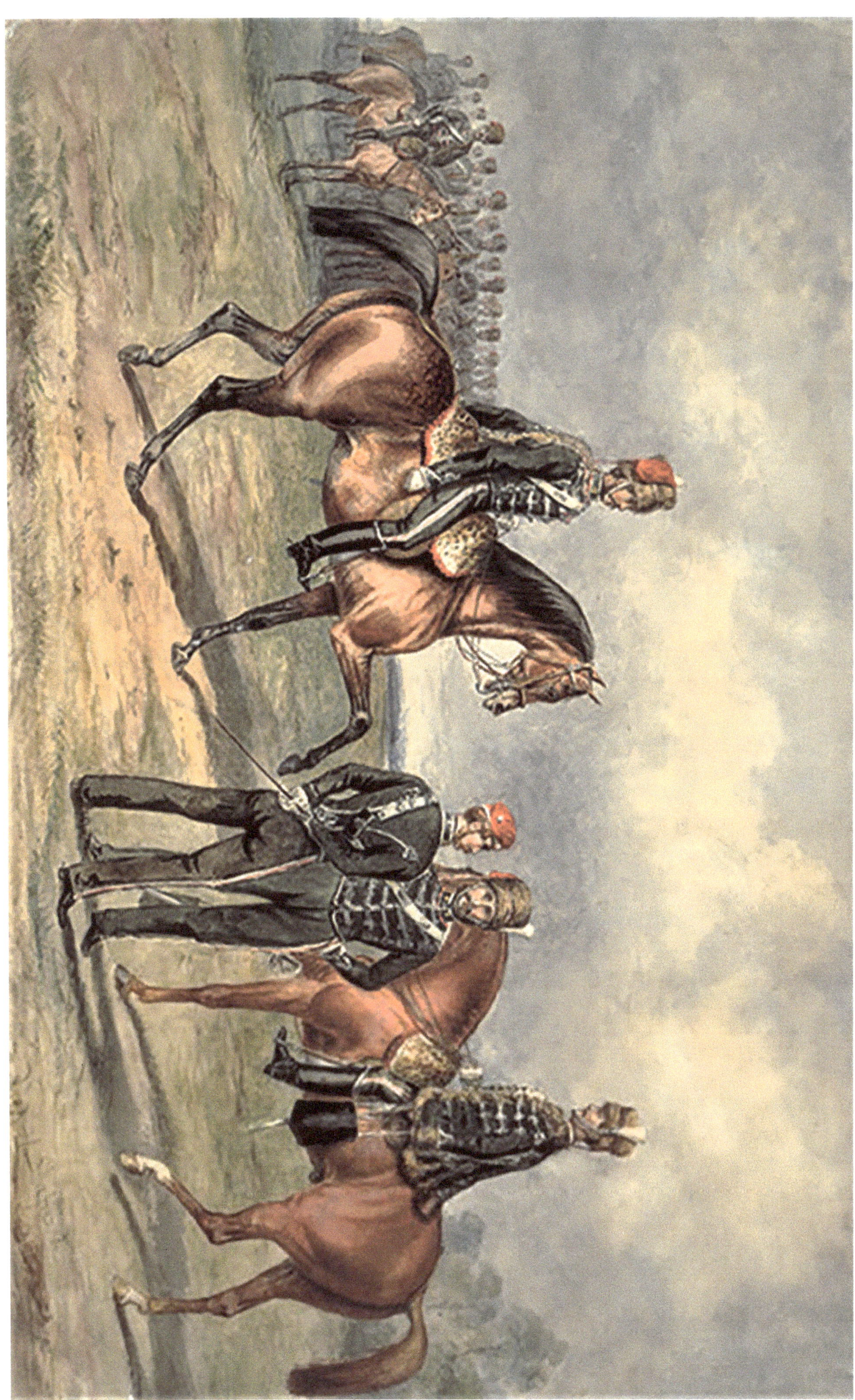

20 – THE VOLUNTEER, 1860

One of a pair (the other featuring a volunteer of 1803) of colour lithographs by G McCulloch after John Absolon and published by Lloyd Brothers & Co of 96 Gracechurch Street with the caption 'The Volunteer 1860' on 1 November 1860. The printing was done by Day & Son, lithographers to the Queen. The volunteer wears a long grey coat with red edging to the collar and shoulder straps, and grey trousers. Red also appears as a backing to the three silver chevrons and a crown worn on the upper arm. The shako, with its green feather plume, is also grey. (*Image courtesy of the Anne SK Brown Military Collection, Brown University Library*)

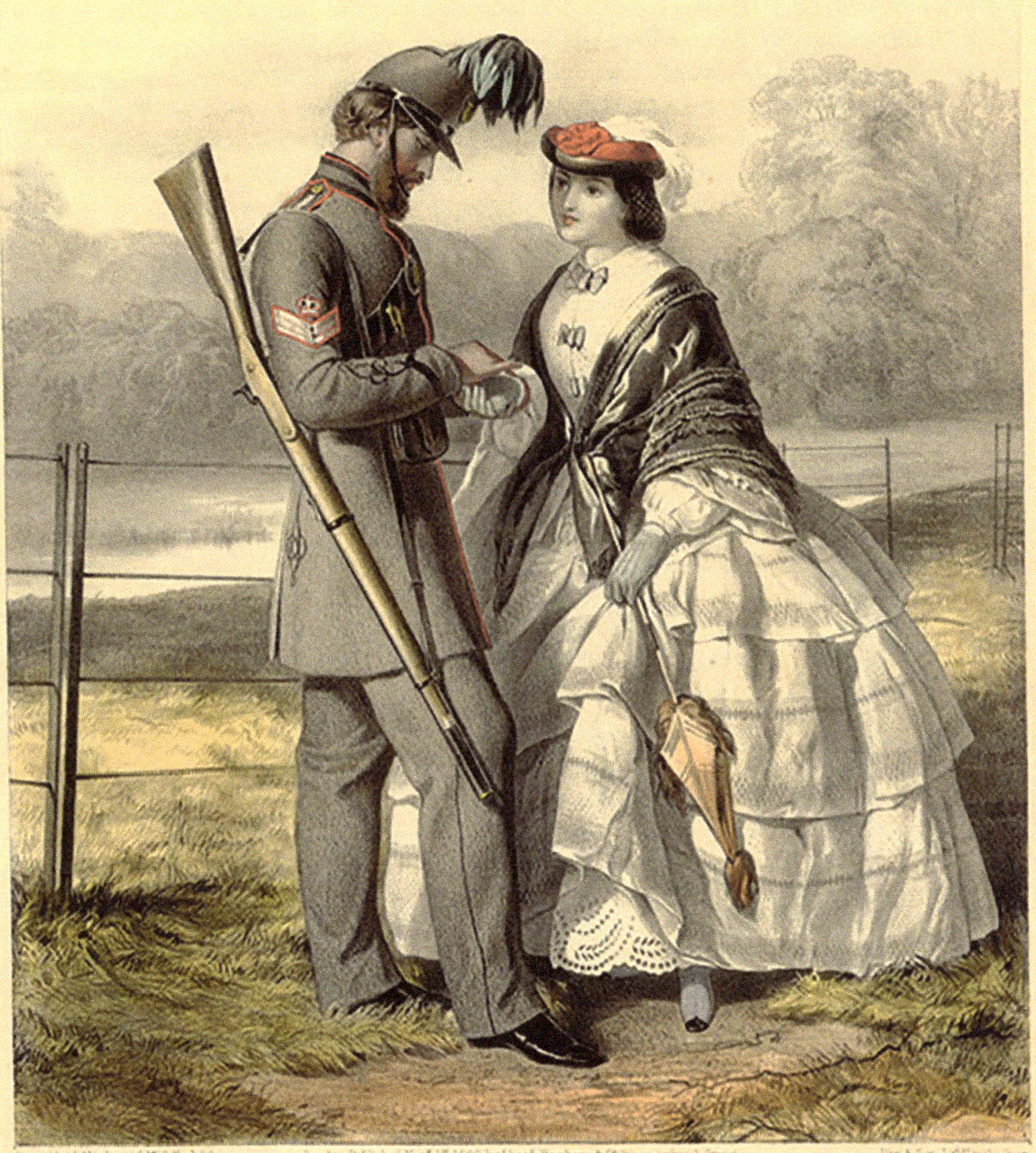

THE VOLUNTEER __ 1860.

21 – THE BORDER RIFLE VOLUNTEER CORPS

Plate XV1 after Lieutenant-General Sir James Moncrieff Grierson from his book, *Records of the Scottish Volunteer Force*, published in 1909 by William Blackwood & Sons. From left to right: a private of the 2nd Roxburgh RVC 1860, bugler 4th Roxburgh RVC 1860, private 1st Selkirk RVC 1860, sergeant 1st Administrative Battalion Roxburgh and Selkirk RVC 1863-1877, captain 1879-1902 and private 1902-1907.

There were 5 numbered corps raised in Roxburghshire: 1st at Jedburgh, 2nd Kelso, 3rd Melrose, 4th Hawick and 5th Hawick. In Selkirkshire there were two, the 1st at Galashiels, the 2nd at Selkirk. All seven corps in November 1861 were placed into the 1st Administrative Battalion of Roxburghshire Rifle Volunteers, the uniforms being of a slate-grey with scarlet collars and black braid and piping. In 1877 the red collars were abolished and in 1879 grey helmets were introduced. The Border Rifles title had been confirmed on the battalion in 1868.

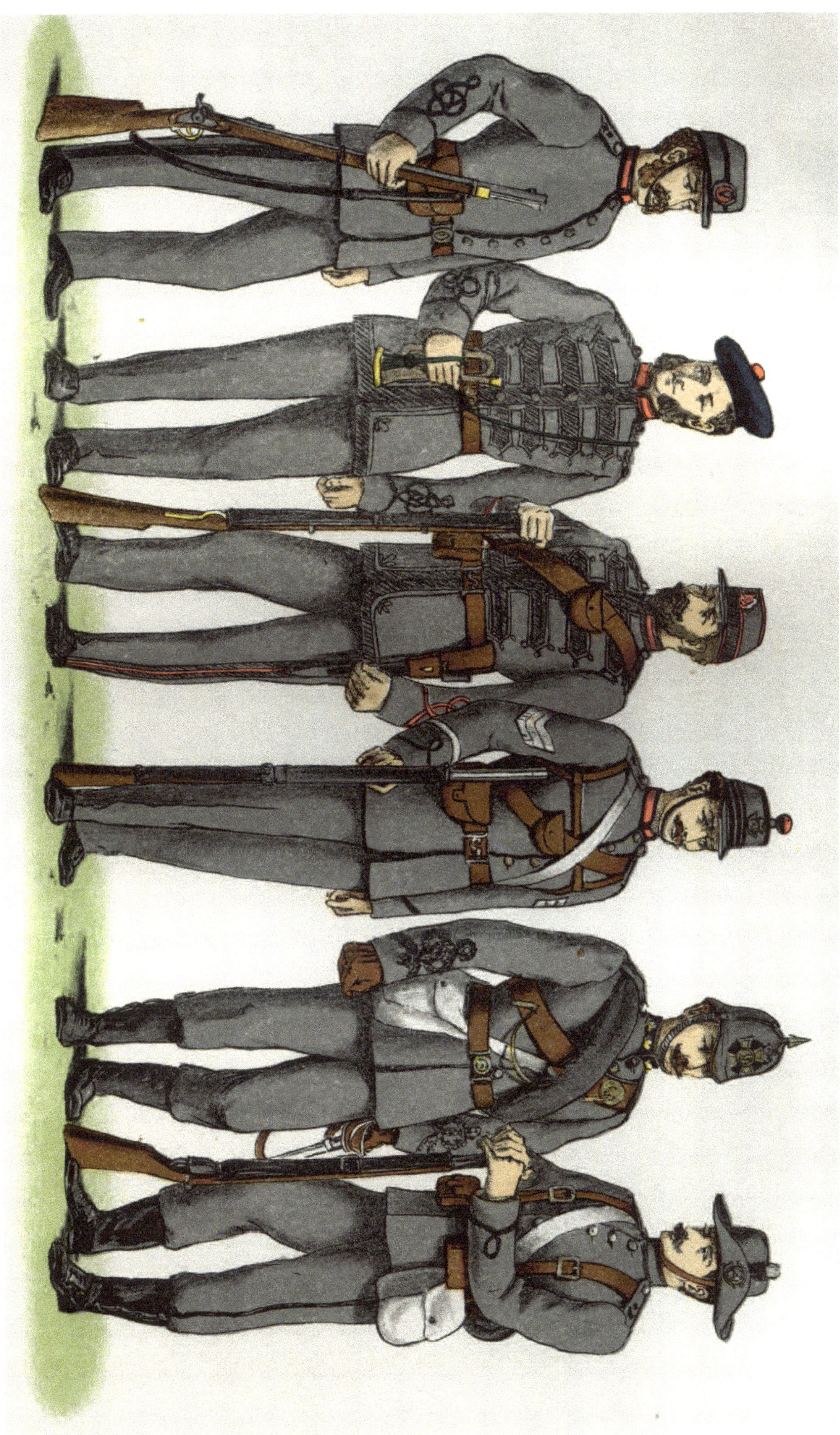

22 – EAST KENT RIFLES

Coloured lithograph by Henry Joseph Fleuss after Robert Thomas Landells and published by SW Silver & Co of Cornhill, City of London c1860. From left to right, the figures are captioned, 'Private Full Dress', 'Private Undress' and 'Officer Full Dress'. The uniforms are grey with red collar, cuffs and piping, the shakos having green plumes.

The several independent companies of rifle volunteers from the East Kent area were located at Canterbury, Sittingbourne, Ash, Ashford and Wingham (*Image courtesy of the Anne SK Brown Military Collection, Brown University Library*)

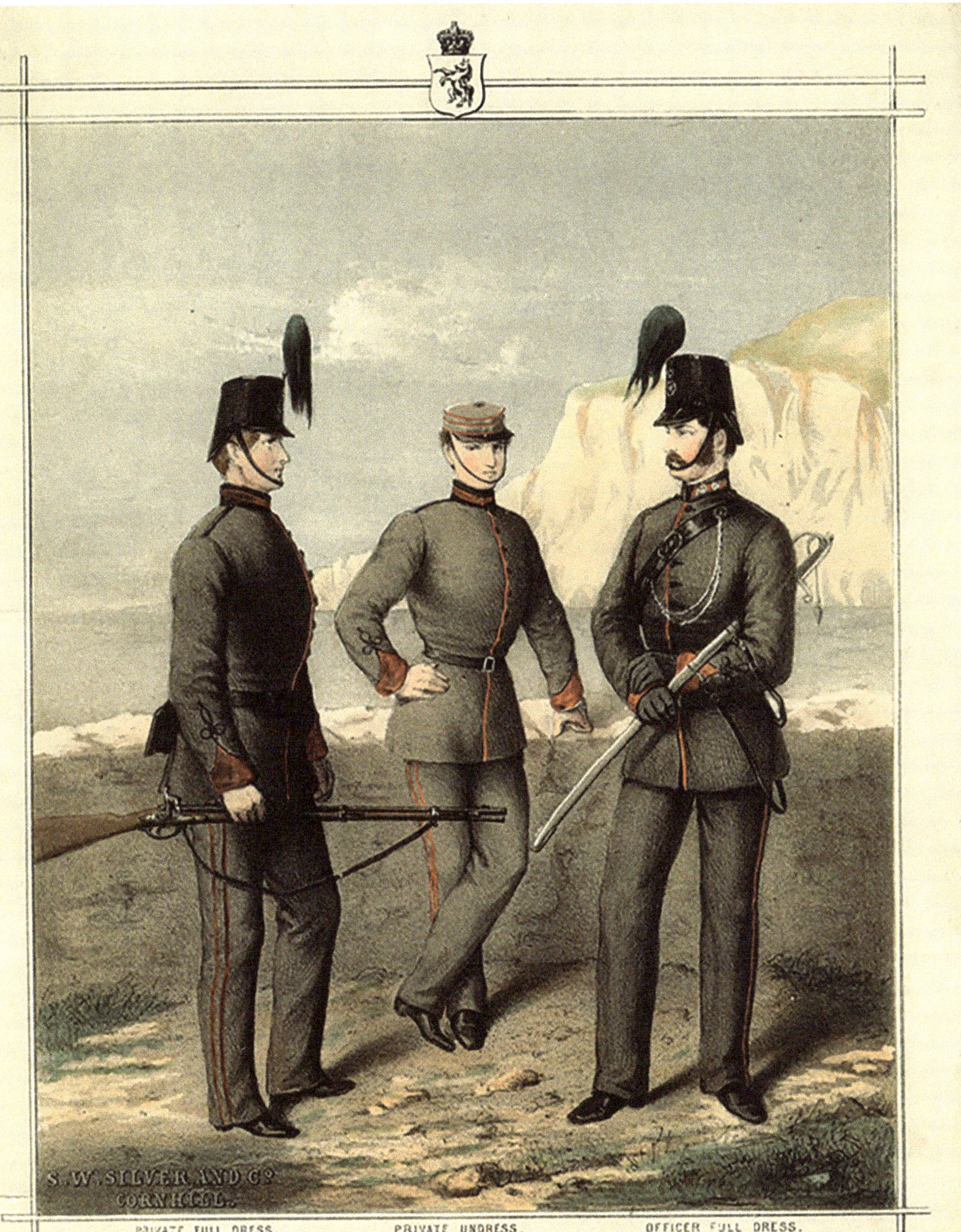

PRIVATE FULL DRESS. PRIVATE UNDRESS. OFFICER FULL DRESS.

R.T. LANDELLS, DEL. M & N. HANHART, IMP. H. FLEUS, LITH.

23 – HALT OF THE LONDON SCOTTISH (7TH MIDDLESEX RIFLE VOLUNTEERS)

Chromolithographic plate signed by Harry Payne and published by Raphael Tuck & Sons of London, Parish and New York with the caption, 'Halt of the London Scottish (7th Middlesex Rifle Volunteers)'. The artist's signature and the date 1893 appear in the bottom righthand corner of the image. Against a skyline of the City of London, the London Scottish are seen resting during a march.

The services of a corps composed of Scotsman living in the London area were accepted by the War Office on 2 November 1859. Originally designated as the 15th Middlesex, the regiment comprised six companies with Lord Elcho (afterwards Earl of Wemyss) in command. Headquarters were established at 8 Adelphi Terrace, Westminster and the companies were located: No1 (Highland) at 10 Pall Mall East, No2 (City) the Oriental Bank, No3 (Northern) Rosemary Hall Islington, No4 (Central) Scottish Corporation House Crane Court, No5 (Southern) 68 Jermyn Street and No6 (Western) at Chesterfield House. After several changes in company organisation, the corps was re-numbered as 7th in 1880.

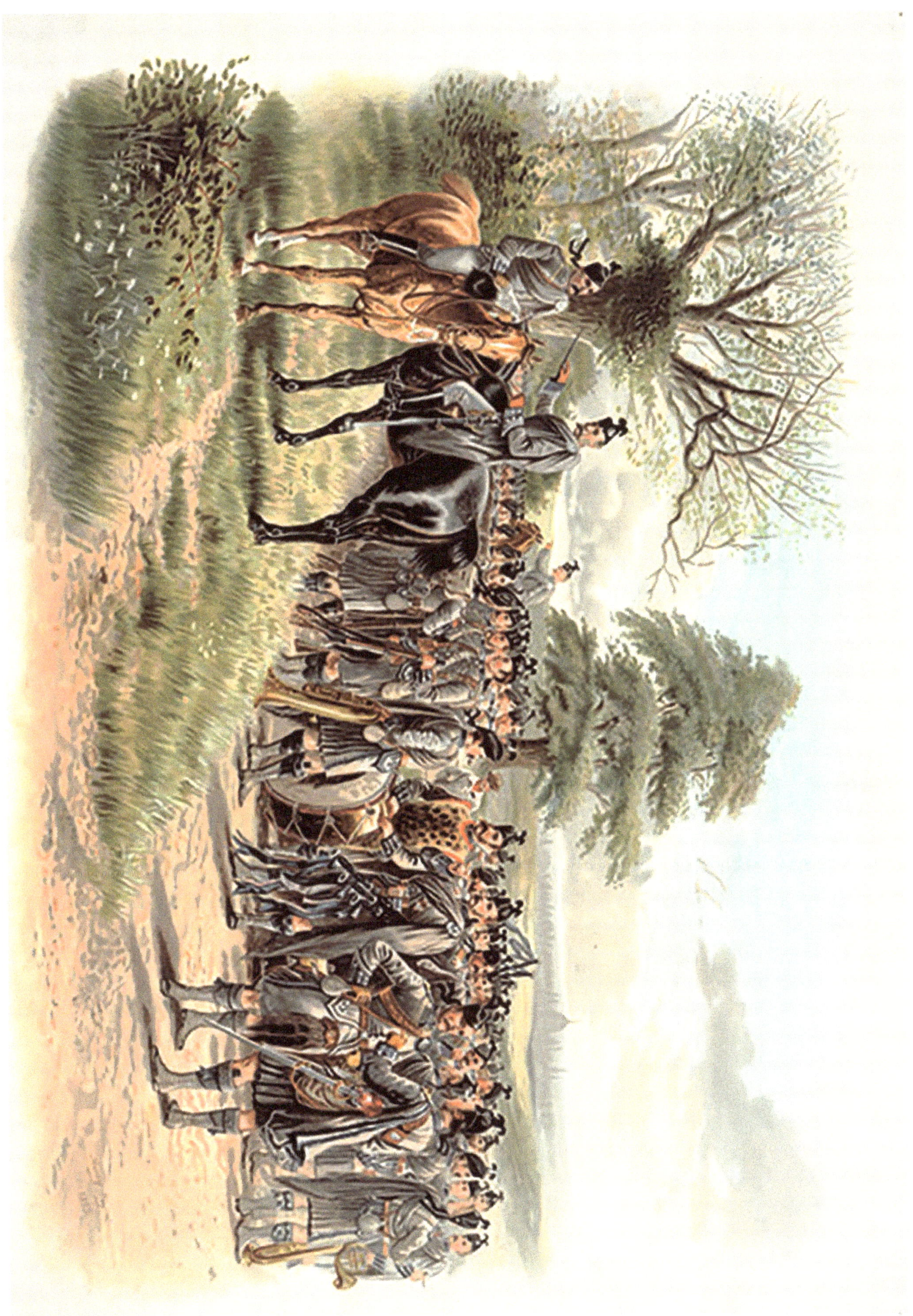

24 – 13TH MIDDLESEX RIFLE VOLUNTEER CORPS (QUEEN'S)

Original watercolour by Frank Feller featuring members of the 13th Middlesex Rifle Volunteer Corps (Queen's). The artist includes in his image the band and a member of the 'S' (Mounted Infantry) Company (right distance) and the regiment's Ambulance Section which can be seen on the high ground to the left. Much detail of the grey uniforms has been included in the painting, including the Maltese cross helmet plates, red facings, brown belts and '13 over Mx' shoulder designations.

Formed in January 1860 as the 22nd Middlesex Rifle Volunteer Corps with headquarters at Pimlico, re-numbering as 13th took place in 1880. Around the time of Frank Feller's picture the several companies were organised and designated as follows: 'A' to 'D' (Pimlico Division), 'E' and 'F (St John's Division), 'G' (St Margaret's Division), 'H' (St James's Division), 'I' and 'K' (St Martin's Division), 'L' (Schoolbread's Company), 'M' (St Clement Dane's Division), 'O' (Royal Welsh), 'R' (Greater Westminster), 'S' (Mounted Infantry) and 'T' (Cyclists). (*Image courtesy of the Anne SK Brown Military Collection, Brown University Library*)

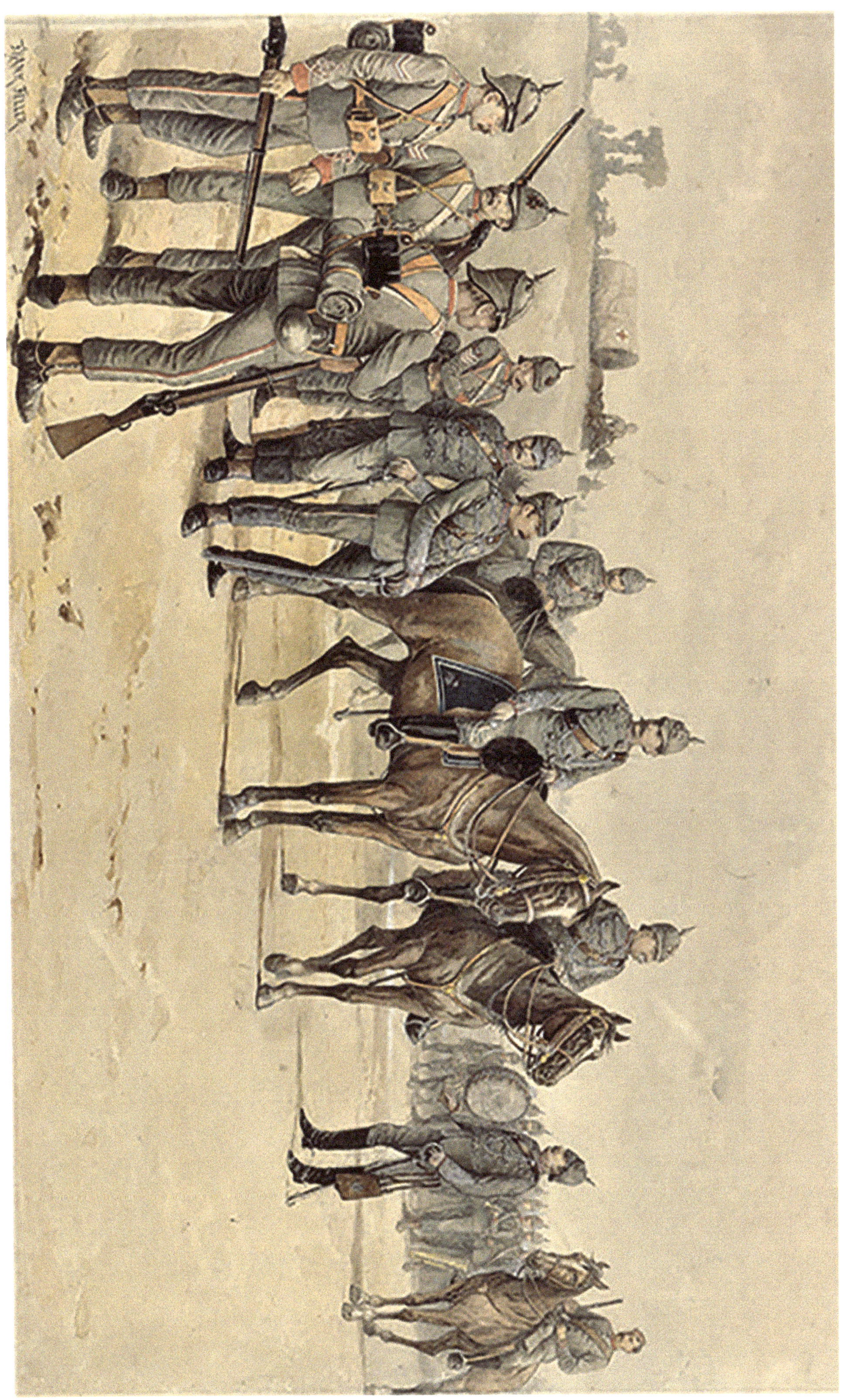

25 – CYCLIST, 13TH MIDDLESEX RIFLE VOLUNTEER CORPS

One of a set of six postcards published by the 13th Middlesex RVC featuring one of its 'T' (Cyclist) Company. An artist's signature of 'SJR' appears on some of the cards. The badge worn on the scarlet collar is a silver portcullis from the arms of Westminster. Note how the rifle is carried on the cycle and the brown leather bandolier worn over the left shoulder.

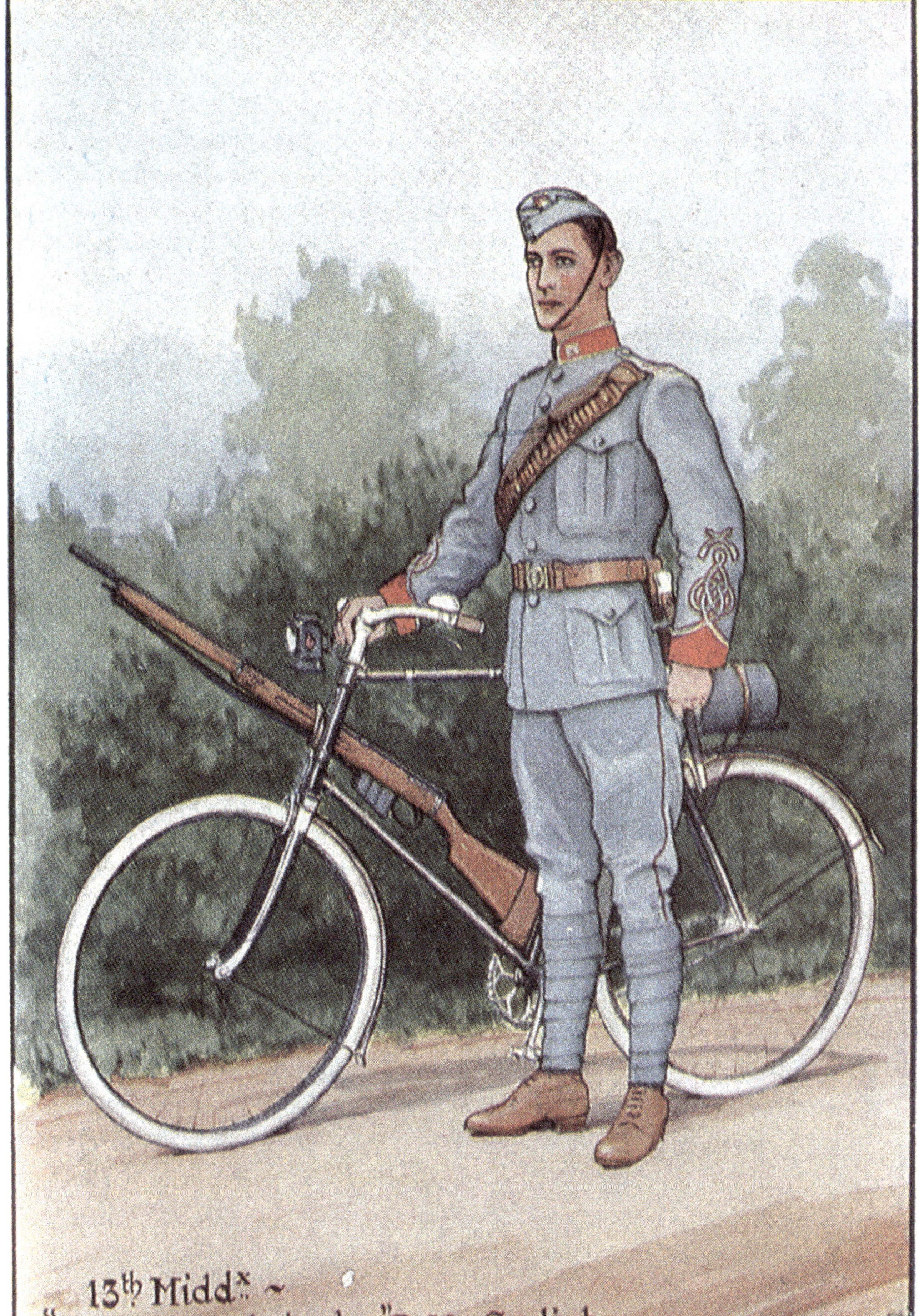

13th Middx. ~
"Queen's Westminster" R.V. Cyclist.

26 – ROYAL ENGINEERS (VOLUNTEERS)

For my 1983 publication, *Royal Engineer (Volunteers) 1859-1908*, I asked the late George Rice to come up with a suitable cover illustration. A talented and obliging artist, George presented me with a group of five figures based on individual photographs from Colonel C Cooper-King's *The British Army and Auxiliary Forces*—published by Cassell and Co in 1893. Here we have volunteer sappers in a variety of headgear. There is an officer with sword, a bandsman with trombone, and with a pickaxe, one of the engineers from the Crewe railway town in Cheshire who wore a representation of a locomotive on their collars. Always providing great detail in his paintings, the artist shows volunteers hard at work in the background.

Royal Engineers (Volunteers)

1859 – 1908

by
R.A. WESTLAKE

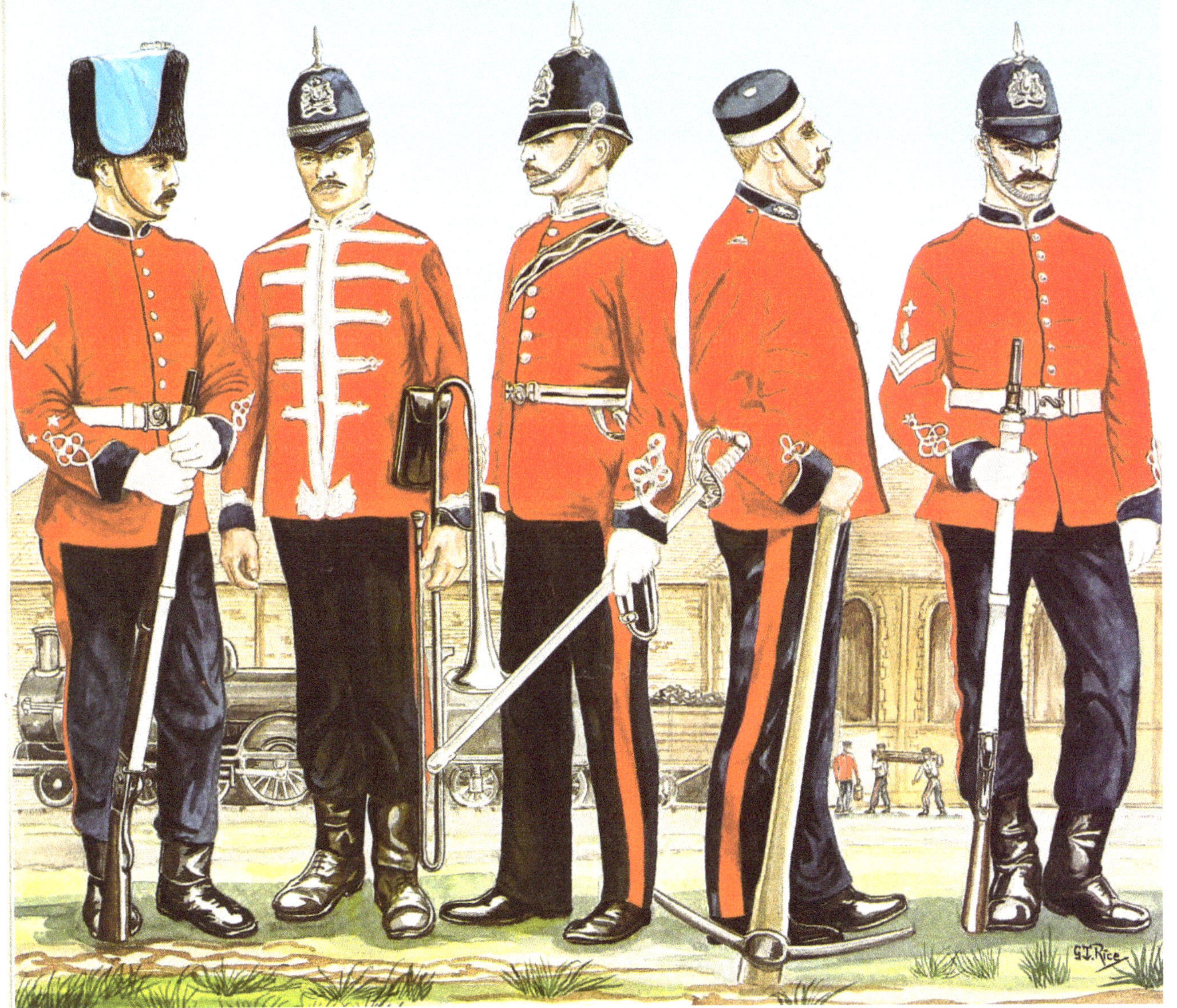

27 – THE GALLOWAY RIFLE VOLUNTEER CORPS

Plate XIX from *Records of the Scottish Volunteer Force 1859-1908*, written and illustrated by Lieutenant-General Sir James Moncrieff Grierson and published by William Blackwood & Sons in 1909. The image features three members of the corps, from left to right a sergeant of 1873-1883, lieutenant in patrol jacket 1883-1905, and a private in service dress of 1905-1908.

The battalion had originated in 1860 from the several independent rifle volunteer corps raised in the counties of Kirkcudbrightshire and Wigtownshire. Together, they were organised into an administrative battalion which in 1880 had been consolidated under the title of the Galloway Rifle Volunteer Corps with headquarters at Newton Stewart. General Grierson records that uniformity in dress was first attained on 5 December 1873 (prior to that the uniforms of each individual corps varied) 'when the whole battalion was clothed in dark grey tunics and trousers, with scarlet cuffs, collars, piping, and Austrian knot (later with black tracing all round), dark grey shakos with black ball-tuft, and black belts.' The shakos were replaced by glengarry caps in May 1883 and the drab service dress seen in the illustration came in for general wear in 1905.

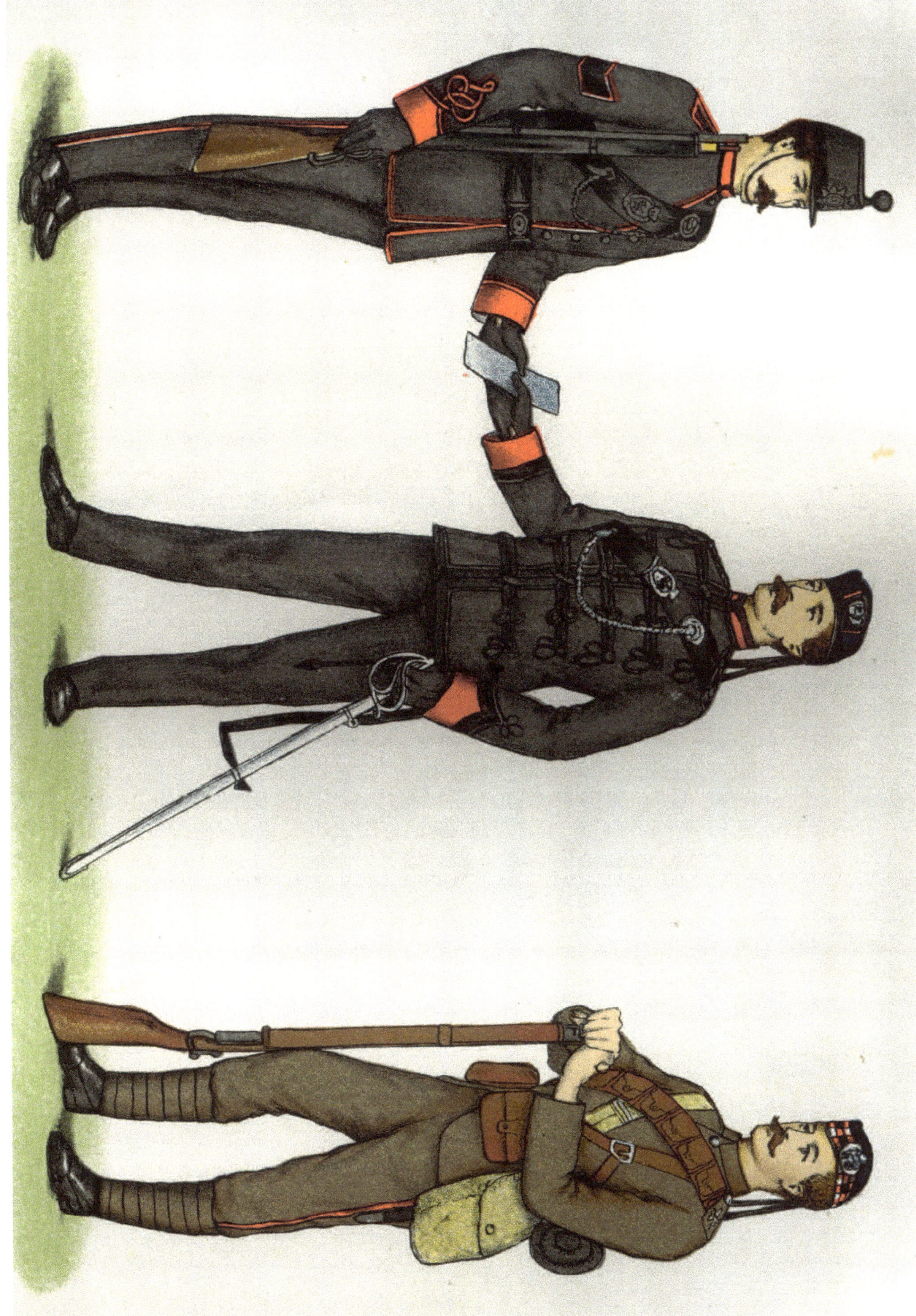

28 – ROYAL SCOTTISH REVIEW AT HOLYROOD PARK, 7 AUGUST 1860

Colour lithograph by C Schacher, printed by Schenck & McFarlane of 19 St James Square, Edinburgh and published by John Menzies of 2 South Hanover Street, Edinburgh with the caption 'Royal Scottish Volunteers Review / Holyrood Park 7th August 1860'. The print also carries the dedication, 'To Colonel McMurdo CB, the Officers and Volunteers of Scotland / this print is respectfully dedicated by their Obt Servants Schenck McFarlane'.

The review was attended by Queen Victoria who can be seen seated in a carriage on the extreme right of the picture. Lieutenant-General Sir James Moncrieff Grierson wrote of the event in 1909 mentioning how the volunteers had been conveyed to Edinburgh by rail, road and sea. Only volunteer corps took part in the event. The ground, however, was kept by the 13th Light Dragoons and 78th Regiment of Foot. A party of the Royal Company of Archers (the Queen's Bodyguard for Scotland) can just be made out standing behind the queen's carriage. Music for the march past was provided by the bands of the 29th and 78th Regiment and that of the 1st West York Rifle Militia. Behind the royal party a stand had been erected to accommodate 4,000 spectators. The total estimate for those attending, many of whom can be seen massed on the slopes of Arthur's Seat to the left, has been recorded as 200,000 to 300,000. General Grierson made a detailed record of the troops present on pages 38 to 42 of his book Records of the Scottish Volunteer Force, the total number taking part, '21,514 in 348 companies'. *(Image courtesy of the Anne SK Brown Military Collection, Brown University Library)*

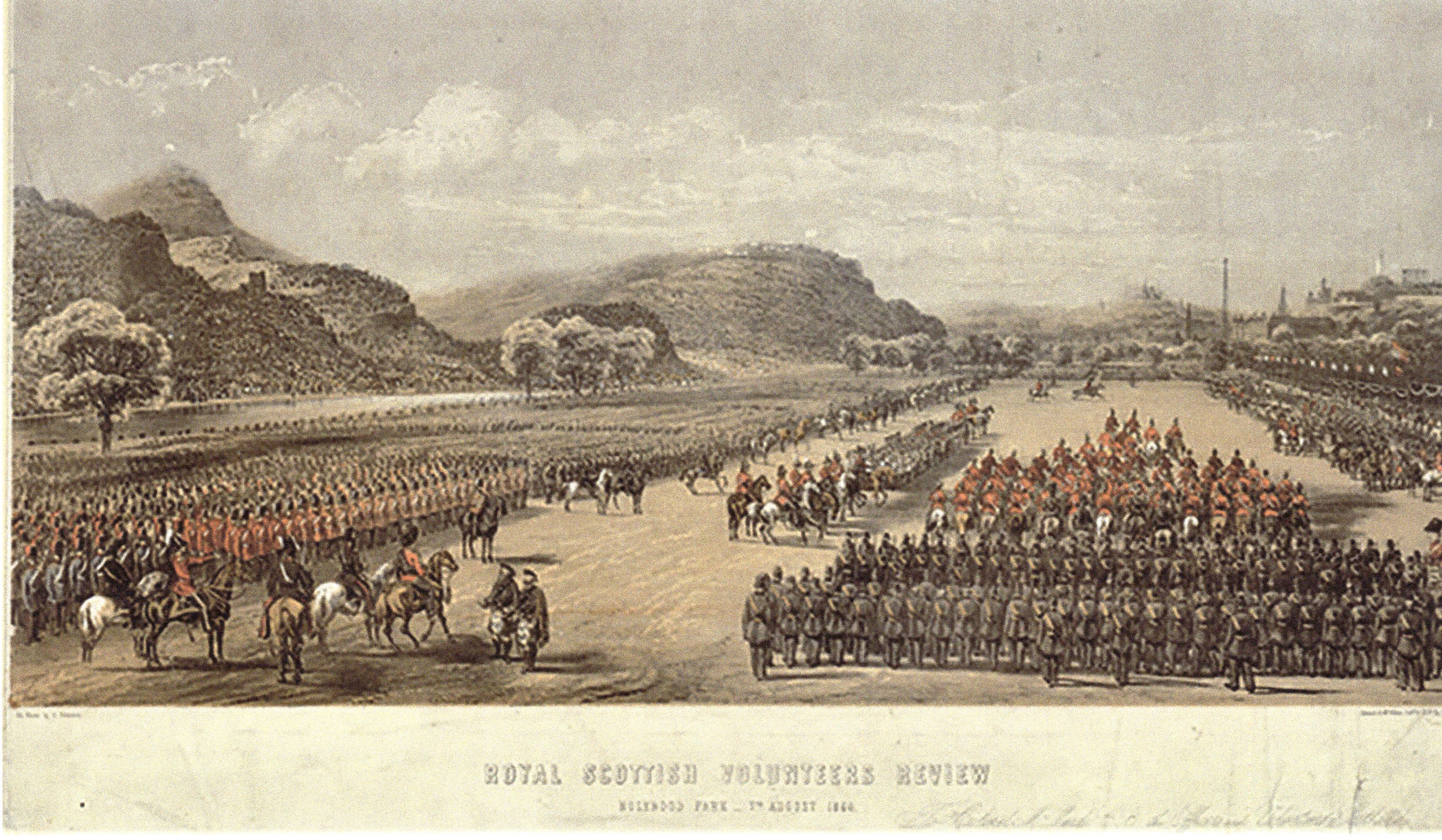

ROYAL SCOTTISH VOLUNTEERS REVIEW

HOLYROOD PARK _ 7th AUGUST 1860

29 – GRAND FIELD DAY OF THE EXETER AND SOUTH DEVON VOLUNTEER RIFLE BRIGADE

Coloured lithograph drawn by Thomas de Pomeroy, litho work by Day & Son, published with the caption, 'The First Grand Field Day Of / The Exeter And South Devon Volunteer Rifle Battalion. / In The Grounds of Torre Abbey, Torquay, July, 1855.' Placed between the wording the arms and supporters of Exeter. With a church steeple and houses of Torquay in the distance, the battalion clothed in dark green carry out numerous exercises before a vast crowd.

Although the creation of the Volunteer Force officially dates from 1859, a battalion of rifle volunteers had in fact been formed and sanctioned in South Devon, as a protection for its coast, some years before, the commissions of its officers being signed and dated by Queen Victoria on 4 January 1853. It was this battalion that in 1859 received the title of 1st Devonshire (Exeter and South Devon) Rifle Volunteer Corps and as such stood as the most senior volunteer corps in the country. (*Image courtesy of the Anne SK Brown Military Collection, Brown University Library*)

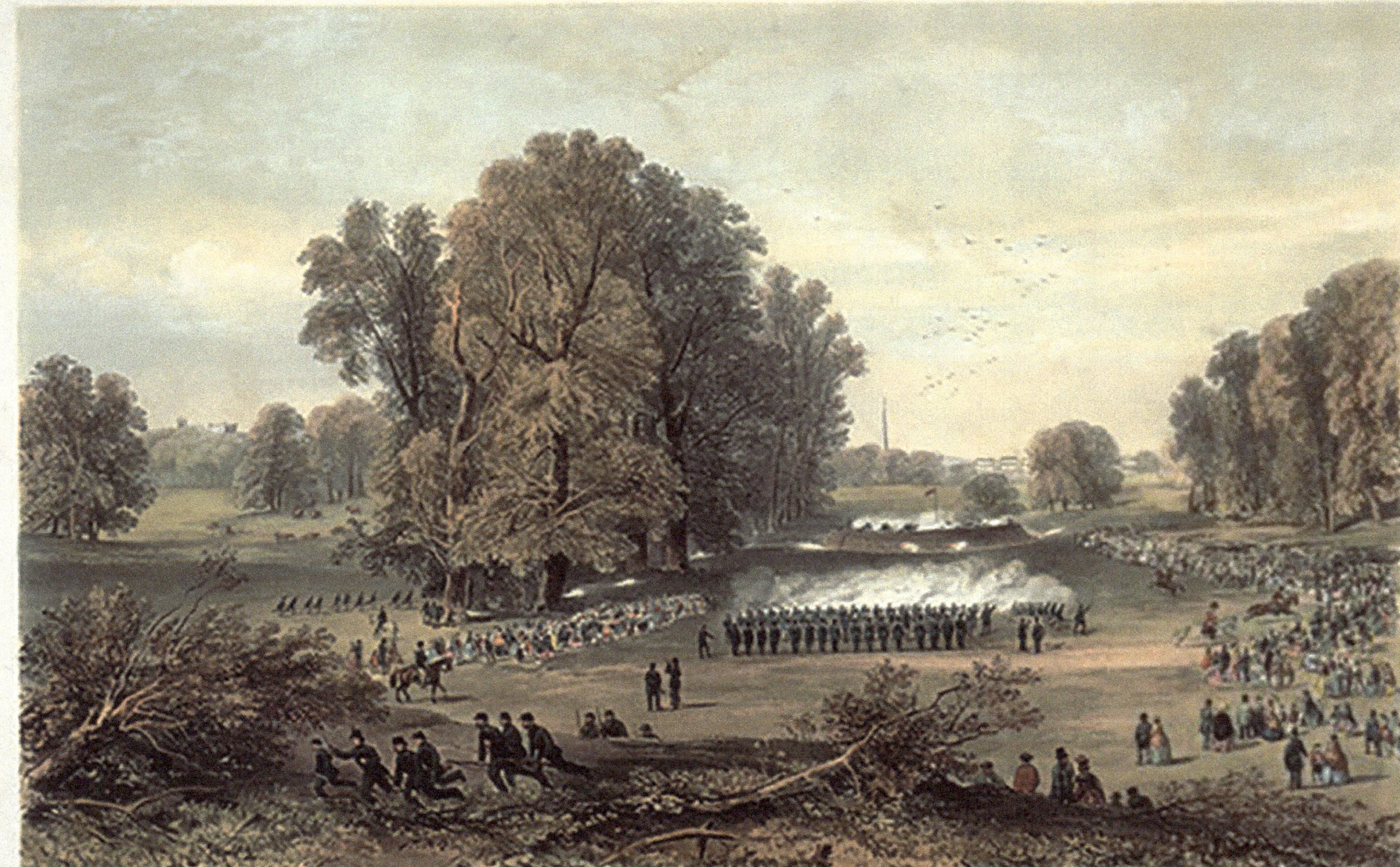
THE FIRST GRAND FIELD DAY OF
THE EXETER AND SOUTH DEVON VOLUNTEER RIFLE BATTALION.
IN THE GROUNDS OF TORRE ABBEY. TORQUAY, JULY,

30 – OXFORD UNIVERSITY RIFLE VOLUNTEERS

Colour lithograph by M & N Hanhart after William Sharpe which appeared with the following caption printed below the image, 'Oxford University Rifle Volunteers'. Between the lettering was a representation of the arms of the university with a crown above and crossed rifles behind.

The 1st (Oxford University) Rifle Volunteer Corps was formed of three companies on 8 August 1859, the establishment being raised to six before the end of the following year.

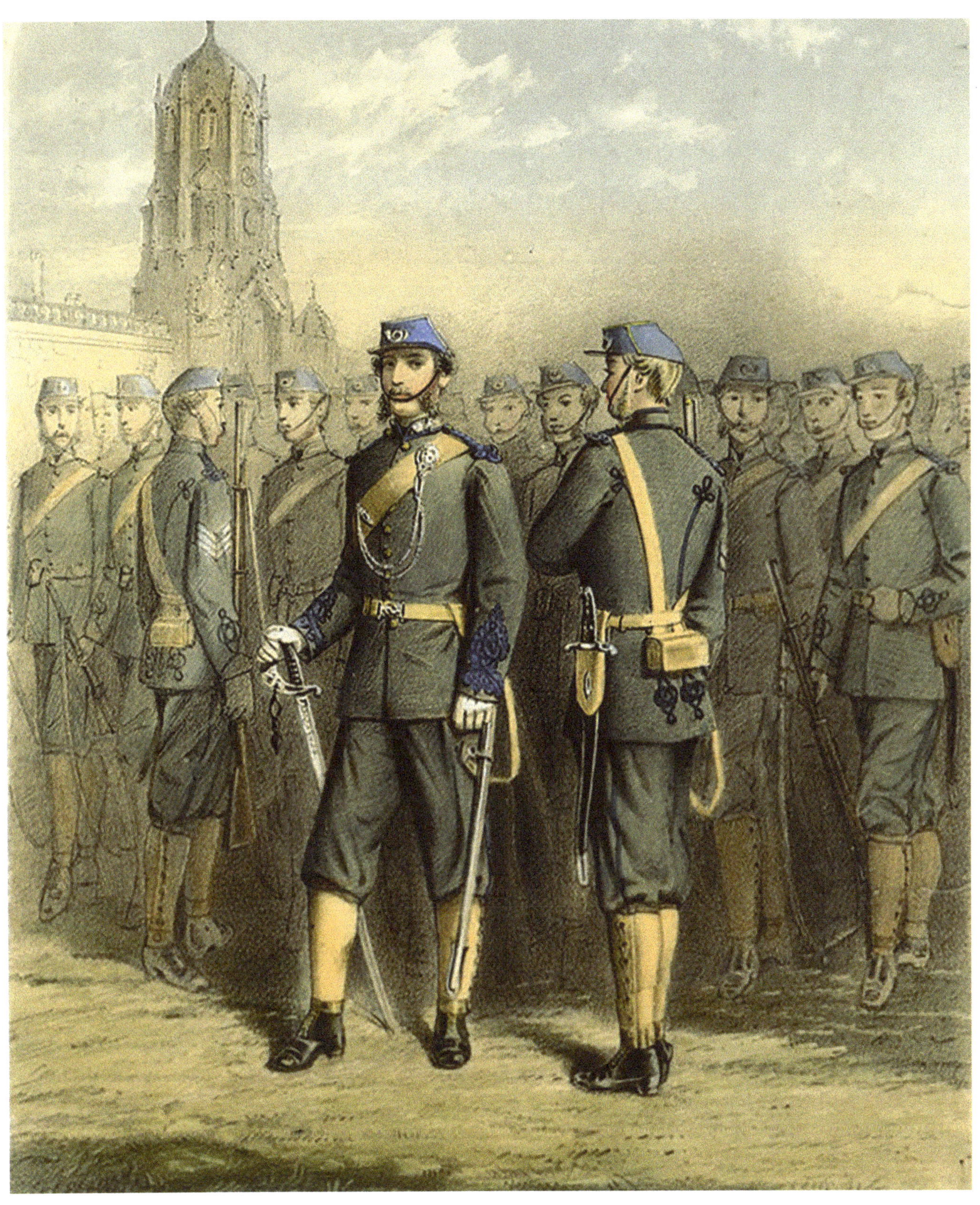

31 – OXFORD UNIVERSITY RIFLE VOLUNTEERS

Original unsigned watercolour, but noted by the Anne SK Brown Military Collection as by RC Davidson. Wearing much the same uniform as above, a shooting party is seen loading and firing across open land towards an unseen target. The artist clearly shows the blue shakos and piping worn by the corps. (*Image courtesy of the Anne SK Brown Military Collection, Brown University Library*)

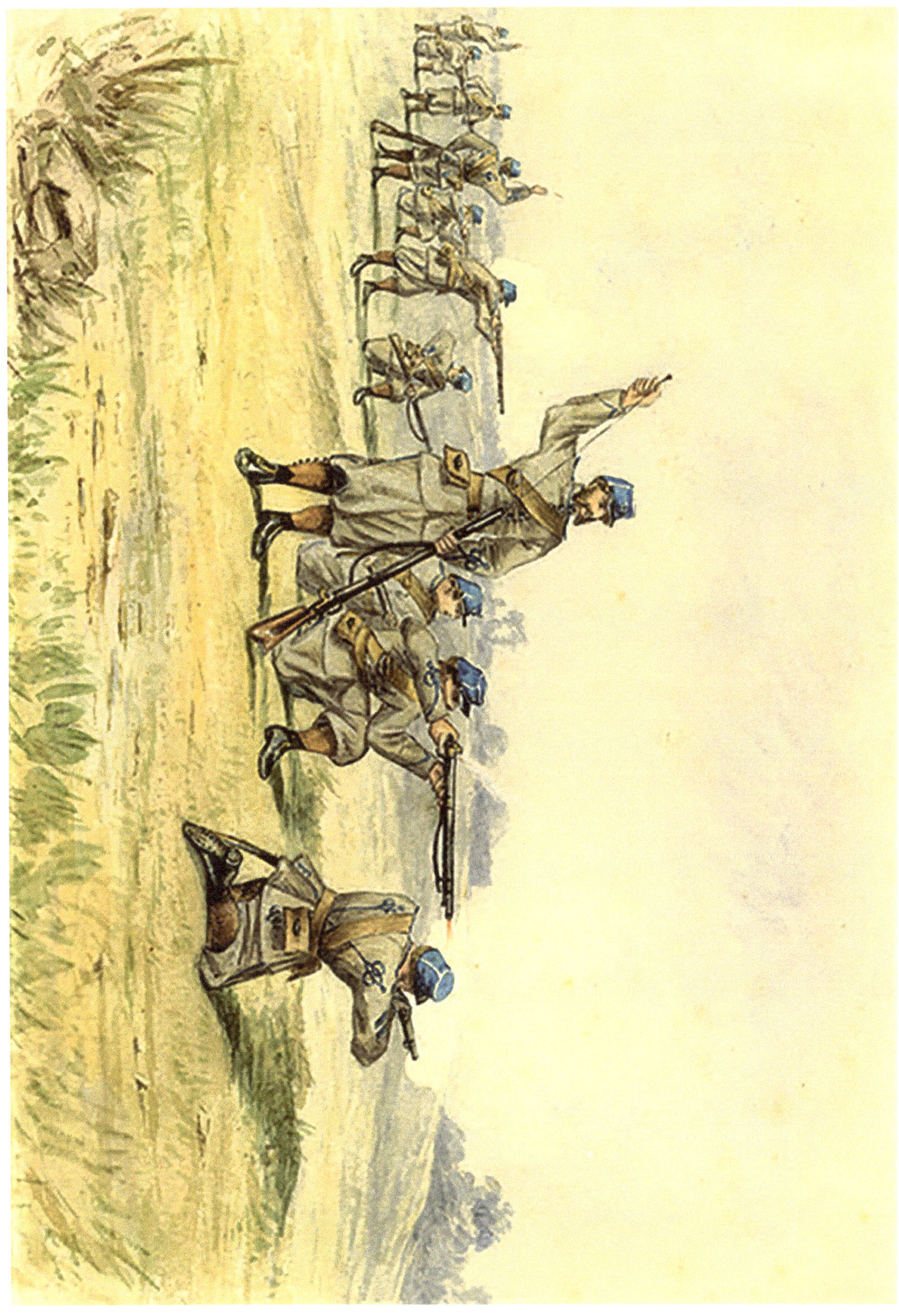

32 – SHOOTING TEAM OF THE 9TH MIDDLESEX RIFLE VOLUNTEER CORPS

Engraving from the *Illustrated London News* of 3 October 1863 published with the caption 'A Battalion Twenty of the West Middlesex Rifle Volunteers.' The signature M Jackson is just visible in the bottom right hand corner, the location identified by the poster on the shed door as Wormwood Scrubs. Behind the party, the embankment that carries the Great Western Railway's main line is just minutes out of the not-yet-a-decade-old Paddington Station. 'The Scrubs', as it is general known, is in West London and had been leased to the War Office as a military training ground in 1812.

The 9th Middlesex (West Middlesex) Rifle Volunteer Corps was formed with headquarters at Lord's Cricket Ground on 14 October 1859. Originally six companies, there were eight by April 1860 under the command of Lieutenant-Colonel Commandant the Rt Hon Granville Augustus William, Baron Radstock. The uniforms were grey with scarlet facings, the headdress also grey and with a wide scarlet band.

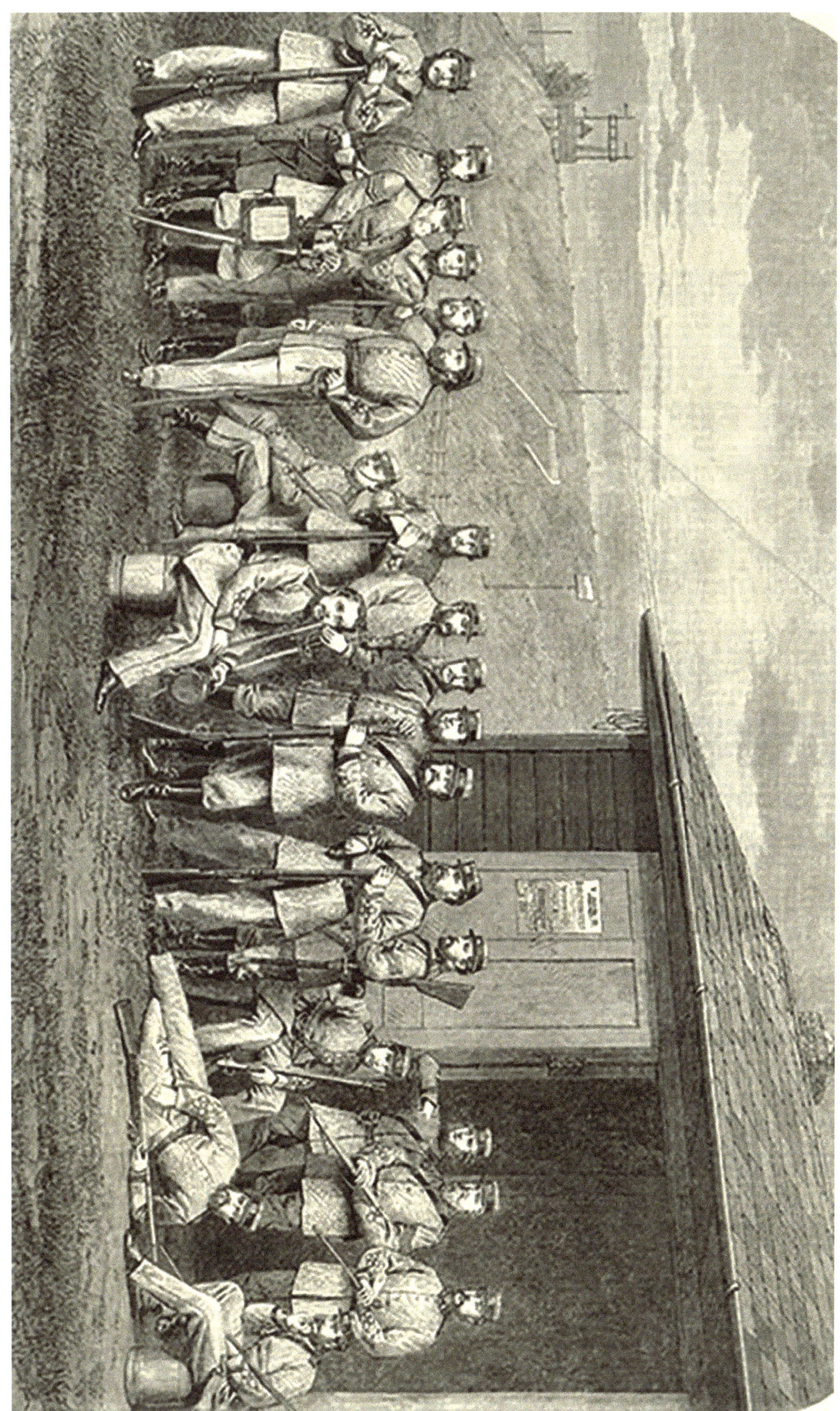

33 – BUT THIS IS MERE DIGRESSION FROM MY PURPOSE

Plate from *Military Misreadings of Shakspeare* by Major Seccombe published c1880 by George Routledge & Sons containing twenty-four colour lithographs linked with one line quotes from the works of William Shakespeare. The spelling of the Bard's name in the title is that of its author who appears on the title page as 'Major Seccombe.' The plates take the form of cartoons, each measuring eight by six-and-half inches; their captions occupy the whole page opposite. Throughout the book a number of images represent no particular formation, just groups of uniformed characters, but many can indeed be associated with certain regiments thanks to the artist's attention to detail. Could members of those regiments possibly be offended? Well, Major Seccombe must certainly have been aware of this as after the contents pages of his book he adds, 'In submitting these Military Caricatures to the public, the artist would disclaim all intention of reflecting upon the powers of equitation, etc., of any particular corps, the uniforms of the regiments represented having been chosen solely for variety.' Major Seccombe was in fact Major Thomas Strong Seccombe (1840-1913), a British Royal Artillery Officer.

No particular regiment can be established in this instance, but the uniform clearly suggests a member of one or other of the many hundreds of grey-clad rifle volunteer units that existed between 1859 and 1908. These were Britain's part-time 'amateur' soldiers, men who after a day's work at office, bank, factory or mine gave up their spare time so as to be on hand should the country be invaded. While learning the skills of soldiering, much fun would be poked as they acquired knowledge in drill, marching and the essential art of musketry. From Major Seccombe's cartoon, it would seem that accuracy at the butts on this occasion had left much to be desired. 'But this is mere digression from my purpose'; the rifleman draws from his knowledge of *Henry IV, Part II, Act iv, Scene 1* in his excuse, as a local farmer holds up blooded evidence of misguided marksmanship.

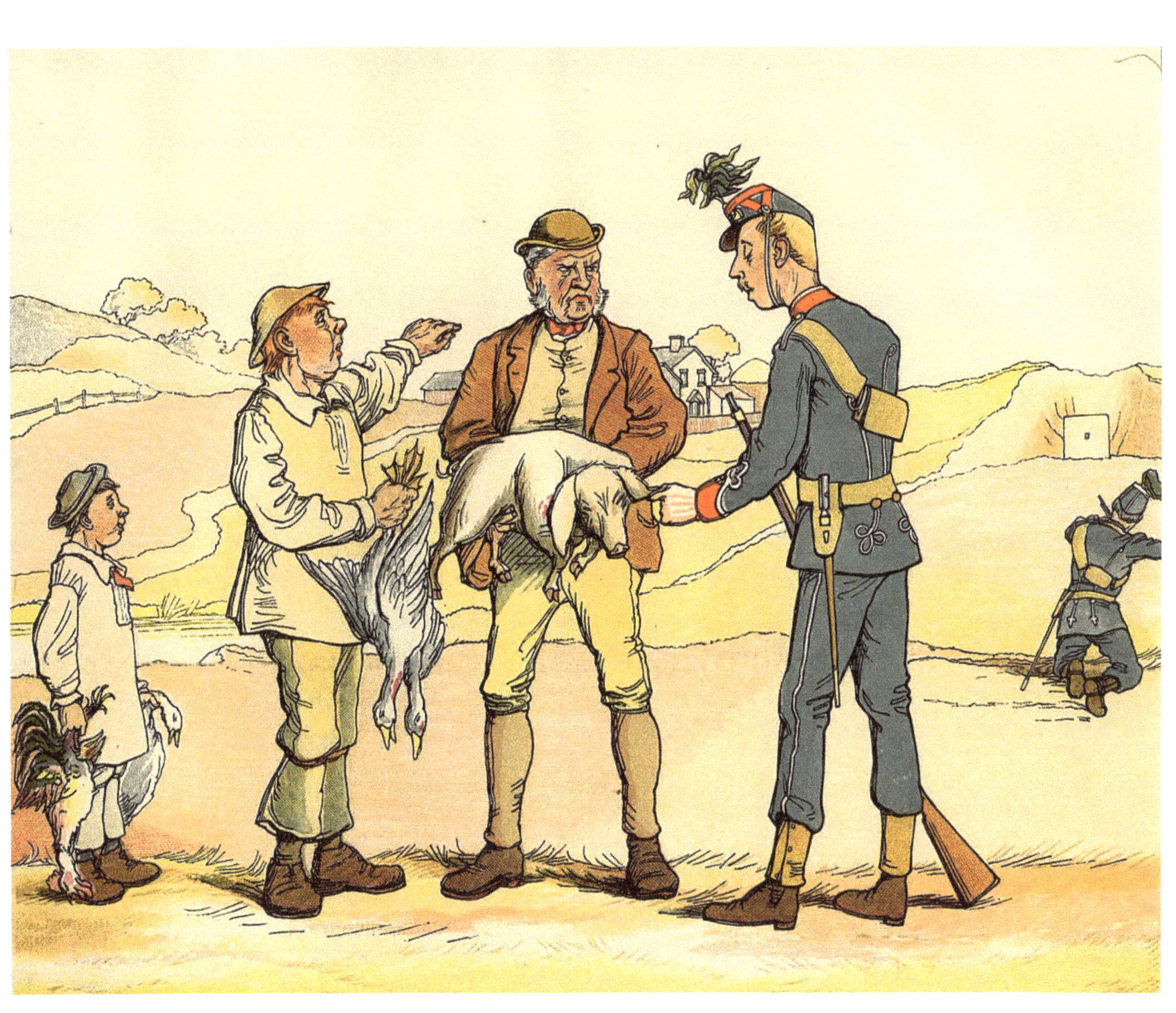

34 – RIFLE UNIFORM (ARTILLERY)

One of two coloured lithographs after Thomas Guerin and printed by M & N Hanhart of 22a Mortimer Street, London c1860, illustrating volunteer uniforms 'Recommended by the War Office'. This one is captioned 'Rifle Uniform (Artillery)'. Featured in this plate is a rifle volunteer, his suggested uniform being dark grey with nine buttons down the front. The collar, edging down the front and along the bottom edge of the coat and the Austrian knot on the sleeves are of a dark colour and edged with yellow. Cord, buttoned, shoulder straps are visible. The trousers have the same colours down the outer seams. The short grey cap has a black peak with yellow piping. Black belts are being worn, one across the left shoulder, the other holding a small ammunition pouch and bayonet frog. The belt is fastened with an oblong plate with bugle horn badge. In the background, a faint figure stands holding a rifle with bayonet fixed.

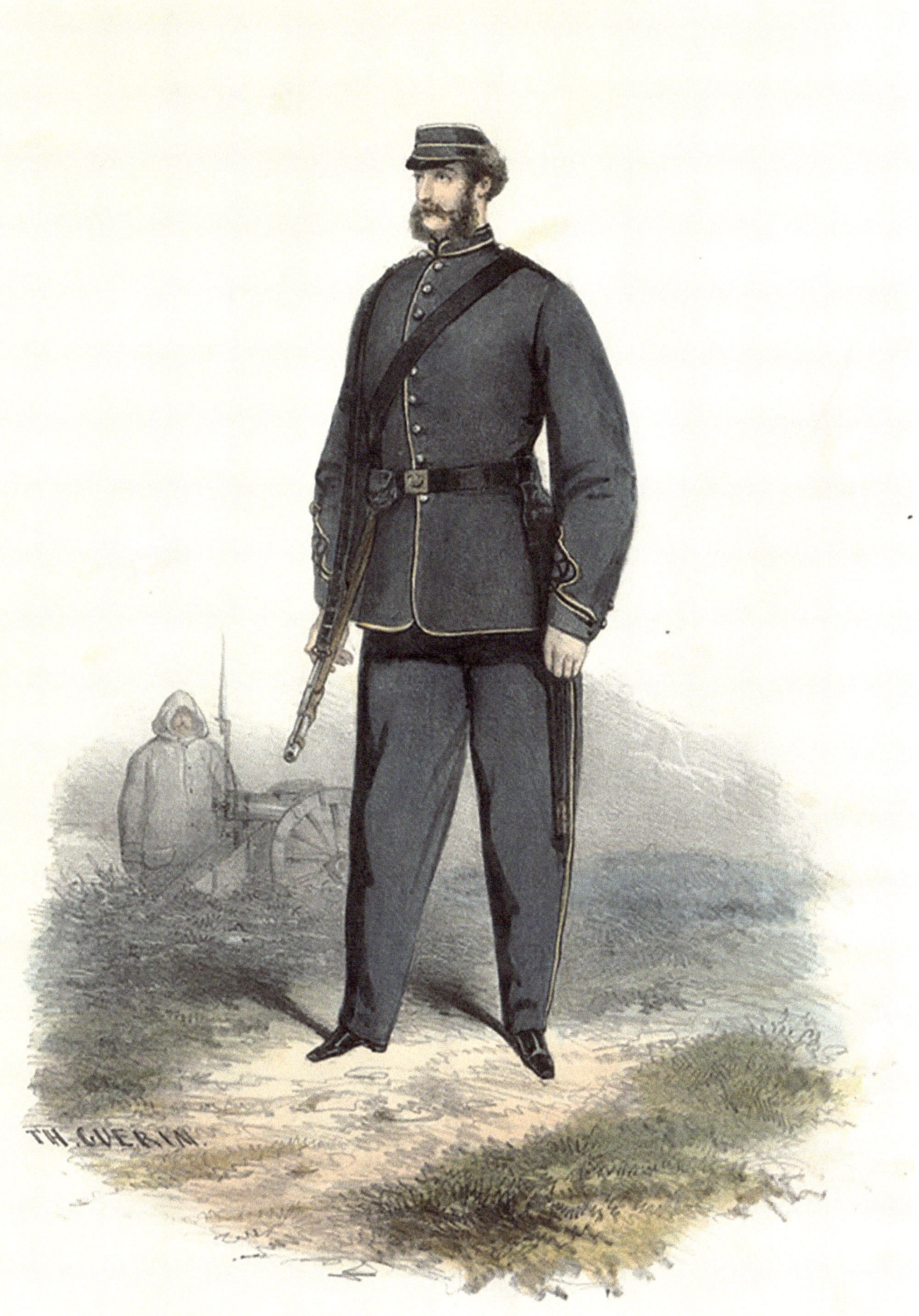
TH. GUERIN.

35 – RIFLE UNIFORM

One of two coloured lithographs after Thomas Guerin and printed by M & N Hanhart of 22a Mortimer Street, London c1860, illustrating volunteer uniforms 'Recommended by the War Office'. This is one captioned 'Rifle Uniform'. Featured in this plate is a rifle volunteer, his suggested uniform being light grey with nine buttons down the front. The collar, edging down the front and along the bottom edge of the coat and the Austrian knot on the sleeves are of a dark colour and edged with yellow. The trousers have the same colours down the outer seams. The short grey cap has a black peak with yellow piping. Brown belts are being worn, one across the left shoulder, the other holding a small ammunition pouch and bayonet frog. One of the figures in the background is similarly dressed, a second pouch visible on the right hip. Another seems dressed for cold weather and wears a short overcoat with six buttons and a cape, together with brown gaiters up to just below the knee. (*Image courtesy of the Anne SK Brown Military Collection, Brown University Library*)

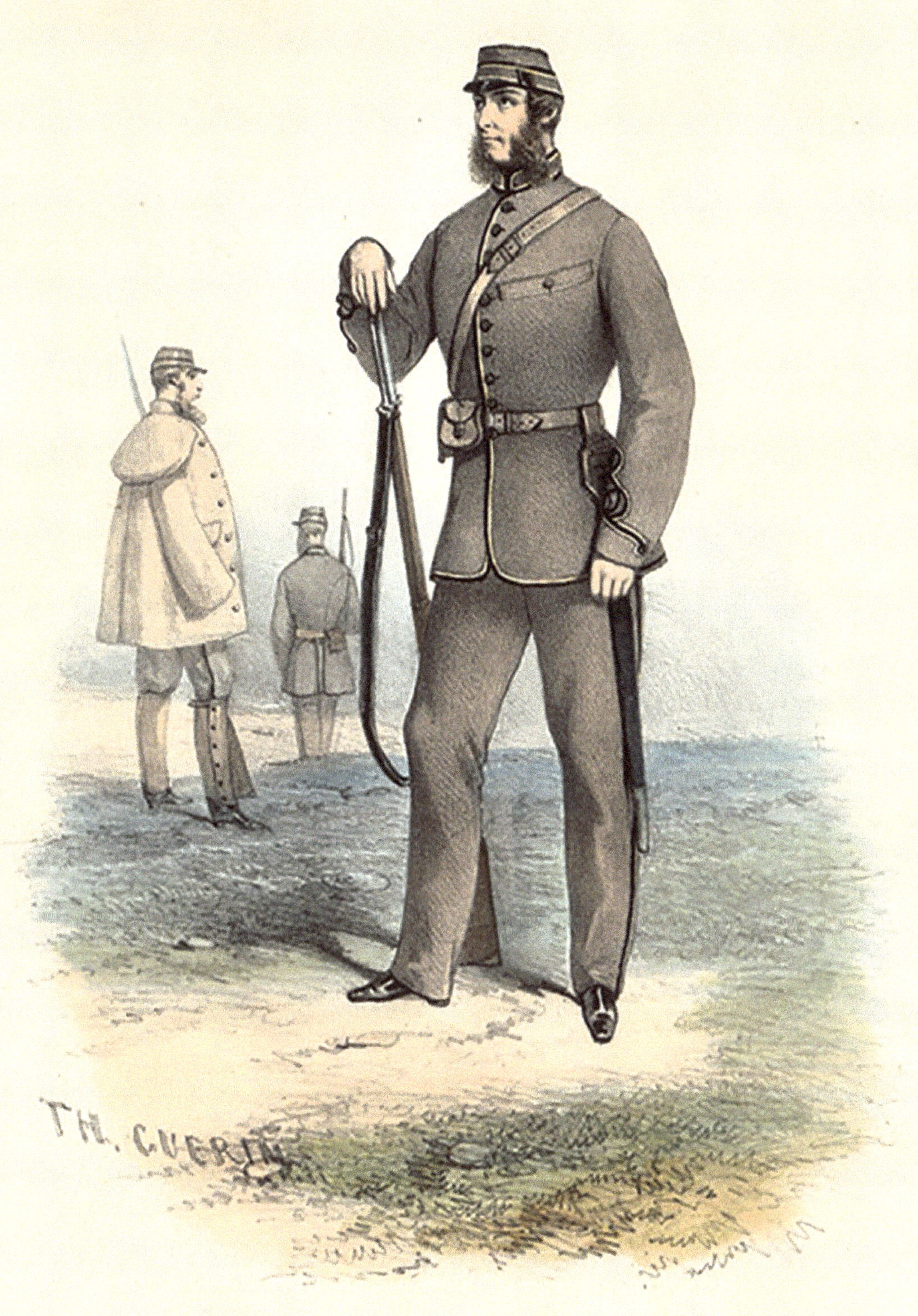

RIFLE UNIFORM.

(RECOMMENDED BY THE WAR OFFICE.)

PUBLISHED 22A MORTIMER ST. LONDON.
M & N. HANHART, IMPT

36 – WEST MIDDLESEX RIFLES

Coloured lithograph after Thomas Guerin and printed by M & N Hanhart of 22a Mortimer Street, London c1860 with the caption 'West Middlesex Rifles (Marylebone)'.

The 9th Middlesex (West Middlesex) Rifle Volunteer Corps was formed with headquarters at Lord's Cricket Ground on 14 October 1859. Originally six companies, there were eight by April 1860 under the command of Lieutenant-Colonel Commandant the Rt Hon Granville Augustus William, Baron Radstock. (*Image courtesy of the Anne SK Brown Military Collection, Brown University Library*)

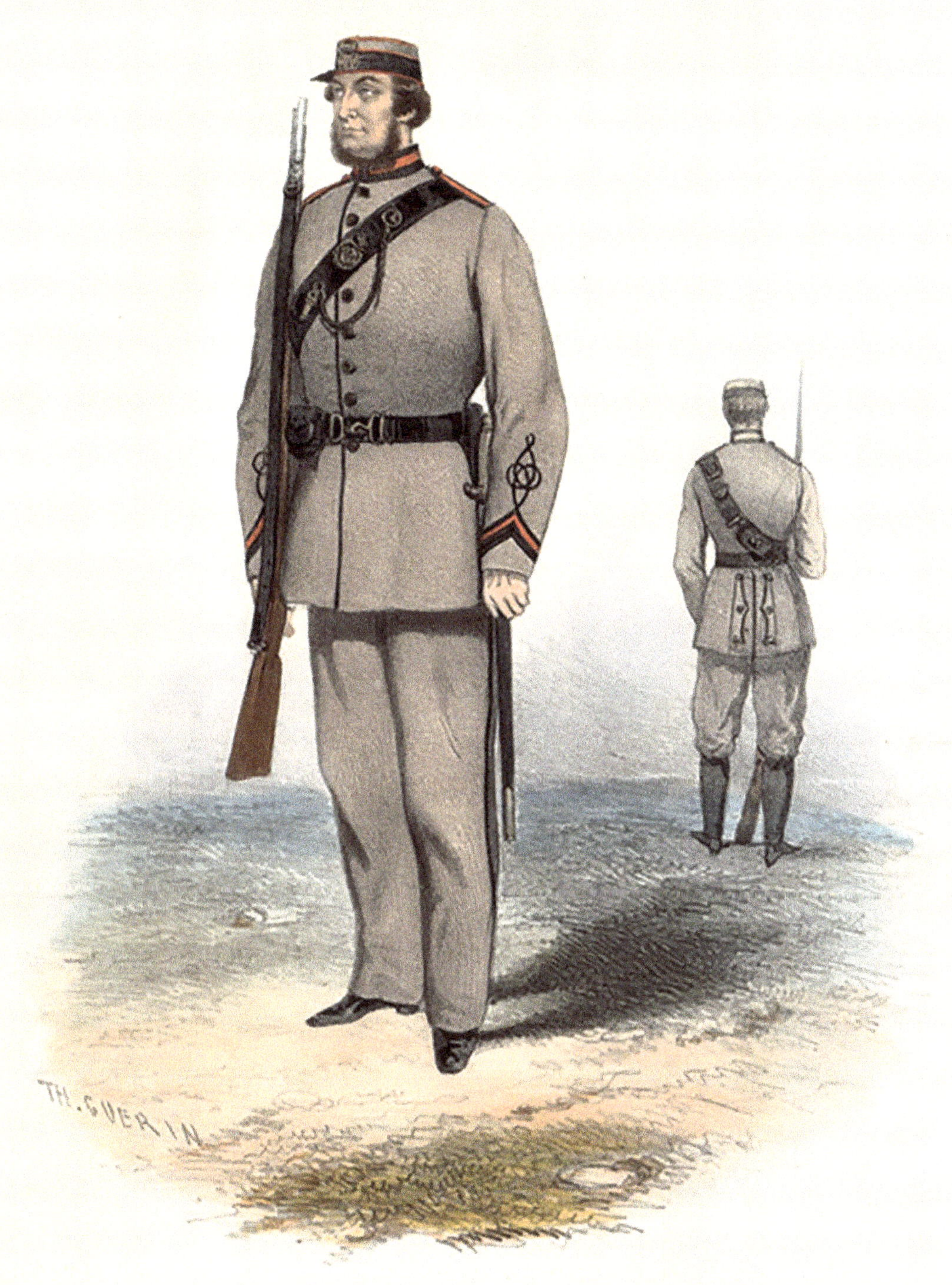

WEST MIDDLESEX RIFLES.

(MARYLEBONE.)

37 – 3rd VOLUNTEER BATTALION KING'S OWN SCOTTISH BORDERERS

Plate XVIII from *Records of the Scottish Volunteer Force 1859-1908* written and illustrated by Lieutenant-General Sir James Moncrieff Grierson, published in 1909 by William Blackwood & Sons. The plate shows from left to right: a private (1860-1876) and lieutenant (1876-1888) of the 1st Administrative Battalion of Dumfrieshire Rifle Volunteers, and a corporal in marching order (1888-1900) and sergeant in review order (1900-1908), both of the 3rd Volunteer Battalion King's Own Scottish Borderers.

All corps formed within the county of Dumfriesshire joined the 1st Admin Battalion which became the new 1st corps in 1880, the 3rd Volunteer Battalion King's Own Scottish Borderers in 1887. Formation and organisation went as follows:

1st (1860-1880)—Formed as one company at Dumfries with Patrick Dudgeon as captain, James Sloan, lieutenant and Henry Gordon, ensign. All three officers held commissions dated 25 February 1860. Increased to two companies in 1872 and became 'A' and 'B' Companies of the new 1st Corps in 1880.

1st (1880-1908)—The 1st Admin Battalion was formed with headquarters at Dumfries on 4 January 1862 and consolidated in April 1880 as the new 1st Corps with ten companies: 'A' and 'B' Dumfries (late 1st Corps), 'C' Thornhill (late 2nd Corps), 'D' Sanquhar (late 3rd Corps), 'E' Penpont (late 4th Corps), 'F' Annan (late 5th Corps), 'G' Moffat (late 6th Corps), 'H' Langholm (late 7th Corps), 'I' Lockerbie (late 8th Corps), 'K' Lochmaben (late 9th Corps).

Became a volunteer battalion (without change of title) of the Royal Scots Fusiliers in 1881 but transferred to King's Own Scottish Borderers with title 3rd (Dumfries) Volunteer Battalion in 1887. The change was notified in General Order 181 of December. In March 1885 'E' Company was absorbed into 'C' as a section and at the same time a new 'E' was formed at Ecclefechan. 'K' Company moved to Canonbie in December 1888.

2nd—Formed as one company at Thornhill with William Maxwell as captain, Thomas Dickson, lieutenant and William Smith, ensign. All three held commissions dated 6 March 1860. Became 'C' Company of the new 1st Corps in 1880.

3rd—Formed as one company at Sanquhar with James Kennedy as captain, Hamilton D B Hystop, lieutenant and William Otto Macqueen, ensign. All three held commissions dated 28 February 1860. Became 'D' Company of the new 1st Corps in 1880.

4th—Formed as one company at Penpont, two miles south-west of Thornhill, with John G Clark as captain, Robert Kennedy, lieutenant and George Dalziel, ensign. All three held commissions dated 29 February 1860. Became 'E' Company of the new 1st Corps in 1880.

5th—Formed as one company at the seaport of Annan with Frederick McConnell as captain, William Dobbie, lieutenant and William Roxburgh, ensign. All three held commissions dated 14 June 1860. Became 'F' Company of the new 1st Corps in 1880.

6th—Formed as one company at Moffat with George G H Johnstone as captain, Thomas Welsh, lieutenant and Walter Johnstone, ensign. All three officers held commissions dated 20 June 1860. Became 1880 'G' Company of the new 1st Corps in 1880.

7th—Formed as one company at Langholm with Captain William E Malcolm commissioned on 1 June 1860. Became 'H' Company of the new 1st Corps in 1880.

8th—Formed as one company at Lockerbie with Osmond de H Stewart as captain, Thomas Stobart, lieutenant and William Wallace, ensign. All three officers held commissions dated 20 June 1860. Became 'I' Company of the new 1st Corps in 1880.

9th—Formed as one company at Lochmaben, eight miles north-east of Dumfries, with John Johnstone as captain, James Watt, lieutenant and James Johnstone, ensign. All three officers held commissions dated 18 February 1861. Became 'K' Company of the new 1st Corps in 1880.

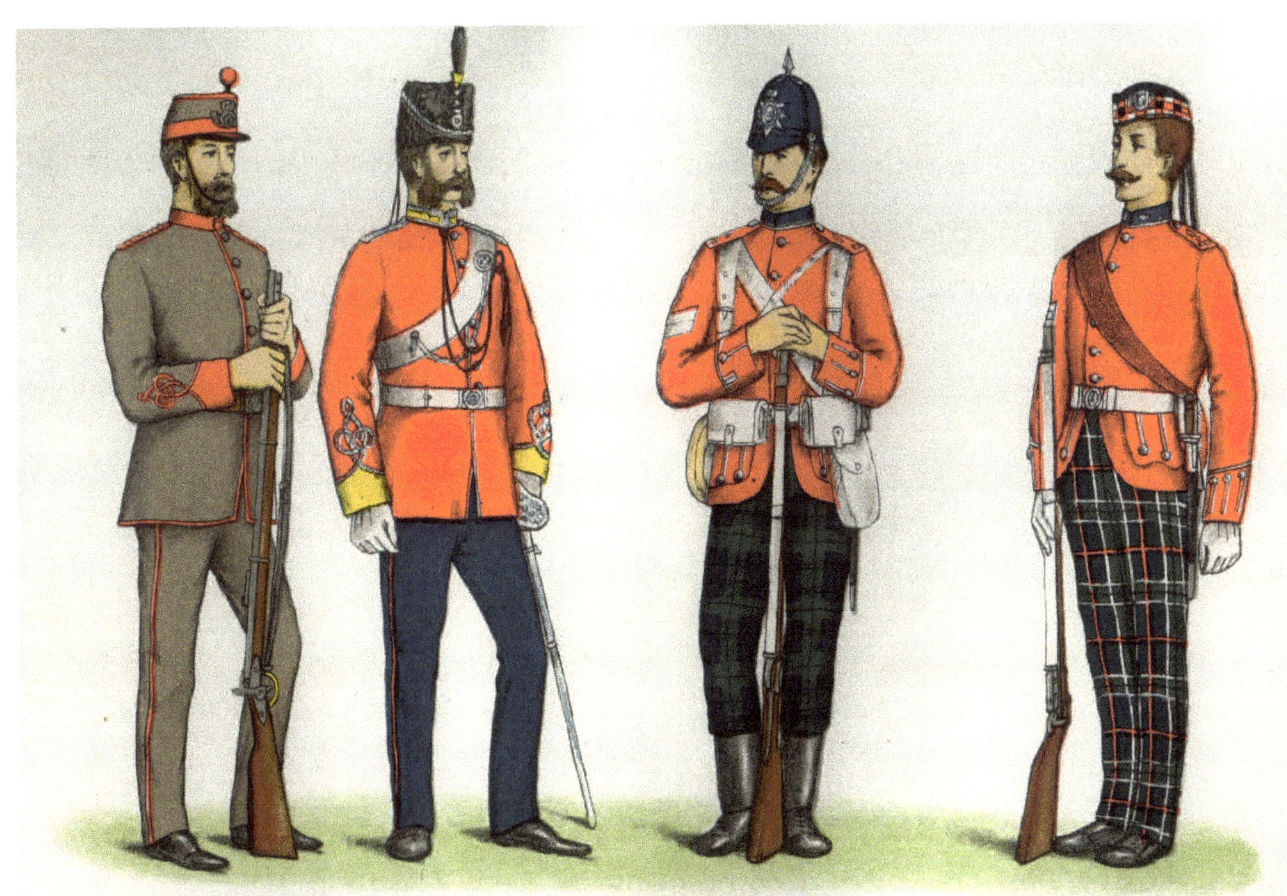

38 – REVIEW AT AINTREE

Colour lithograph published by Thomas Morgan Jr & Co entitled 'Review at Aintree'. The print carries the name of Colonel McMurdo, CB, inspector general of volunteer reviewing officer, Lieutenant-Colonel James Bourne of the 4th Lancashire Artillery Volunteers and Major Harman, assistant inspector of volunteers. Also shown is a list of the corps present, together with the names of their commanding officers and mention is made of the several artillery and rifle volunteers from Cheshire who were there keeping the ground. Below this, the following dedication: 'This Print is by permission dedicated to Lieut. Col. James Bourne, 4t L.A.V. / by his very obedient Servants / Thomas Morgan Junr. And Co.' Watched by large crowds packing the stands, the 4th Lancashire Artillery Volunteers in their blue uniforms, black busbies and red plumes, head the parade. (*Image courtesy of the Anne SK Brown Military Collection, Brown University Library*)

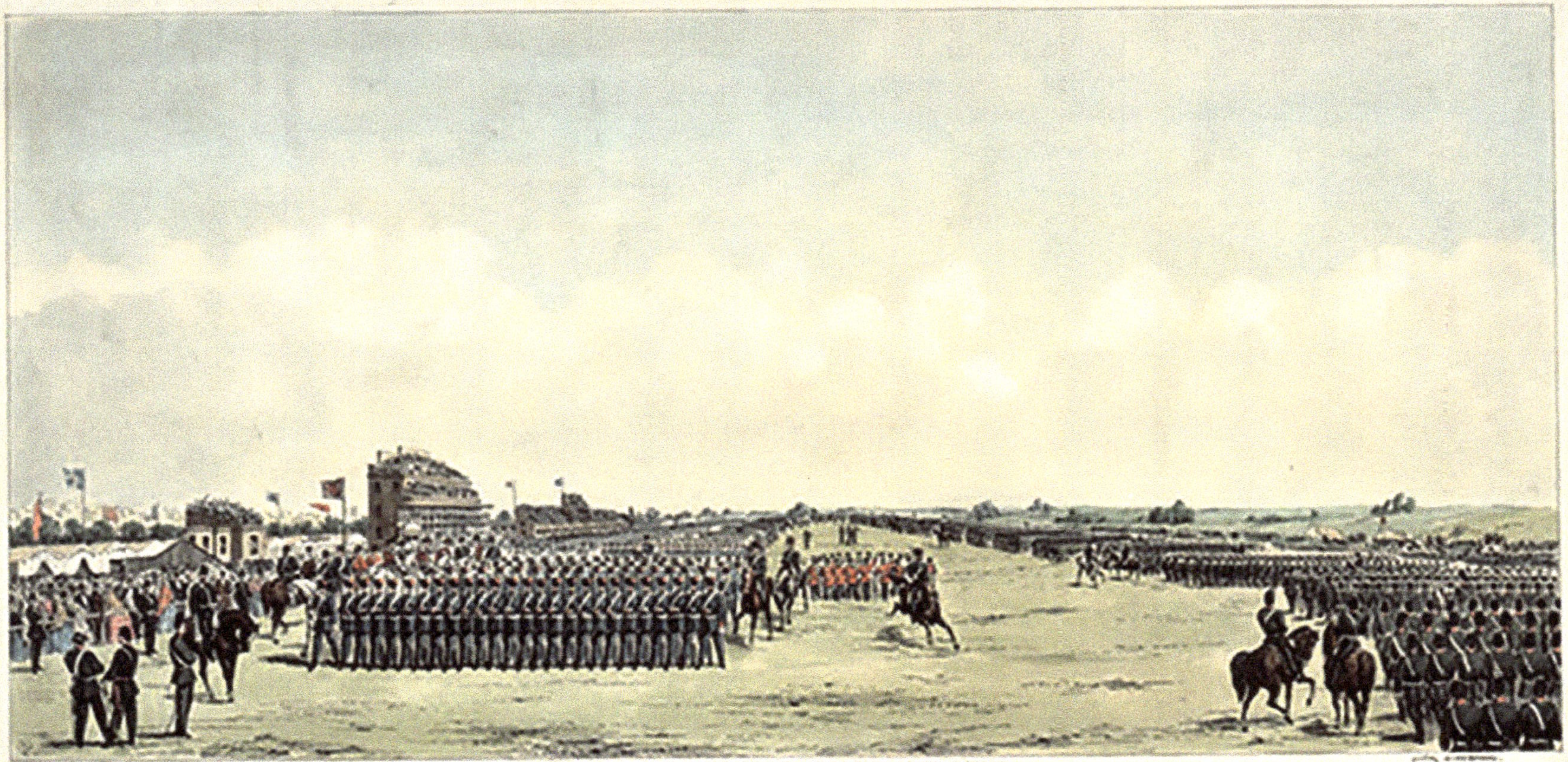

COL. [illegible] C.B. INSPECTING GENERAL OF VOLUNTEERS REVIEWING OFFICER.

LIEUT. COL. JAMES BOURNE 4TH LANCASHIRE ARTILLERY VOLUNTEERS COMMANDING.

MAJOR [illegible] ASSISTANT INSPECTOR OF VOLUNTEERS.

REVIEW AT AINTREE

Artillery Brigade.

Rifle Brigade.

This Print is by permission dedicated to Lieut. Col. James Bourne 4th L.A.V. by his very obedient Servants Thomas Morgan Junr. and Co.

39 – PATTERN OF ARTILLERY UNIFORM

Colour aquatint from Rudolph Ackermann's 'Costumes of the Volunteer Corps, drawn by Orlando Norie, engraved by James Harris and published by Rudolph Ackermann at his Eclipse Sporting & Military Gallery, 191 Regent Street 16 February 1860. Below the print, 'Pattern of Artillery Uniform. / Recommended by the Committee on Volunteer Clothing.' The print shows three figures dressed in dark blue jackets and trousers with scarlet piping and black gaiters. (*Image courtesy of the Anne SK Brown Military Collection, Brown University Library*)

Rr. Ackermann's Costumes of the Volunteer Corps No. 4.

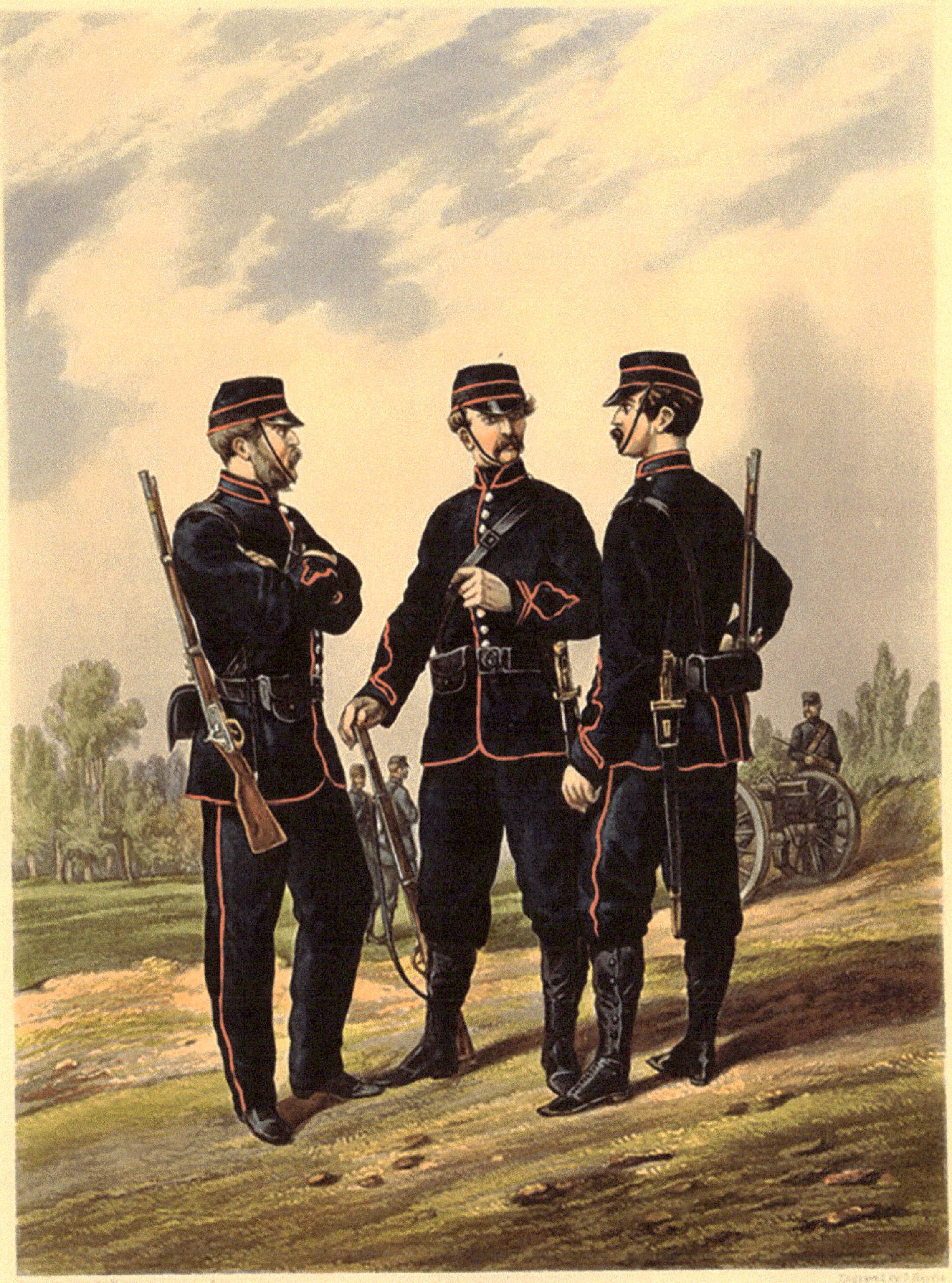

Pattern of Artillery Uniform.

Recommended by the Committee on Volunteer Clothing.

40 – ROBERT LOYD LINDSAY, VC

Colour lithograph drawn from life on stone by Henry Joseph Fleuss and engraved by Vincent Brooks. The print was published with the following caption, 'Robert Loyd Lindsay, V.C. / Late Lt. Col Scot Fus. Gds. / Lieut. Col. Commandant of the Berkshire V.R.C. and / Lt Commt. Of the Overstone Moulton mounted V.R.C.'

Formed with headquarters at Reading on 10 September 1859, the 1st Berkshire Rifle Volunteer Corps soon comprised three companies under the overall command of Major Commandant Robert James Loyd-Lindsay, former lieutenant colonel Scots Fusilier Guards and winner of the Victoria Cross at the Crimea. Loyd-Lindsay later took command of the 1st Admin Battalion, the three 1st Corps companies after that being commanded by Captains Sir Claudius S Paul Hunter, Charles Stephens and William Martin Atkins.

The Overstone and Moulton Mounted Rifles had been formed by Lieutenant-Colonel Robert Lloyd Lindsay in March 1860 and was raised mainly from local farmers and members of the Pytchley Hunt. With just forty volunteers on the strength, the colonel's commission was only as a lieutenant. As Lord Wantage, he noted in his memoir that the corps was drilled in his park at Overstone in 'their scarlet Norfolk jackets and grey breeches'. The corps was disbanded in November 1869.

The colonel is seen wearing a grey unform with scarlet piping all around a green collar, on the shoulder straps, cuffs and trouser seams. The grey cap has a green band edged with scarlet. Several medals are being worn, the crimson ribbon of the Victoria Cross just visible behind a black pouch-belt.

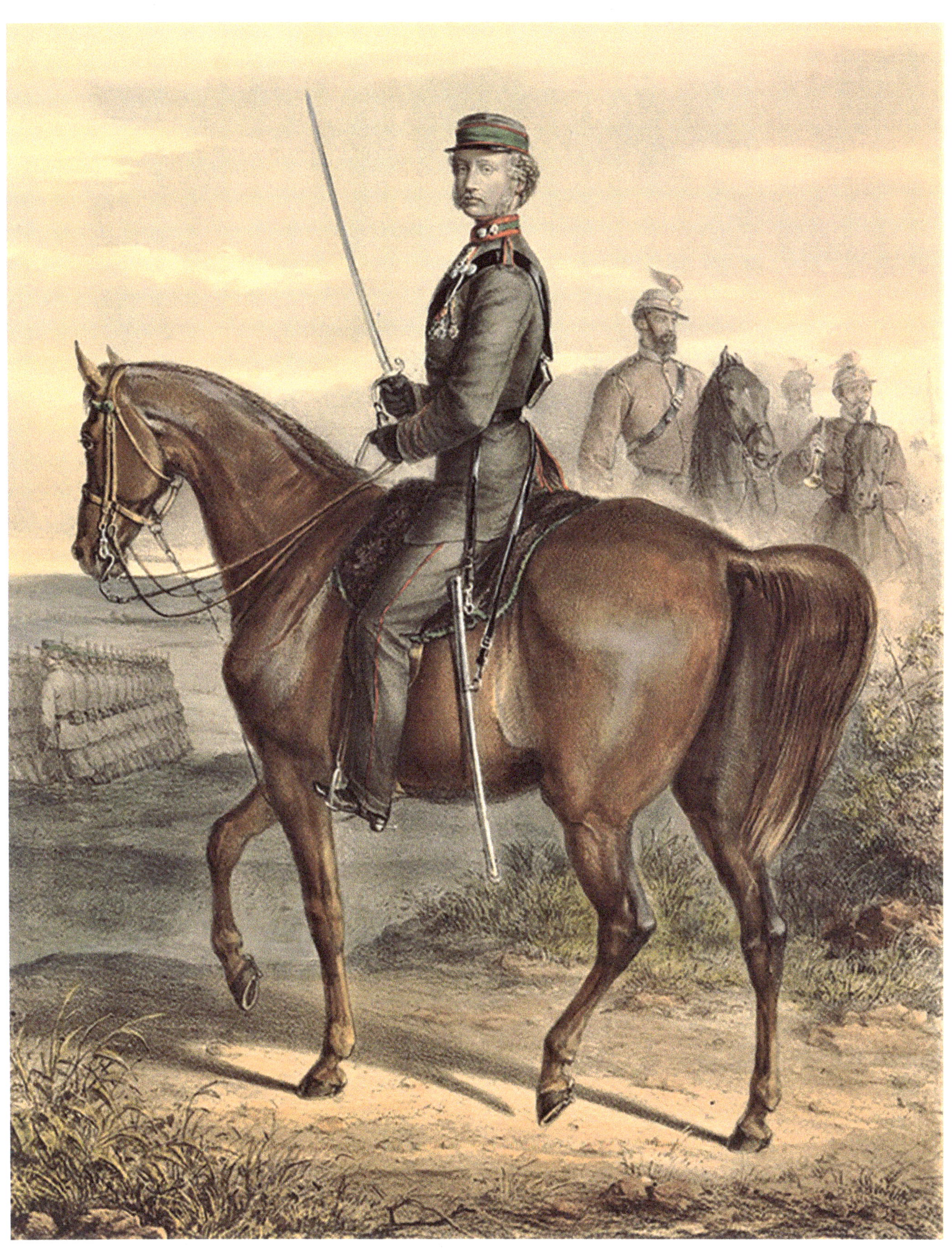

41 – 1st MIDDLESEX LIGHT HORSE VOLUNTEERS

Original watercolour painting by Orlando Norie features two officers of the 1st Middlesex Light Horse Volunteers wearing green uniforms with scarlet facings. Formed at Tattersall's Horse Sale Yard at Hyde Park Corner in January 1861, the 1st within a few months had absorbed the 2nd Middlesex Light Horse at St James's Place. Unofficially the corps was known as the 1st Metropolitan Light Horse. Disbandment was in 1866. (*Image courtesy of the Anne SK Brown Military Collection, Brown University Library*)

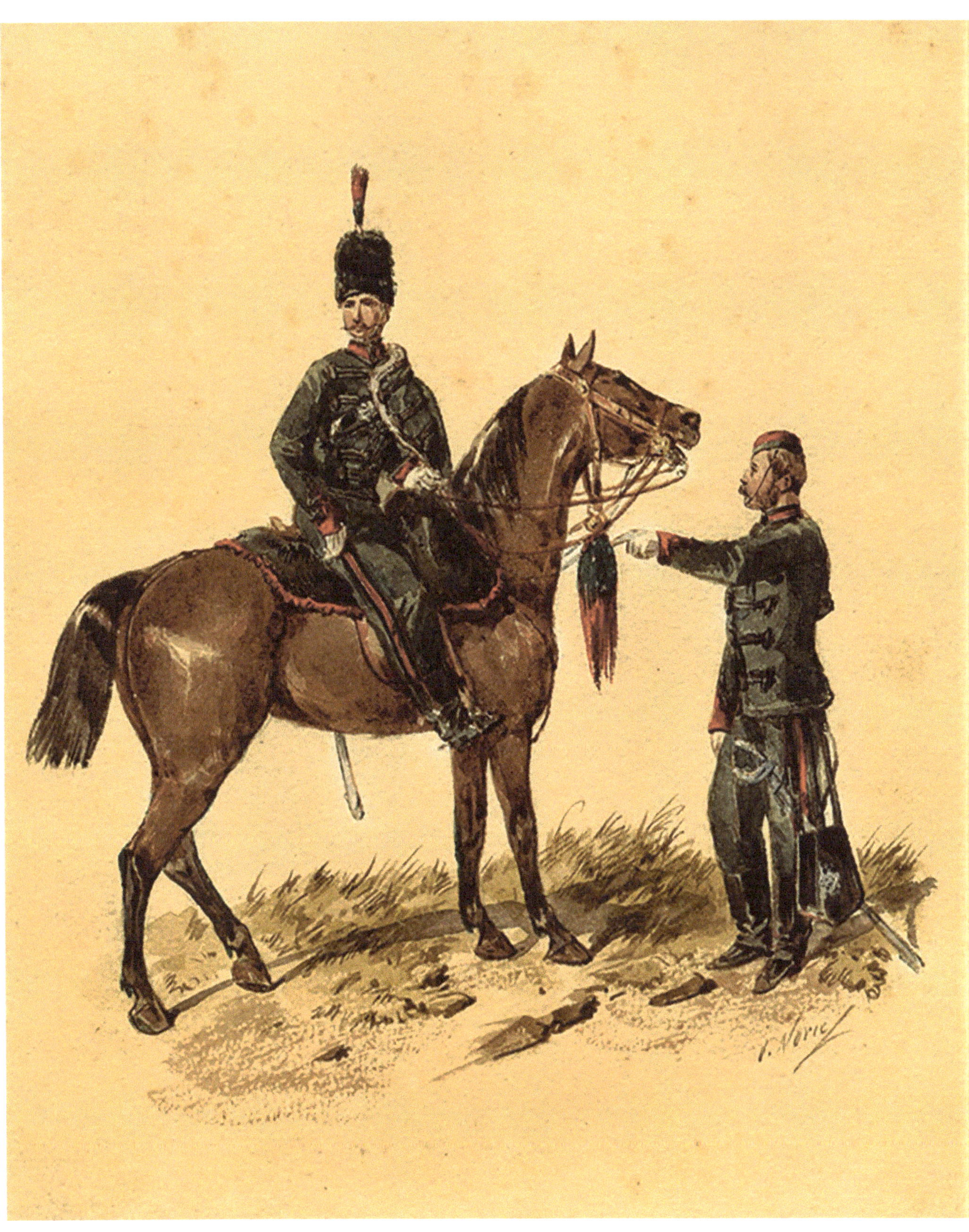

42 – 1st LANARKSHIRE VOLUNTEER RIFLE CORPS

Plate XX from *Records of the Scottish Volunteer Force* written and illustrated by Lieutenant-General Sir James Moncrieff Grierson and published in 1909 by William Blackwood & Sons.
The six figures are captioned from left to right as: 'Private 1st (1st Western) LRC 1859', 'Private 1864', 'Field Officer 1868', 'Private 1874', 'Private 1890' and 'Private 1908'.

Sir Archibald Islay Campbell, Bt was gazetted as lieutenant-colonel in command of the 1st Lanarkshire RVC with effect of 6 March 1860, this having been formed by the amalgamation of the following Glasgow corps: 1st, 2nd, 9th, 11th, 15th, 17th, 18th, 33rd, 39th, 50th, 53rd, 63rd, 72nd, 76th, 77th and 79th, a total of sixteen companies that in June 1860 were formed into two battalions of eight each: 1st Battalion: No 1 Company (late 1st Corps), No 2 Company (late 9th Corps), No 3 Company (late 11th Corps), No 4 Company (late 15th Corps), No 5 Company (late 17th Corps), No 6 Company (late 33rd Corps), No 7 Company (late 39th Corps), No 8 Company (late 79th Corps). 2nd Battalion: No 9 Company (late 2nd Corps), No 10 Company (late 18th Corps), No 11 Company (late 50th Corps), No 12 Company (late 53rd Corps), No 13 Company (late 63rd Corps). No 14 Company (late 72nd Corps), No 15 Company (late 76th Corps), No 16 Company (late 77th Corps).

In 1863 No 11 Company was disbanded and in the same year No 14 was absorbed into No 15. In 1864 No.7 was absorbed by No 3 and the remaining companies were lettered: 'A' to 'G', for the 1st Battalion and 'K' to 'Q' for the 2nd. The latter only numbered six companies, the letter 'O' not being used. There was a reduction in strength in 1870, 'K', the old University Company, being absorbed into 'Q' which had originated as the old 77th Corps and in part made up from university members. A new 'K' and an 'O' Company were added in 1878, but the former was re-lettered as 'I' and another 'K' formed in 1881. 'H' Company was formed and added in 1881, the 1st Corps then becoming (without change of title) a volunteer battalion of the Cameronians (Scottish Rifles). The corps carried out its first drills on the Burbank ground in Great Western Road, building there in 1866-67 a drill hall at the cost of £1250. Later, new headquarters were built at 261 West Princess Street, the cost this time being £16,000. Associated with the 1st Corps since its formation in 1902 was the High School Glasgow Cadet Corps.

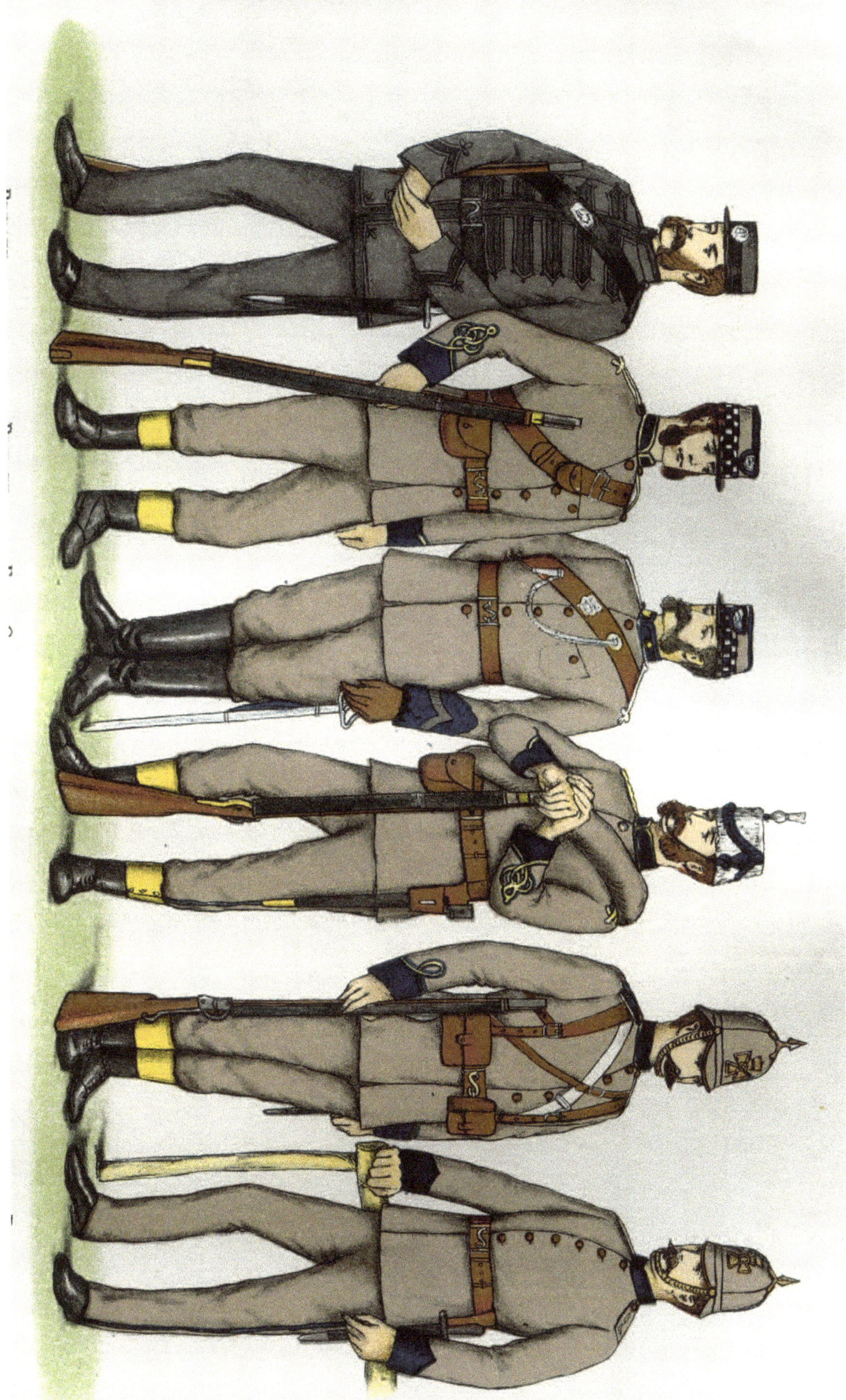

43 – THE BRITISH VOLUNTEERS MARCH

Music sheet illustration for 'The British Volunteers March' composed, arranged and dedicated to members of the Volunteer Force by Alfred Cobby. The work was published in London by Robert Cocks & Co of New Burlington Street off Regent Street, the illustration Concanen & Lee, printing by Stannard & Dixon. Three examples of volunteers are illustrated.

Composer Alfred Cobby from Bognor in Sussex was a well-known organ builder and music teacher and for a number of years was the organist at Christ Church in St Marylebone, London. Robert Cocks & were also well known and are noted as being of 'special appointment' to Queen Victoria and the Emperor Napoleon III.

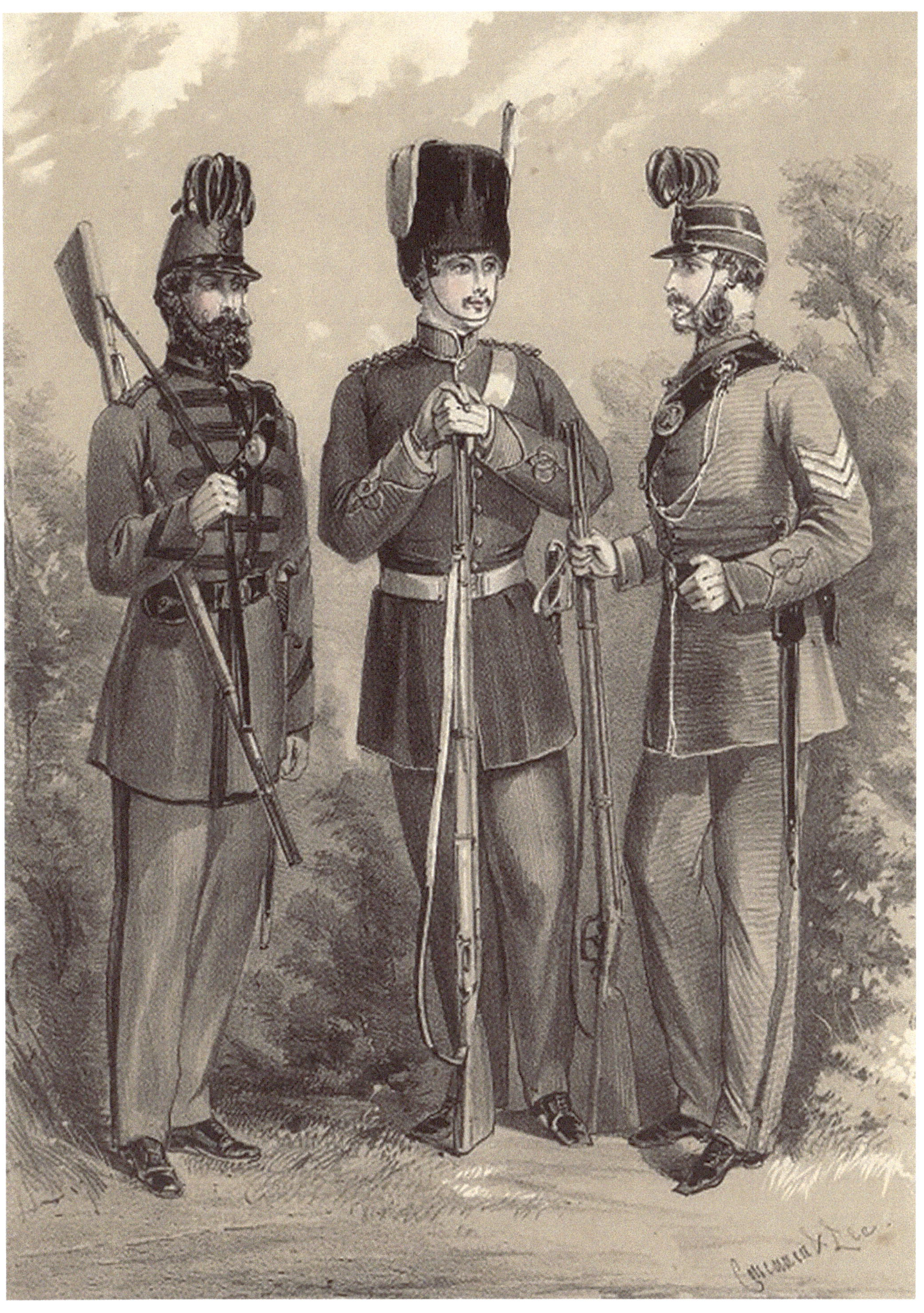

44 – THE VOLUNTEER GUARDS

Music sheet illustration for William Henry Montgomery's tune, 'The Volunteer Guards', published c1865 by Richard Cook & Co. Litho by Thomas Packer, printing by Stannard & Dixon.

The 'Volunteer Guards' were in fact the 32nd Middlesex Rifle Corps, known to the public as the Six-foot Volunteer Guards. The corps was formed in February 1860 with a view to meet the requirements of men whose stature rendered their appearance in the ranks of ordinary-sized corps somewhat awkward. More than one hundred and fifty gentlemen of the required standard, including several military officers and six-footers from other corps, have been enrolled.

The corps carried on their drills at either St George's Barracks or Hungerford Hall. The military artist Lady Butler mentions in her autobiography how 'I stuffed my sketch books with British Volunteers…there was a very short-lived corps called the Six-foot Guards.' The 32nd Middlesex Rifle Volunteer Corps, with its scarlet coats and black belts, was disbanded in 1868.

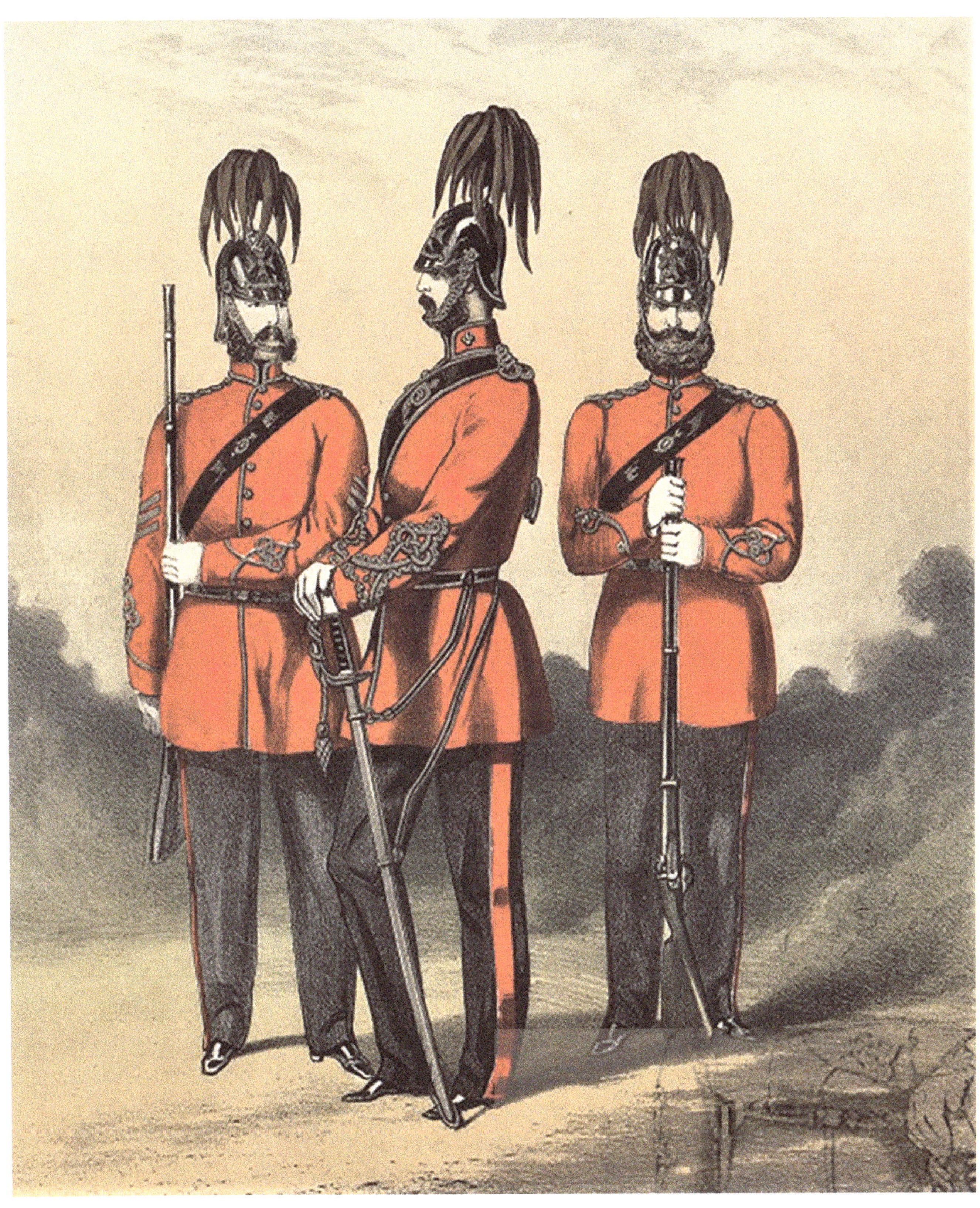

45 – BRISTOL VOLUNTEERS

Thanks to the Anne SK Brown Military Collection at Brown University, USA the illustration has been identified as being from the cover of a music sheet entitles 'Bristol Volunteer March'. Below the image were the words, 'Composed and Inscribed To / Lieut. Colnl. Bush. Major Saville, / The Officers And Members Of The / Bristol Volunteer Corps.' The picture features two volunteers, one dressed in the blue uniform of an volunteer artilleryman, the other in the green of a rifle volunteer. The background shows other volunteers, some working large mortars.

The 1st Gloucestershire Artillery Volunteer Corps was formed at Bristol on 21 December 1859, the 1st Gloucestershire Rifle Volunteer Corps, commanded by Lieutenant-Colonel Robert Bush late of the 96th Foot, around the same time. The battalion had comprised ten companies by June 1860 and was permitted to include City of Bristol as part of its official title.

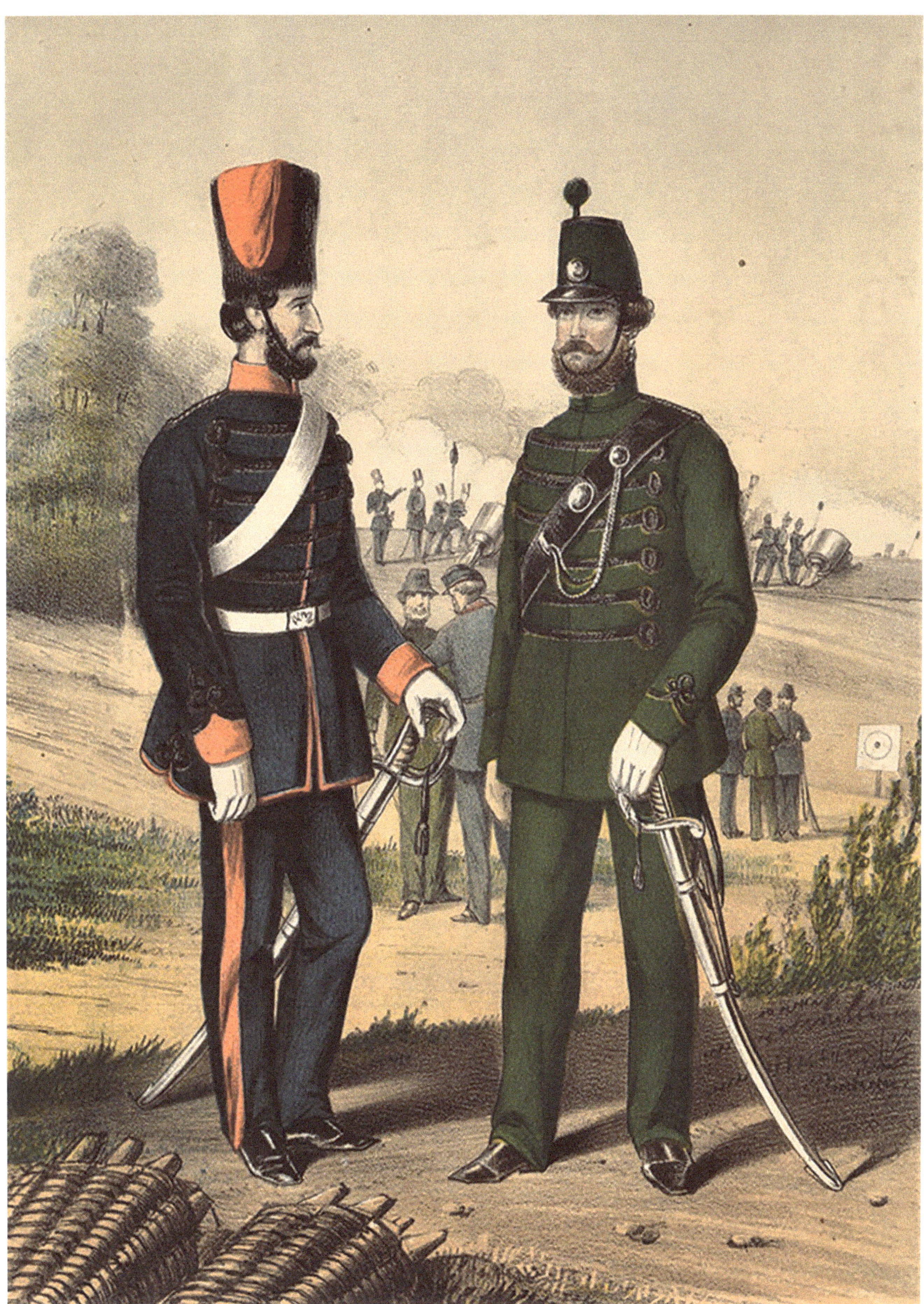

46 – THE RIFLE VOLUNTEER'S MARCH

Illustration from 'The Rifle Volunteer's March' composed by W Smallwood and published by B Williams of Paternoster Row, City of London in 1862. The artwork by Thomas Packer features four volunteers in various uniforms, the one on the right wearing a scarlet coat being one of the 32nd Middlesex Rifle Volunteer Corps, perhaps better known as the 'Six Foot Guards'.

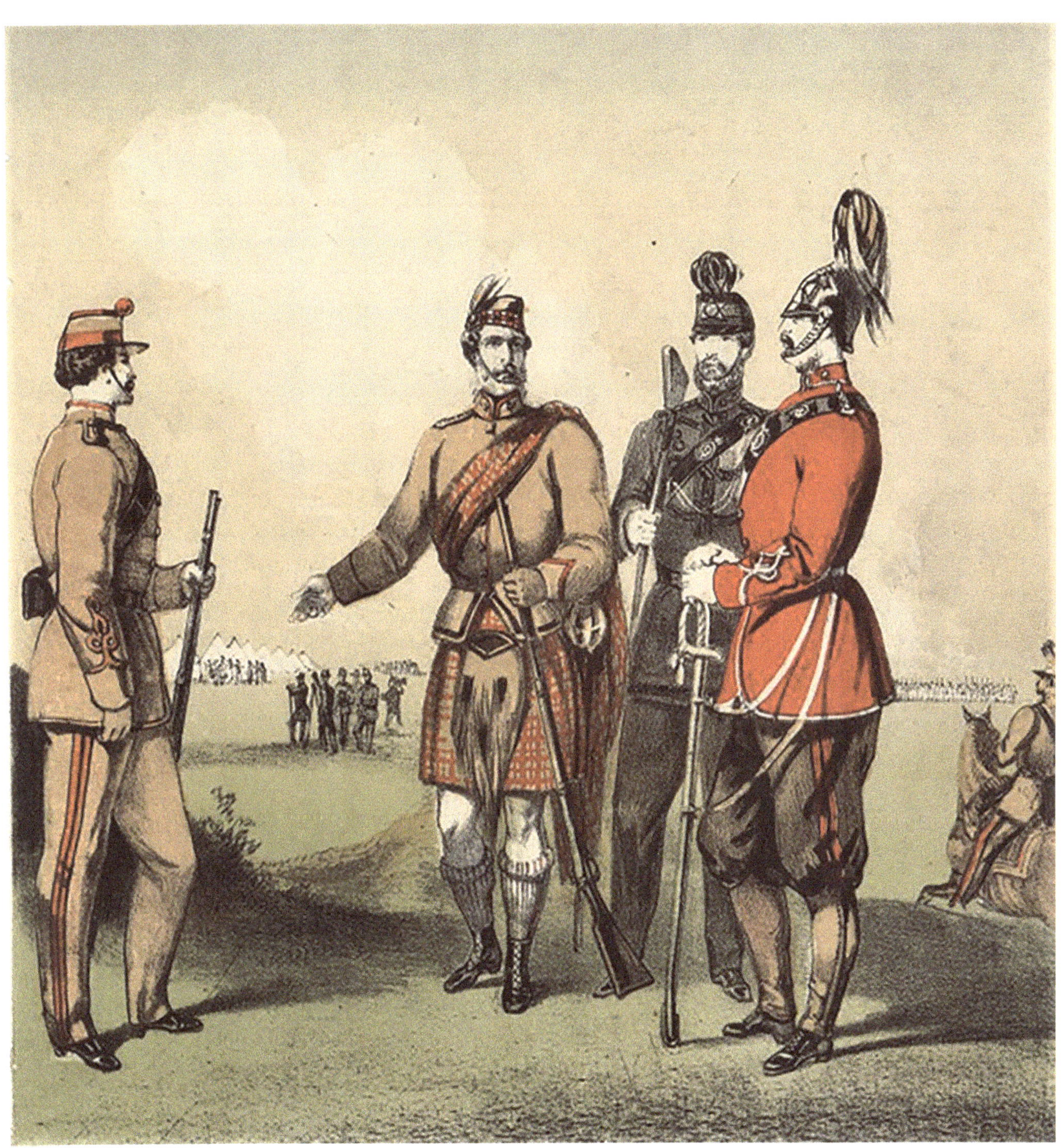

47 – SERGEANT, 6TH LANCASHIRE (1ST MANCHESTER) RIFLE VOLUNTEER CORPS

Colour lithograph by Mansfield after C Black of the 6th Lancashire (1st Manchester) Rifle Volunteers Corps used on the cover of a music sheet, 'The First Manchester Volunteer Rifle Corps', published by R Andrews of 4 Oxford Street, Manchester.

Formed as twelve companies in Manchester on 25 August 1859, the Viscount Grey de Wilton was appointed as Lieutenant-Colonel Commandant on 19 February 1860. A number of large Manchester firms such as Messrs JP and E Westhead, and Messrs J and N Phillips provided whole companies. No 12 Company (headquarters in Eccles) was absorbed into the 46th Corps at Swinton in October 1860, the 43rd at Fallowfield being absorbed in 1861. The 6th Corps for many years occupied headquarters at Wolstenholm's Court, Market Street, Manchester and afterwards at 3 Stretford Road, Hulme.

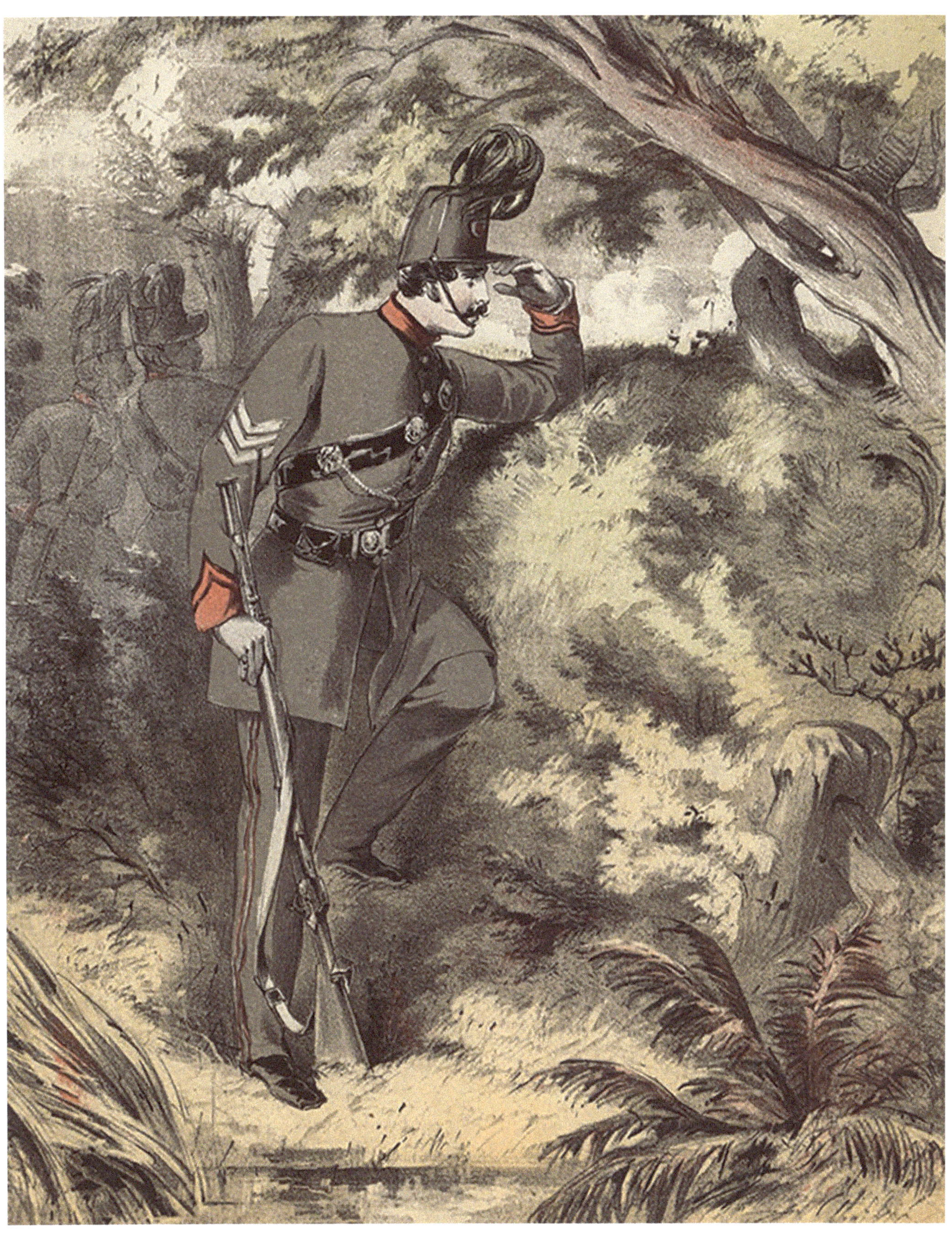

48 – VOLUNTEER REGIMENTS

Colour lithograph by Thomas Wales Lee of Grosvenor Mews, Bond Street, London published by W Jones & Company of 236 Regent Street, London. The Anne SK Brown Military Collection at Brown University Library, USA holds a complete copy of this trimmed print which carries the title of 'Volunteer Regiments'. Printed below each of the six figures are the following unit identifications, from left to right: 'London Scottish', '1st Middlesex Artillery', 'Colonel London Rifle Brigade', 'Queen's Westminster' and 'St Georges'. The publisher's name and address appear below the image together with a note that they were 'Wholesale Manufacturers of Chacos, Caps, Belts, Busbys, and all Accoutrements for Army & Volunteers.' At the top of the print is the company's trade mark of crossed Union flags, one with the letter 'W', the other with 'J', and a cavalry helmet with plume.

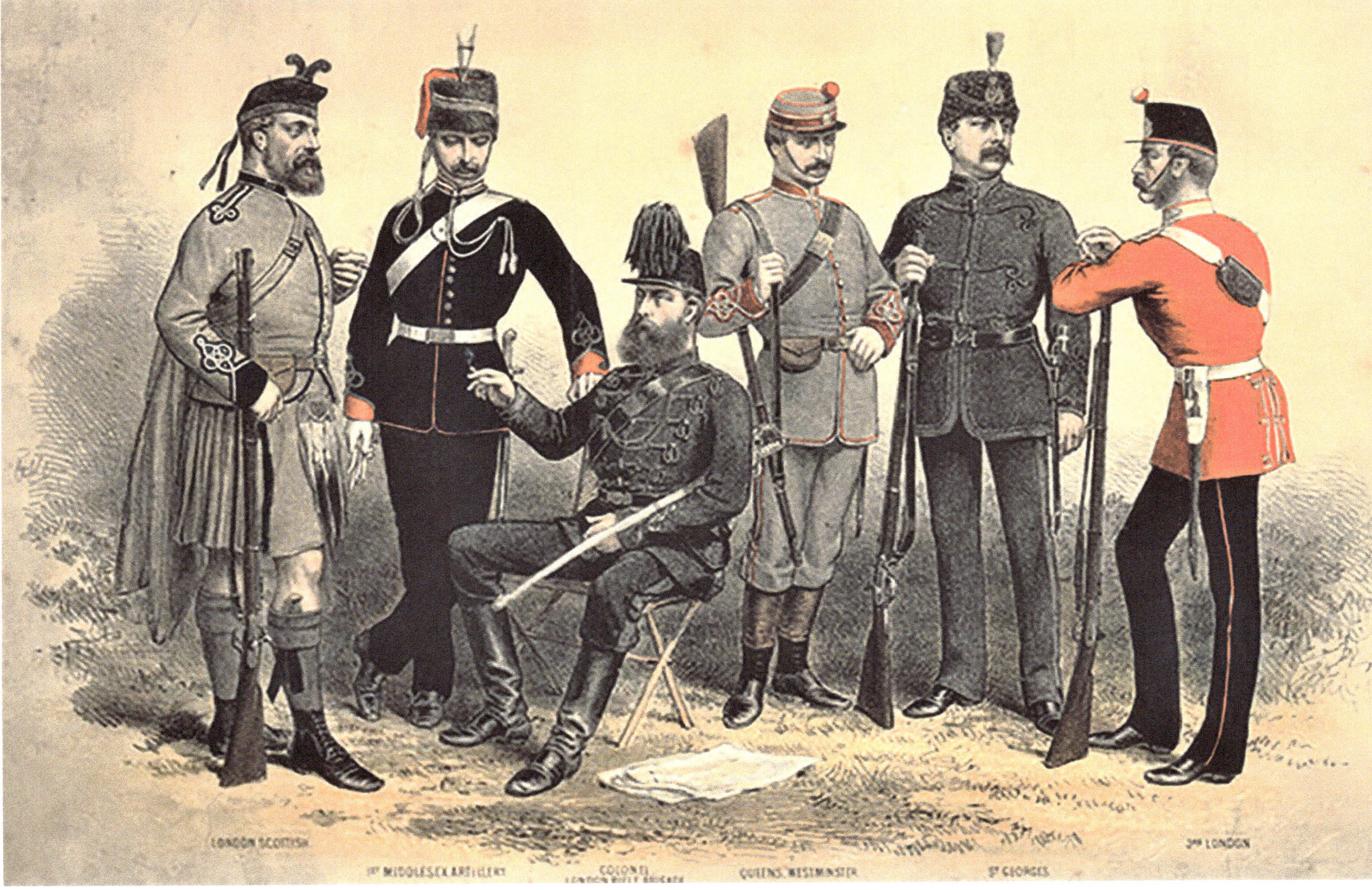
LONDON SCOTTISH
1st MIDDLESEX ARTILLERY
COLONEL
LONDON RIFLE BRIGADE
QUEENS WESTMINSTER
St GEORGES
3rd LONDON

49 – GENERAL OFFICER REVIEWING VOLUNTEERS AT MANOEUVRES

Original watercolour signed 'RS' from the Anne SK Brown Military Collection who credit the painting as possibly the work of Richard Simkin. The general officer, seen in a scarlet jacket and black cocked hat, looks on as a volunteer corps dressed in light grey uniforms with blue facings load and fire their rifles. (*Image courtesy of the Anne SK Brown Military Collection, Brown University Library*)

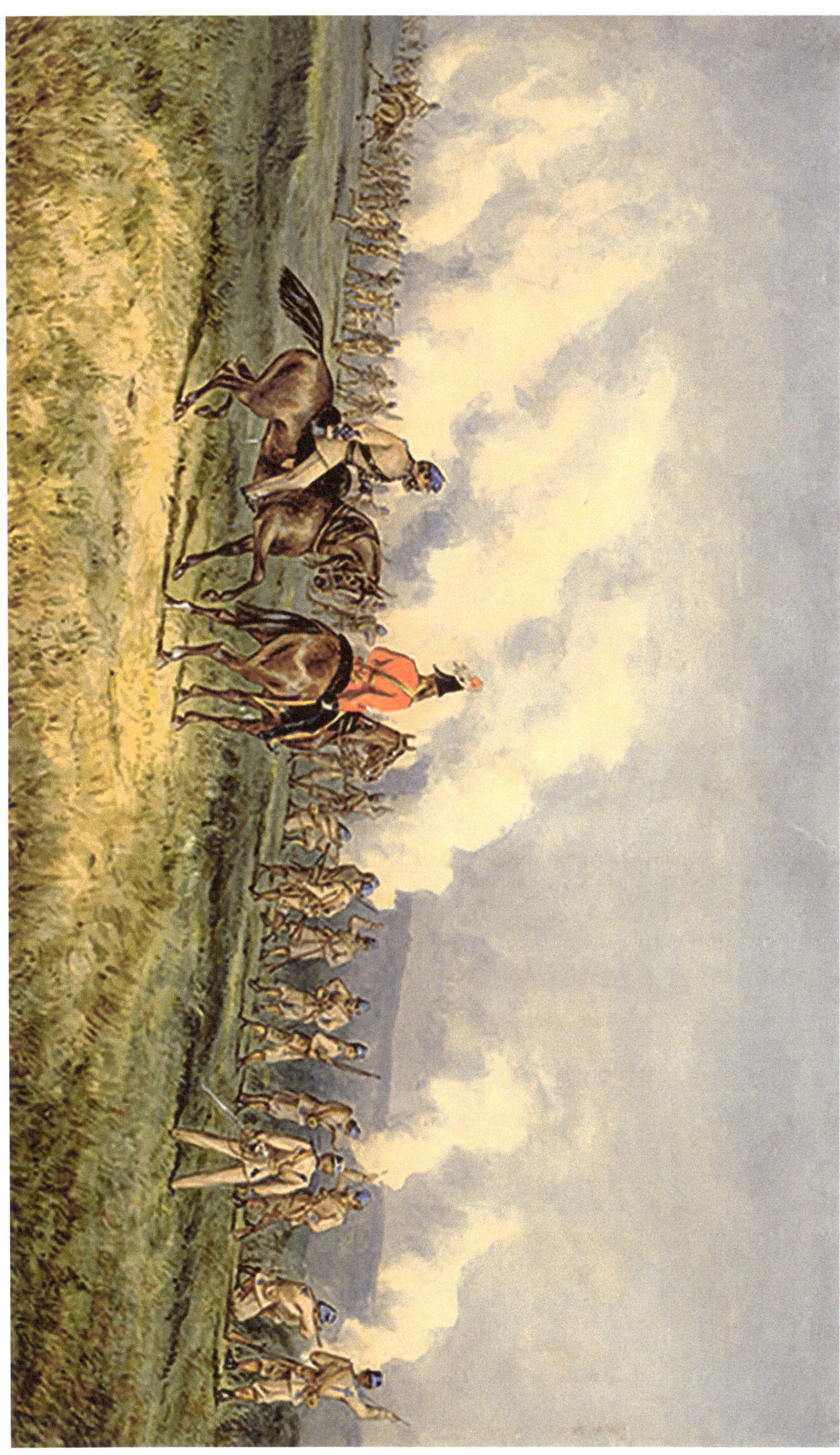

50 – THE VOLUNTEER GALLOP

Colour lithographic music sheet cover by E Bates for 'The Volunteer Gallop', 'Composed and dedicated to the Gloucestershire Volunteers by Tewksbury Goodfellow. (Gloucester City Rifles)'. Priced 2/6, the music was published 'In Air OfThe Gloucester City Rifle Company's Band Fund.'

In the City of Gloucester the 2nd Gloucestershire Rifle Volunteers Corps was formed as one company at Gloucester Dock with the following officers: Captain William Vernon Guise, Lieutenant John Jones and Ensign Theodore Aylmer Preston. All three held commissions dated 21 October 1859. Also with headquarters at Gloucester Dock and of one company was the 3rd Corps with Captain Thomas De Winton, Lieutenant Henry Dowling and Ensign Richard T Smith. (*Image courtesy of the Anne SK Brown Military Collection, Brown University Library*)

THE

VOLUNTEER GALOP.

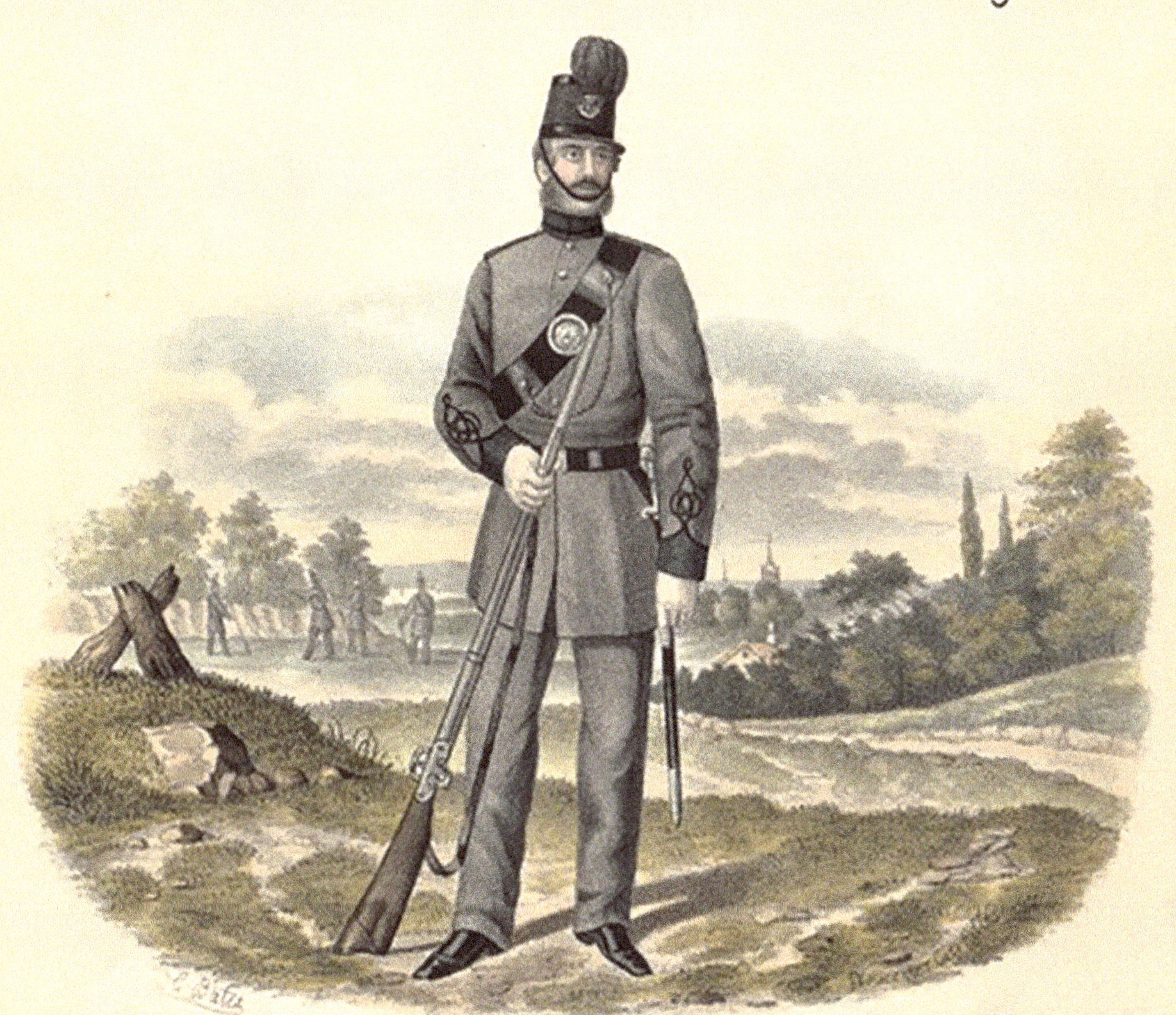

COMPOSED AND DEDICATED

TO THE

GLOUCESTERSHIRE VOLUNTEERS.

BY

TEWKSBURY GOODFELLOW.

(Gloucester City Rifles.)

PRICE 2/6.

I AID OF THE GLOUCESTER CITY RIFLE COMPANY'S BAND FUND.

51 – FORFARSHIRE RIFLE VOLUNTEERS

Plate XXV from *Records of the Scottish Volunteer Force 1859-1908* written and illustrated by Lieutenant-General Sir James Moncrieff Grierson and published by William Blackwood & Sons in 1909. The first three figures are connected with the 2nd Volunteer Battalion Black Watch and are from left to right: a private of the 5th Forfarshire Rifle Volunteer Corps wearing the grey uniform of 1860-64, a private of 1872-82 and a sergeant 1882-1908. The cap, General Grierson dates as 1864-72. The remaining two figures are, an ensign of the 10th Forfarshire Rifle Volunteer Corps and a private of the 3rd Volunteer Battalion Black Watch in review order, 1887-1908.

The 1st Administrative Battalion of Forfarshire Rifle Volunteers was formed with headquarters at Montrose in May 1861 and included the 3rd, 5th, 7th and 13th Corps of the county. Headquarters moved to Friockheim by Arbroath in 1874 and in same year the 2nd Forfarshire Admin Battalion was broken up and its corps transferred to 1st Admin Battalion. The battalion then became known as 1st Admin Battalion of Forfarshire or Angus Rifle Volunteers which, in 1880, was consolidated as the new 2nd Corps with fourteen companies: 'A' and 'B' Forfar (late 2nd Corps), 'C' to 'F' Arbroath (late 3rd Corps), 'G' and 'H' Montrose (late 5th Corps), 'I' and 'K' Brechin (late 7th Corps), 'L' Newtyle (late 8th Corps), 'M' Glamis (late 9th Corps), 'N' Kirriemuir (late 12th Corps), 'O' Friockheim (late 13th Corps).

The new corps at first also included Forfarshire or Angus in its title, but this was changed to just Angus in 1883. Next came the re-designation in 1887 as 2nd (Angus) Volunteer Battalion Black Watch.

The 10th Corps Forfarshire Rifle Volunteer Corps was formed of one company at Dundee on 10 April 1860 with Edward Guild as captain, J Cunningham Kilgour, lieutenant and Hugh Ballingail, ensign. A second company was added on 29 June 1867. The 10th was amalgamated with the 14th Corps, also at Dundee, in September 1868, the new formation comprising six companies under the title 10th Forfarshire (Dundee Highland) RVC with Lieutenant Colonel David Guthrie of Carlogie in command. Re-numbered in March 1880 as 3rd (Dundee Highland), then designated as 3rd (Dundee Highland) Volunteer Battalion Black Watch under General Order 181 of December 1887.

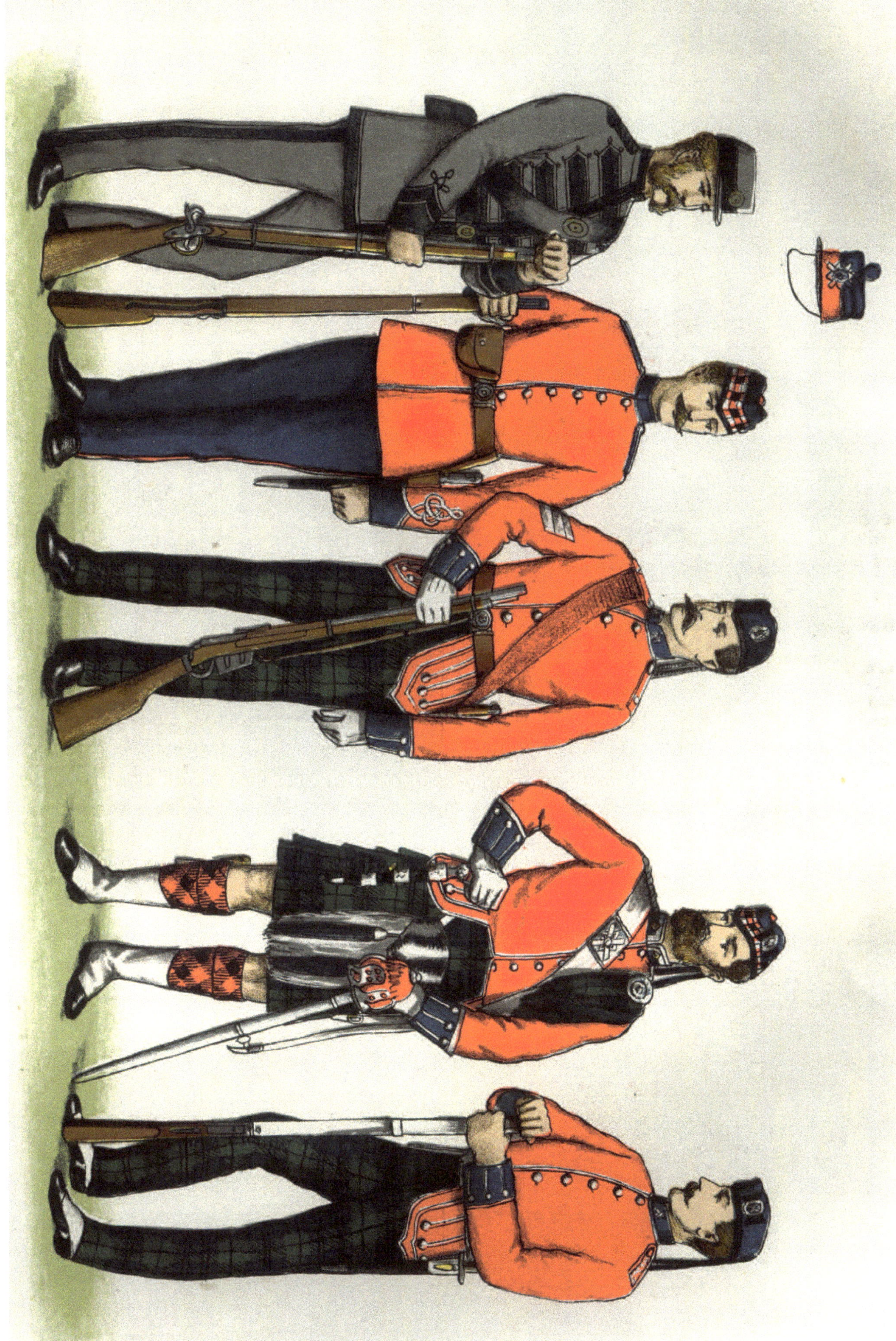

52 – 1st FIFESHIRE ARTILLERY VOLUNTEERS

From plate 1V of *Records of the Scottish Volunteer Force 1859-1908*, written and illustrated by Lieutenant-General Sir James Moncrieff Grierson and published by William Blackwood & Sons in 1909. General Grierson's three figures are from left to right: a gunner of the 3rd Fifeshire Artillery Volunteer Corps, a Captain of the 1st Stirlingshire Artillery Volunteer Corps, both of 1860, and a gunner of the Fifeshire Royal Garrison Artillery Volunteers in 1907.

The 1st Administrative Brigade of Fifeshire Artillery Volunteers was formed with headquarters at Kirkcaldy in November 1860. All eleven of the county's artillery corps were included, the 1st and 2nd Stirlingshire AVC being added in 1863. Brigade headquarters were moved to St Andrews in the same year.

The brigade was consolidated in 1880 as the 1st Fifeshire AVC with headquarters remaining at St Andrews. There were thirteen batteries: Nos 1 to 11 (from the Fifeshire corps in order of seniority), Nos 12 and 13 (from the 1st and 2nd Stirlingshire). In 1882 No 7 Battery at Anstruther was disbanded and in its place a new No 7 raised at St Andrews. The next move was in 1888 when No 2 Battery transferred its headquarters to Newport. A position battery of 16-pounder guns was issued to the corps in 1889 which was manned by No 3 Battery, this in 1892 being designated as No 1 Position. At the same time No 1 Company became No 2 and No 2, No 3. A new battery, numbered as 14th, was formed at Kirkcaldy in 1900 and in 1906 corps headquarters were moved to that town.

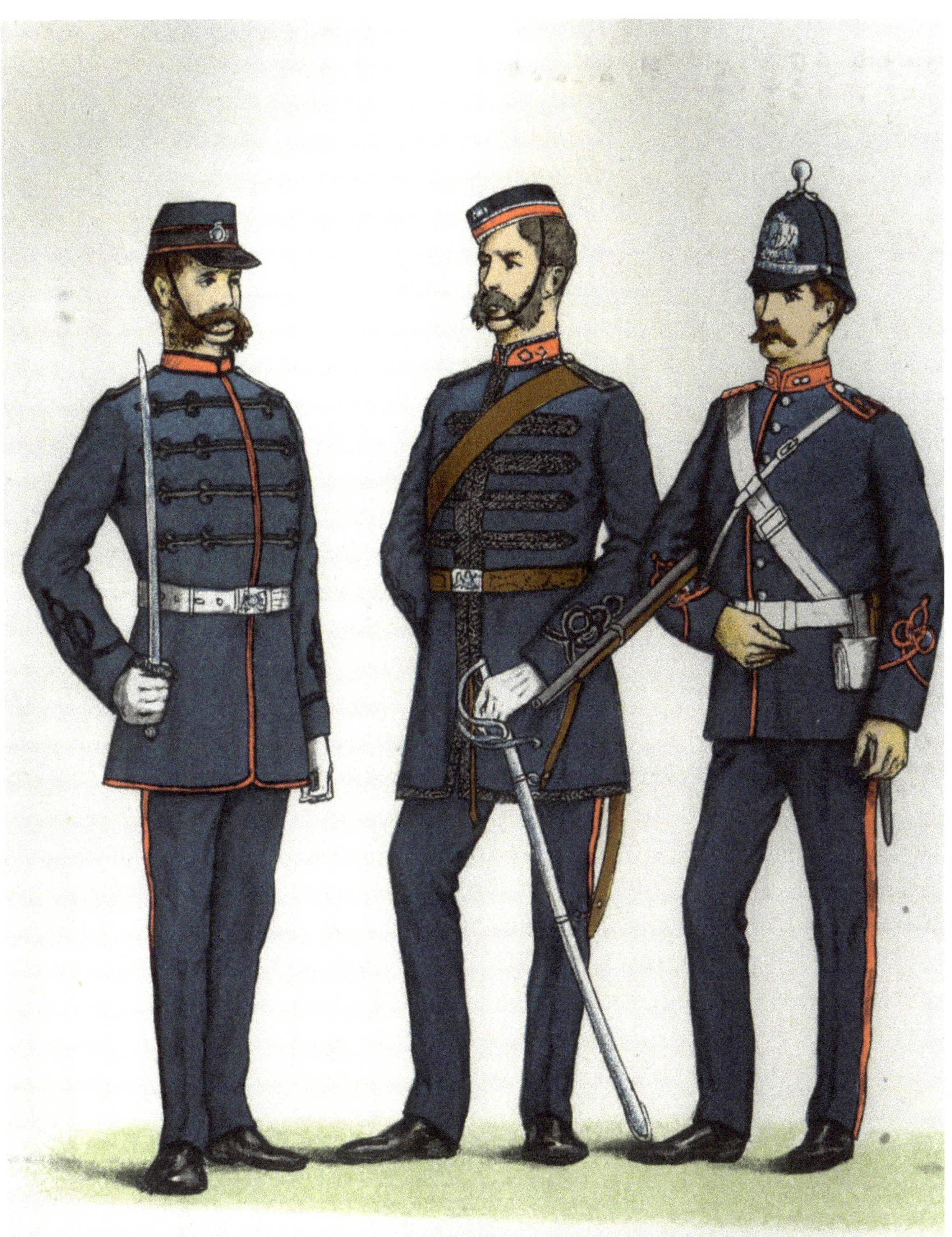

53 – GRAND VOLUNTEER FIELD DAY AT SEFTON PARK, 5 OCTOBER 1867

Colour lithograph by and after John McGahey, published by McGahey of 18 School Lane and T Greenall & Co of 20 North John Street, Liverpool. The following text appeared below the image: 'Grand Volunteer Field Day, Sefton Park, Liverpool, 5th October, 1867, / Under the Inspection of His Royal Highness The Duke of Cambridge, Commander in Chief of the British Forces, / This Print is most respectfully Dedicated by permission to Major Gen. Sir John Garrock HCB, Commanding / By His obliged and very humble Servant, / John McGahey, The Artist.'

The scene shows a mock battle involving volunteers from Liverpool and its surrounding areas. Cavalry can be seen charging, scattering the infantry before it, as the artillery moves forward and riflemen wearing grey uniforms fire a volley. Onlookers occupy crowded stands in the distance, many other civilians mingling among the troops. The number of volunteers involved amounted to 12,023.

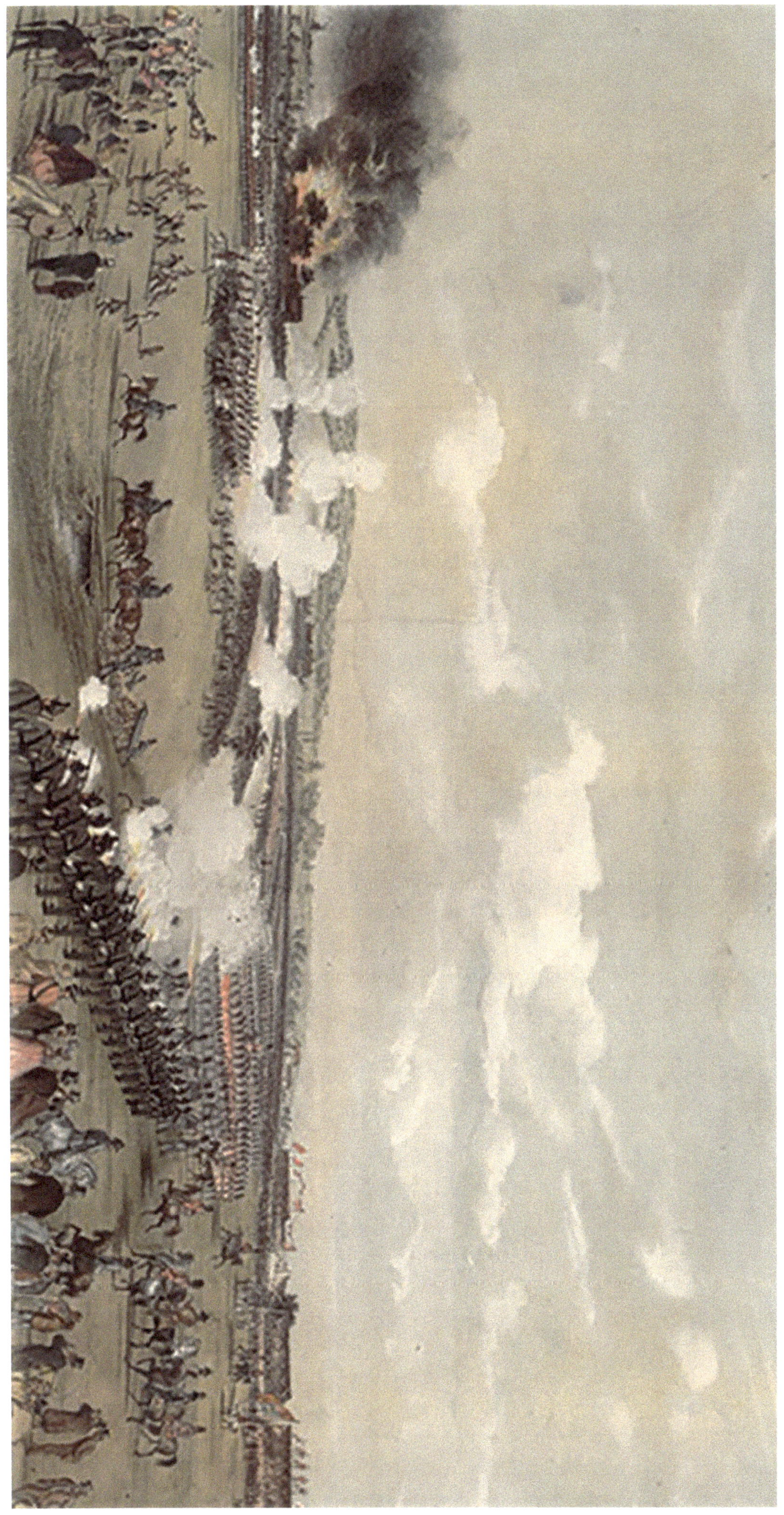

54 – GEORGE HAMILTON CHICHESTER MARQUIS OF DONEGALL

Colour lithograph by Vincent Brooks after Henry Joseph Fleuss and published c1861 with the following caption printed below the image: 'Geo Hamilton Chichester Marquis Of Donegal. / K.P. G.C.H. &c. &c. / Lieut. Col. Of the London Irish V.R.C.' The print shows the colonel standing by his horse. He wears a grey uniform with green facings, his black patent leather pouch-belt having a silver plate with a harp in the centre of a crowned wreath. The black waist-belt also displays a harp in its locket-type fastening. The grey trousers have a broad green stripe, the shako sporting a cock's feather plume, green band and harp badge.

The London Irish was raised as a result of a meeting arranged by Mr GT Dempsey, an Irishman resident in London, at his rooms in Essex Street, Strand in the latter weeks of 1859. Headquarters were placed at Burlington House and the first officers' commissions were dated 28 February 1860. It is of interest to note that out of the nineteen officers recorded in the Army List for December 1860, no less than five held tiles: the Marquis of Donegal (lieutenant-colonel), Lord Otho A Fitzgerald (captain), Lord Ashley (captain), Lord Francis N Conynhham (lieutenant) and the Earl of Belmore (ensign). Headquarters were transferred to York Buildings, Adelphi in 1866, Leicester Square in 1869, King William Street in 1873 and Duke Street, Charring Cross in 1897. The corps had been designated as 28th Middlesex RVC, but was renumbered as 16th in 1880.

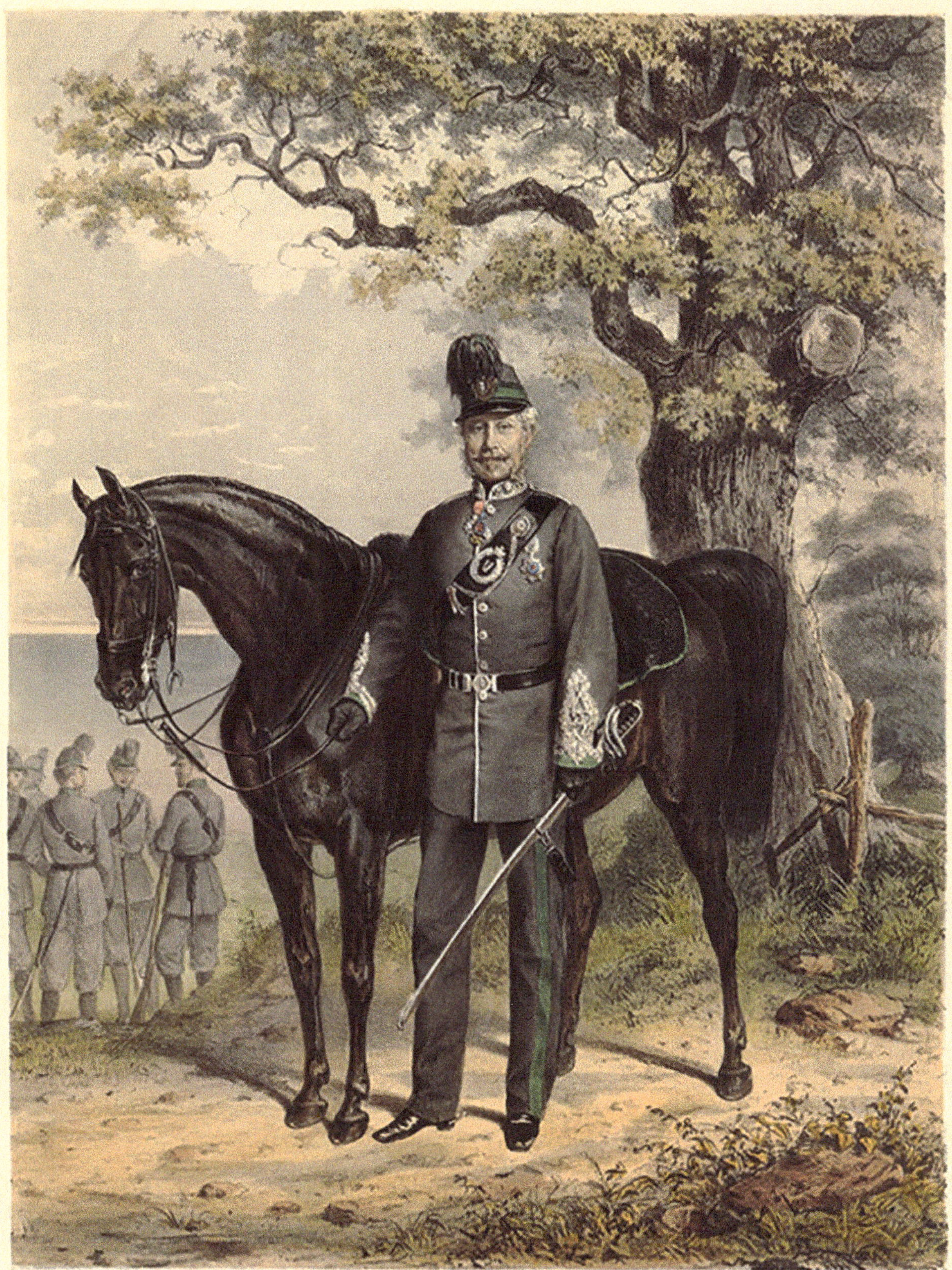

Drawn from Life on Stone by [illegible]

Vincent Brooks, Imp.

GEO. HAMILTON CHICHESTER MARQUIS OF DONEGALL.

K.P. G.C.H. &c. &c.

Lieut. Col. of the London Irish V.R.C.

55 – LIEUTENANT-COLONEL JOSEPH WALKER PEARSE, 1st YORKSHIRE (EAST RIDING) RIFLE VOLUNTEER CORPS

Mezzotint by Thomas Lewis Atkinson after Francis Grant and published by Henry Graves & Co of 6 Pall Mall, London on 5 December 1876. Colonel Pearse is seen posing in a studio with his right hand holding a cap at his right side, the other grasping his gloves and sword. A sabretache hangs from a black waist-belt, his rank clearly identified by the elaborate silver decoration on each sleeve.

The 1st Yorkshire (East Riding) Rifle Volunteer Corps had been formed at Hull on 9 November 1859 and absorbed the 2nd, 3rd, 4th, 7th and 9th Corps, also in Hull, before the end of 1860. The Hull Rifles, as the 1st Corps became known, now comprised eight companies with Joseph Walker Pearce appointed as lieutenant-colonel on 11 August. Colonel Pearce was to hold his position for the next sixteen years. Walter Richards, in his book *His Majesty's Territorial Army*, noted that the 1st Corps owed much to Colonel Pearse, in particular the use of the Cyclops Foundry, in which he had an interest, for drill purposes.

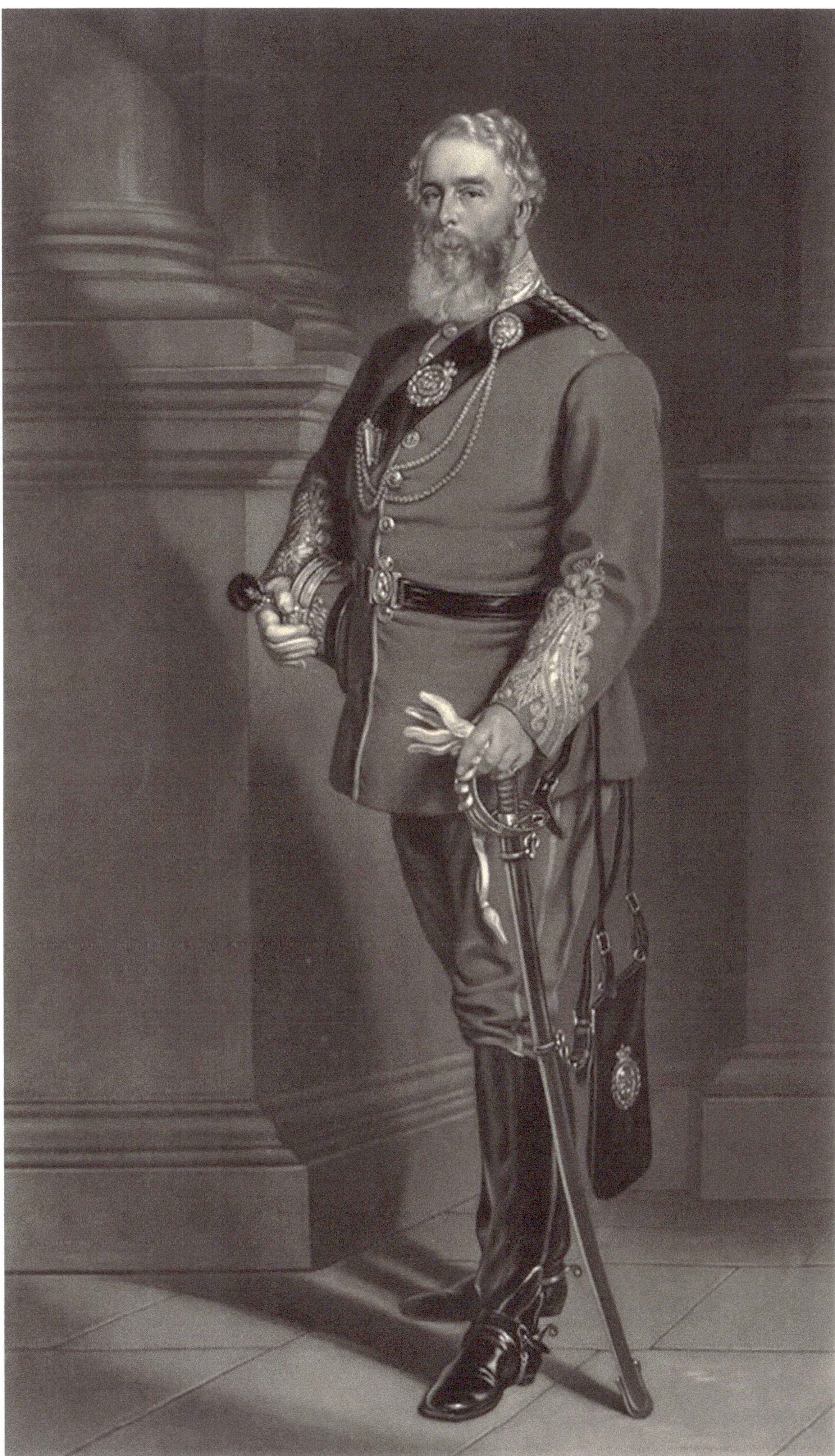

56 – LONDON SCOTTISH RIFLE VOLUNTEER CORPS

Colour lithograph by M & N Hanhart after Henry Joseph Fleuss, published by Rudolph Ackermann of 191 Regent Street, London on 15 June 1860. Below the image is the tile 'London Scottish Volunteer Rifle Corps' on a scroll. Sprigs of oak and laurel are placed at the sides of a crowned shield charged with a thistle and below this, the words 'Lord Elcho, M.P. / Lieut. Colonel Commandant.' Three figures are featured wearing grey ('Elcho Grey') uniforms with light blue collars, cuffs and piping. The central figure of an officer standing on a rock wears a grey cap with blue and white diced band, brown leather belts and holds a basket-hilted sword in his left hand. To his right a volunteer holding a rifle ascends a slope and on the left, a kilted bugler wearing a plain glengarry cap sounds a call.

The services of a rifle corps composed of Scotsmen living in the London area were accepted by the War Office on 2 November 1859. The corps consisted of six companies and was designated as the 15th Middlesex (London Scottish) RVC, Lord Elcho (afterwards Earl of Wemyss) being appointed as lieutenant-colonel in command. Headquarters were established at 8 Adelphi Terrace, Westminster and the six companies were located: No 1 (Highland) 10 Pall Mall East, No 2 (City) at the Oriental Bank, No 3 (Northern) at Rosemary Hall Islington, No 4 (Central) Scottish Corporation House Crane Court, No 5 (Southern) 68 Jermyn Street and No 6 (Western) Chesterfield House West London. *(Image courtesy of the Anne SK Brown Military Collection, Brown University Library)*

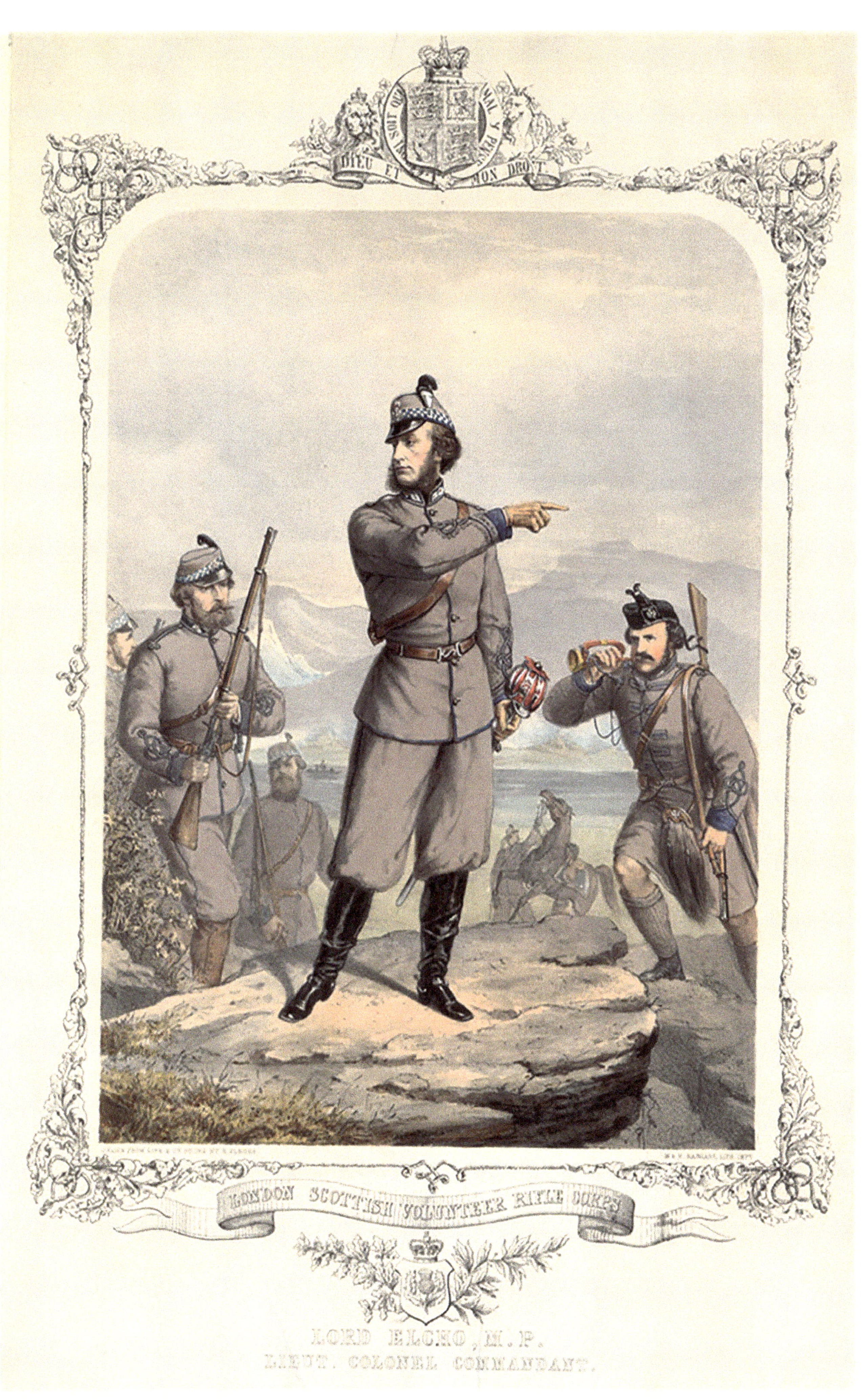
DIEU ET MON DROIT
LONDON SCOTTISH VOLUNTEER RIFLE CORPS
LORD ELCHO, M.P.
LIEUT. COLONEL COMMANDANT.

57 – THE RIGHT HONOURABLE VISCOUNT RANELAGH

Steel engraving by Daniel John Pound after a photograph by John and Octavius Charles Watkins of Parliament Street, London. The image was published with a caption below reading, 'The Right Honourable / Viscount Ranelagh / Lieut. Coll. South Middlesex Rifle Volunteers'. Colonel Ranelagh is seen sitting casually in a chair, his sword sloping off from his left side to the floor. Clearly seen on both the cap and waist-belt clasp is the Middlesex arms badge worn by the corps—the 2nd Middlesex (South Middlesex) Rifle Volunteers.

The 2nd (South Middlesex) was formed with headquarters at Beaufort House, Waltham Green on 14 October 1859. Raised by Viscount Ranelagh, the 2nd Corps included among its first officers: Evan Macpherson, late major in the 68th Regiment of Foot, the Hon WE Fitzmaurice, major 2nd Life Guards, FH Atherely of the Rifle Brigade and long-time MP for the Isle of Wight, John Walrond Clark of the 10th Dragoons, and Charles Smyth Vereker who had served as lieutenant-colonel in the Limerick Artillery Militia. Among the junior officers were Lord Ashley and the Hon Robert Bourke, afterwards Earl of Mayo and Governor General of India. Recruitment went well and within a few months the strength of the corps, one of the largest in the country, stood at sixteen companies. By the end of March 1860 some 1,261 members had subscribed twenty-one shillings each on being enrolled. In addition every man paid the cost of his uniform and equipment, besides an annual regimental subscription of twenty-one shillings.

As founder of the 2nd Middlesex, Viscount Ranelagh's crest of a dexter arm embowed in armour and grasping a dart was used on the later uniforms as a collar badge. His Lordship was to command the corps until his death in November 1885.

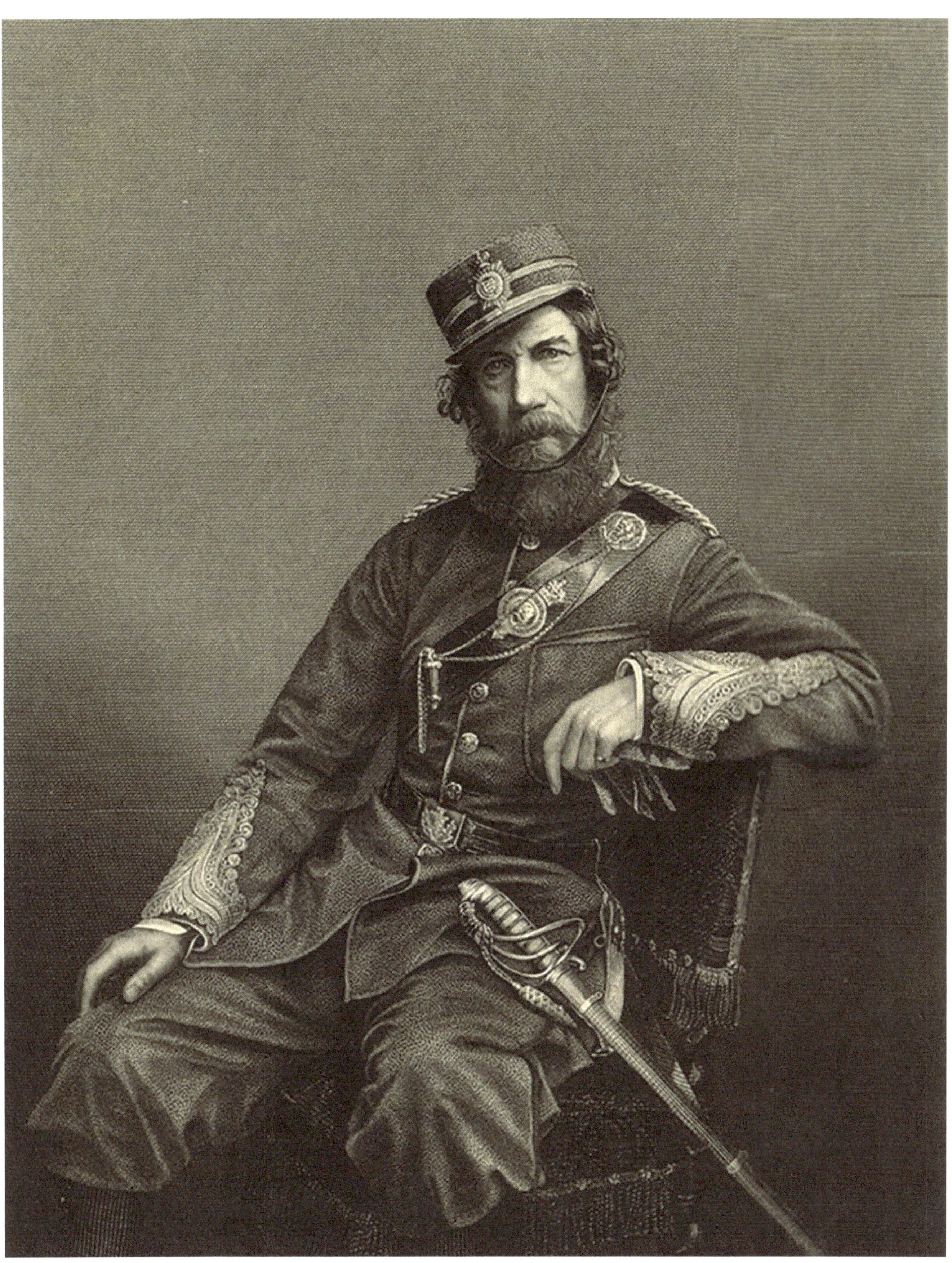

58 – THE LADIES DARLING

Sheet music cover signed by T [Thomas] Packer for 'The Ladies Darling', a comic ballad written and arranged by Henry Walker, published by B Williams of 11 Paternoster Row, City of London. The image shows a volunteer rifleman in a light brown uniform with red cord, a light brown shako with red band and pom-pom, and black gaiters. He walks with his rifle slung over his shoulder, two ladies following on behind. (*Image courtesy of the Anne SK Brown Military Collection, Brown University Library*)

THE LADIES DARLING,

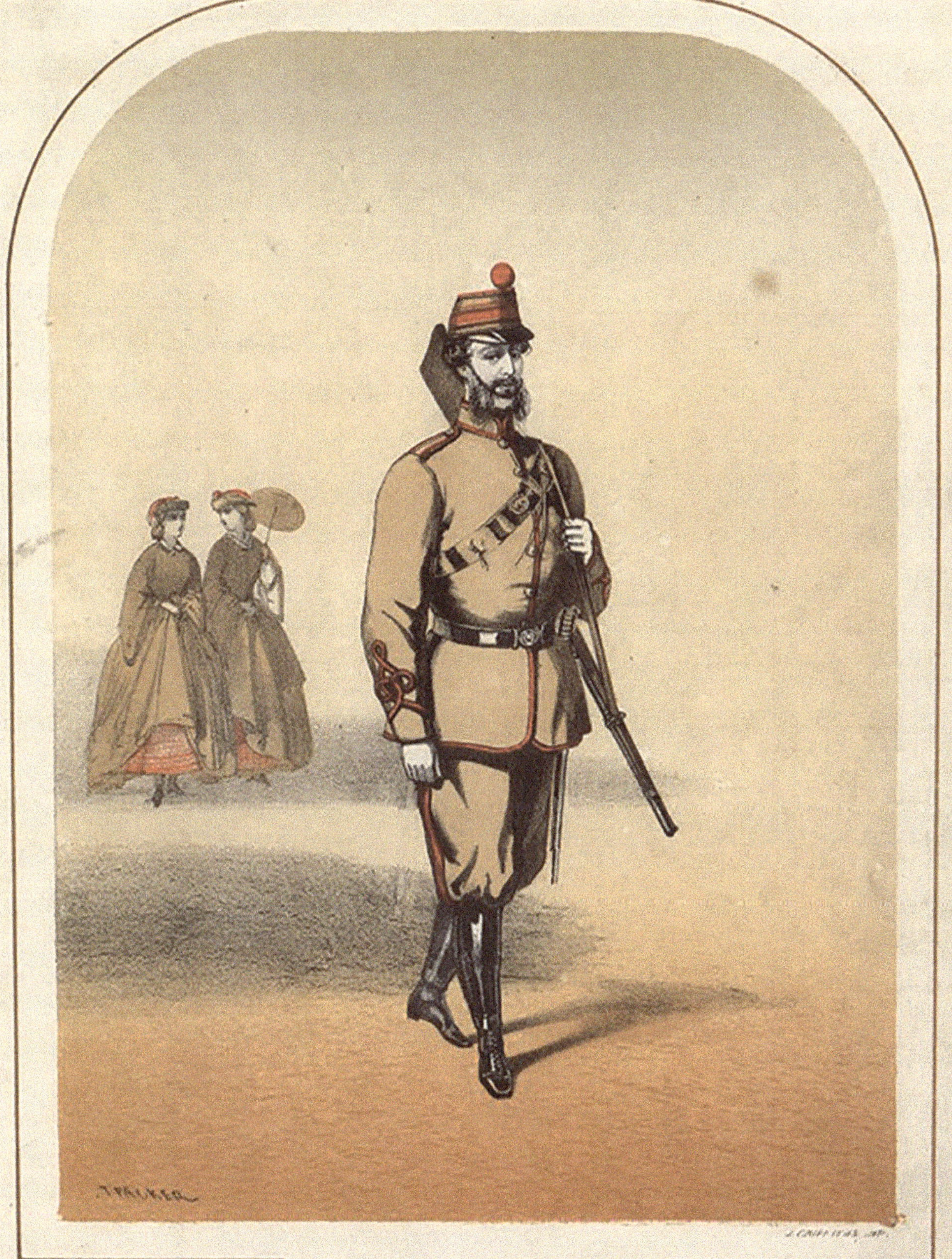

COMIC BALLAD,

SUNG BY

MISS POOLE, MISS KATE HARLEY, MISS WILSON, &c.&c.

THE POETRY WRITTEN & MUSIC ARRANGED BY

HENRY WALKER.

ENT, STA, HALL, — PRICE 2/6

LONDON, PUBLISHED BY, B. WILLIAMS, 11 PATERNOSTER ROW.

WHERE MAY BE HAD THE FOLLOWING LADIES COMIC SONGS, PRICE 2/- EA.

ONLY FOR ONCE IN A WAY, POETRY BY CARPENTER, MUSIC BY C. W. GLOVER | NO I'M NOT IN A HURRY TO MARRY, POETRY & MUSIC BY H. WALKER.

I GUESS YOU'LL BE THERE do GODFREY do HARROWAY | A SHAKE IN THE GRASS do BY CAULFIELD

59 – GRAND REVIEW IN HYDE PARK ON 23 JUNE 1860

Colour lithograph by CJ Culliford of 22 Southampton Street, Strand, London published by WHJ Carter, print seller of 12 Regent Street, Pall Mall, London with the title, 'The Grand Review of The Volunteer Rifle Corps By Her Majesty The Queen, / In Hyde Park, On The 23rd Of June, 1860.' With Matthew Cotes Wyatt's statue of the Duke of Wellington seated on his horse Copenhagen looking down from Hyde Park Corner, rifle corps after rifle corps pass by Queen Victoria who can be seen seated in a carriage to the left of the image. Foot guards and hussars keep the ground, the vast crowd seated in stands to the left and standing. Some have even found their way up to the high bough of a tree to view this spectacular event. Beyond Wellington, an unimaginable, uninterrupted view to the south of Crystal Palace in its cast iron and plate glass. (*Image courtesy of the Anne SK Brown Military Collection, Brown University Library*)

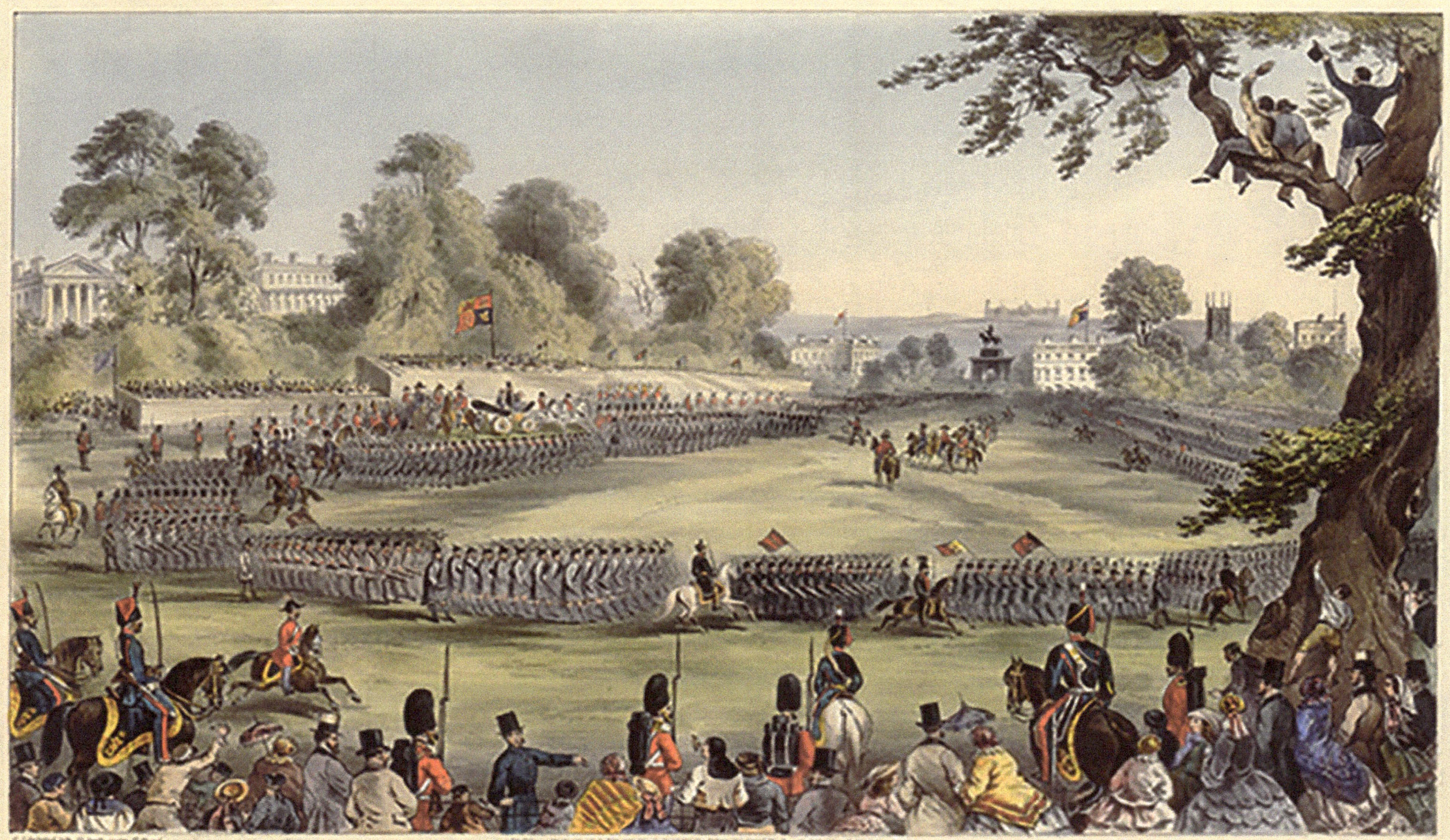

THE GRAND REVIEW OF THE VOLUNTEER RIFLE CORPS BY HER MAJESTY THE QUEEN,

IN HYDE PARK, ON THE 23RD OF JUNE, 1860.

60 – A RIFLE VOLUNTEER

Tinted lithograph signed 'CA' and dated 1860 showing a single figure standing with his rifle at his right side. Against a background of white cliffs and rolling hills, he wears a dark uniform decorated with five rows of cord across the chest and Austrian knots on the sleeves. The black pouch-belt has a circular, crowned plate with the cypher VR in the centre and two chains fixed to a lion mask and terminating with a silver whistle. The black waist-belt holds a small ammunition pouch and is fastened by a lion mask locket. A bugle horn forms the centre of the shako which has a black peak and black cock's tail feathers.

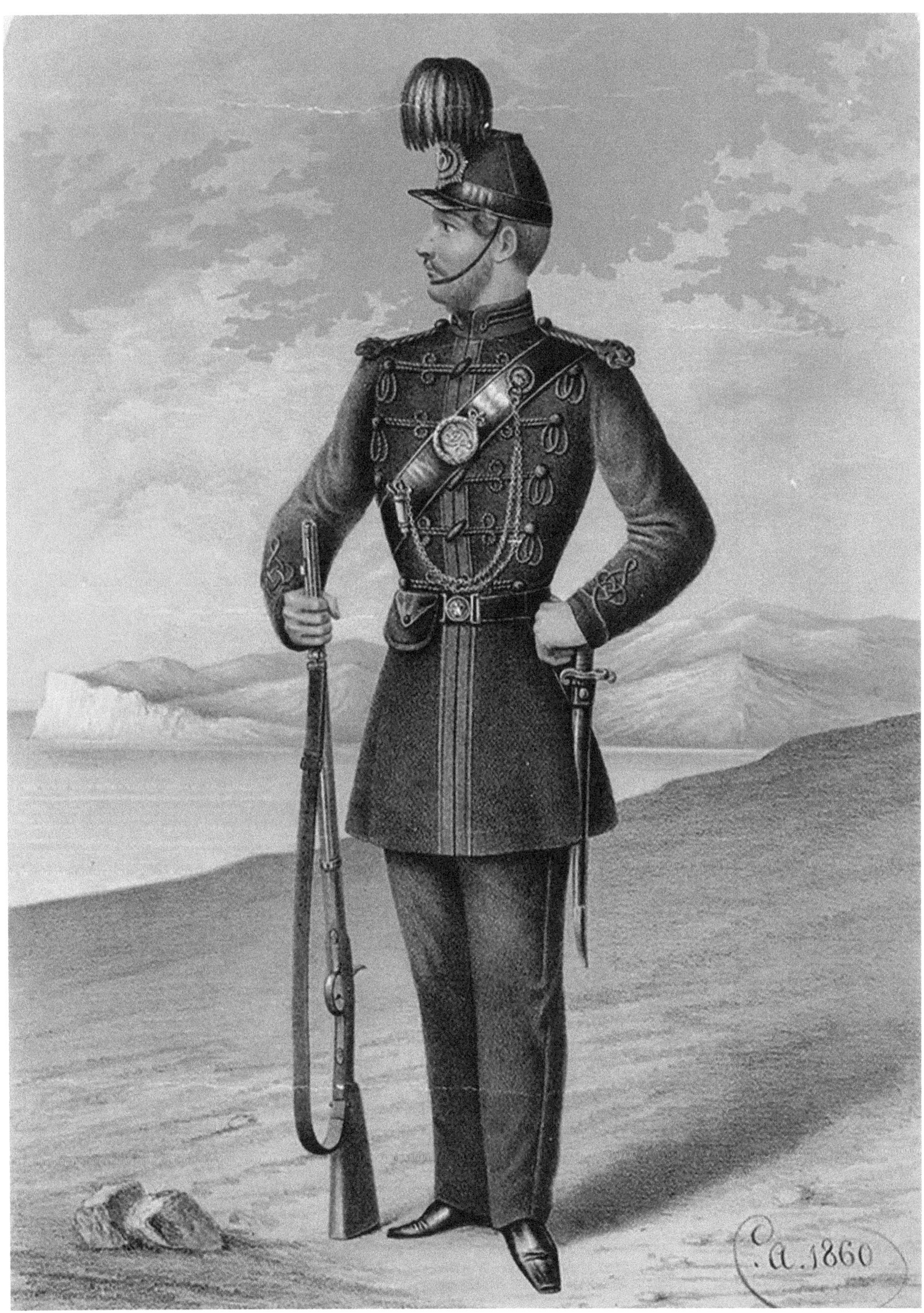

61 – 2nd VOLUNTEER BATTALION GORDON HIGHLANDERS

From Plate XXXVI of *Records of the Scottish Volunteer Force 1859-1908*, written and illustrate by Lieutenant-General Sir James Moncrieff Grierson and published in 1909 by William Blackwood & Sons. Three figures, from left to right: a lieutenant of the 6th Aberdeenshire Rifle Volunteer Corps wearing the uniform of 1860-64, a private of the 2nd Administrative Battalion of Aberdeenshire Rifle Volunteers 1864-75, and a captain of the 2nd Volunteer Battalion Gordon Highlanders.

The 2nd Admin Battalion was formed with headquarters at Tarves in June 1861 and to it were added the 2nd, 5th, 6th, 12th, 13th, 15th, 16th and 18th Aberdeenshire Corps. Headquarters were transferred to Old Meldrum in 1868, then to Aberdeen in 1877. The battalion was consolidated as the new 2nd Corps in 1880 with seven companies: 'A' Methlick (late 2nd Corps), 'B' Ellon (late 6th Corps), 'C' Newburgh (late 12th Corps), 'D' Turriff (late 13th Corps), 'E' Fyvie (late 15th Corps), 'F' Old Meldrum (late 16th Corps), 'G' Tarves (late 18th Corps), then re-designated as 2nd Volunteer Battalion Gordon Highlanders in 1884.

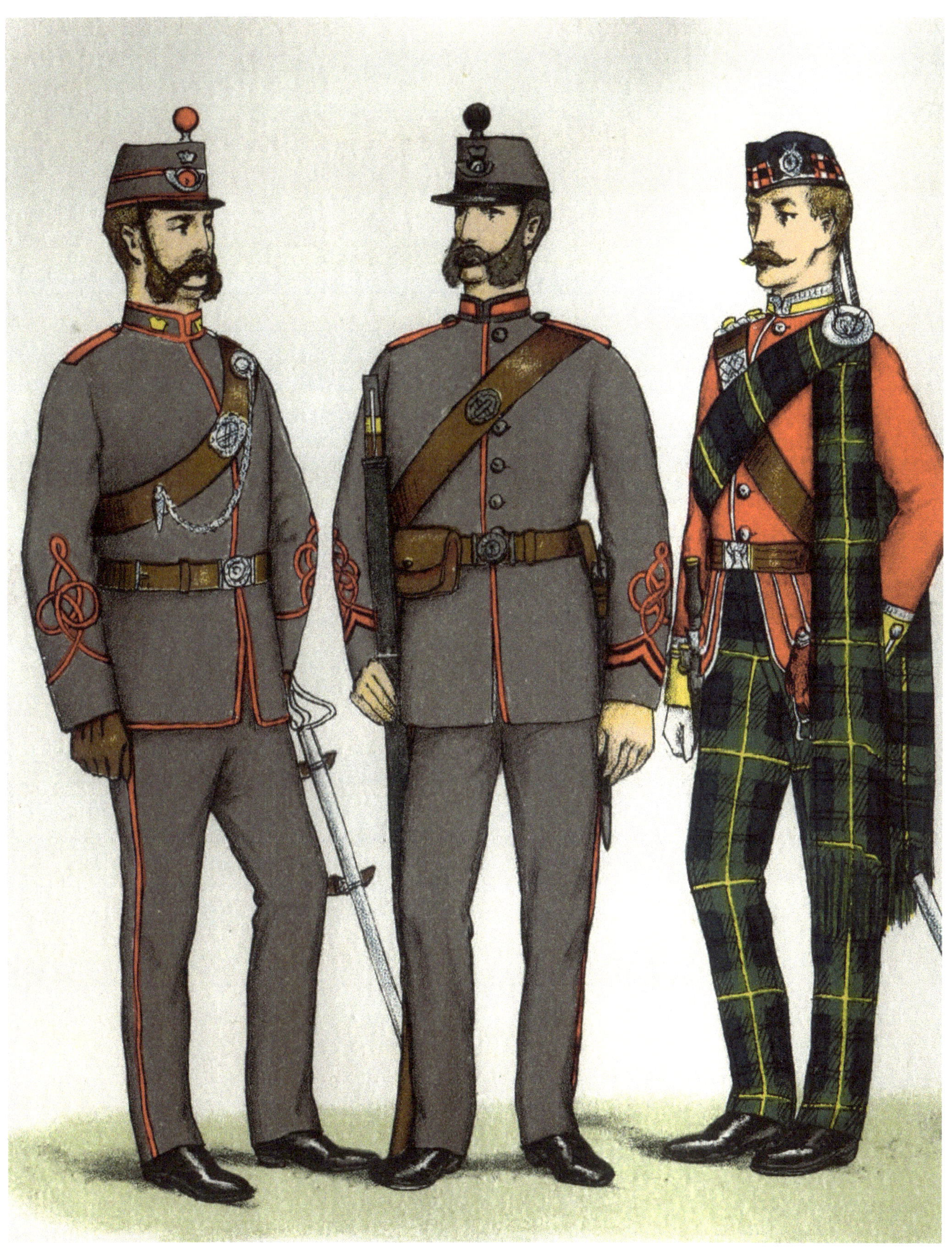

62 – 1ST VOLUNTEER BATTALION CAMERON HIGHLANDERS

Plate XL from *Records of the Scottish Volunteer Force 1859-1908*, written and illustrate by Lieutenant-General Sir James Moncrieff Grierson and published in 1909 by William Blackwood & Sons. The image represents some of the several Inverneshire Rifle Volunteer Corps that provided companies of the 1st Volunteer Battalion Cameron Highlanders. From left to right: a lieutenant of the 5th for 1860-63, sergeant of the 1st for 1860-63, private of the 6th in the dress of 1863-80, a captain of the 2nd for 1863-80, private of the 1st in 1880-93 and a private wearing the uniform of 1893 to 1908.

The 1st Administrative Battalion of Inverness-shire Rife Volunteers was formed with headquarters at Inverness on 18 June 1860 and from 1864 included 'Inverness Highland' as part of its title. The battalion was consolidated in 1880 as the new 1st Corps with ten companies: 'A' Inverness (late 1st Corps), 'B' Inverness (late 3rd Corps), 'C' Inverness (late 4th Corps), 'D' Inverness (late 5th Corps), 'E' Fort William (late 2nd Corps), 'F' Kingussie (late 6th Corps), 'G' Beauly (late 7th Corps), 'H' Portree (late 8th Corps), 'I' Ardersier (late 9th Corps), 'K' Roy Bridge (late 10th Corps). It then became a volunteer battalion of the Seaforth Highlanders in 1881, but transferred to the Cameron Highlanders in 1883 with the title 1st (Inverness Highland) Volunteer Battalion authorized under General Order 181 of December 1887.

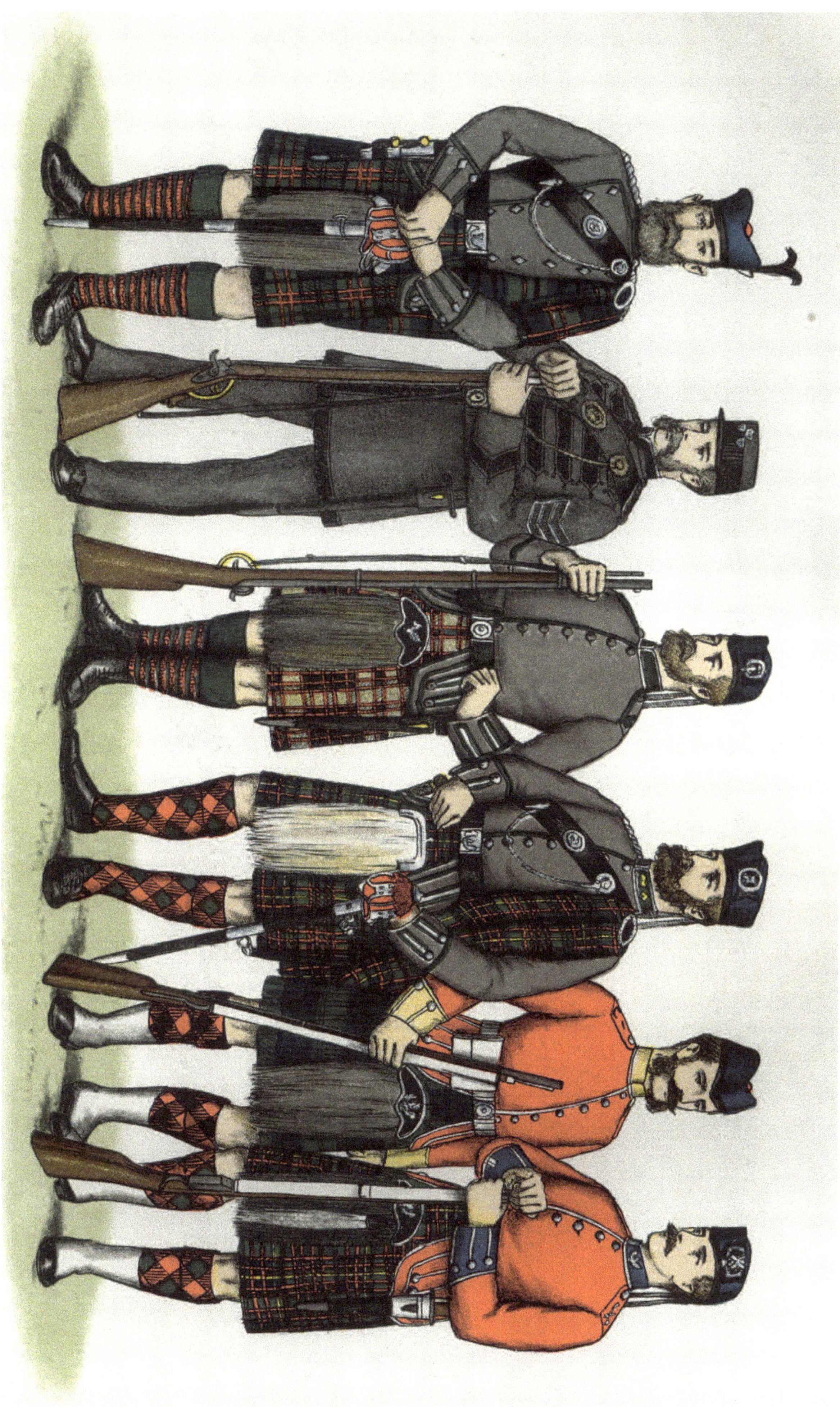

63 – THE FUNERAL CORTEGE OF SERGEANT MONGER

Colour lithograph by and after William Burgess published by John King & Co of 63 Queen Street, London with the following caption below the image: The Funeral Cortege Of Sergeant Monger Of The Dover Volunteer Artillery, / Who with Lieut. G. Thompson was killed at Arch Cliff Fort by the bursting of a Gun during Target Practice on the Evening of the 9th August, 1860.' After this, the following dedication: 'To the Officers and men of the Cinque Port and other Volunteer Corps who with the Royal Artillery, Royal Engineers, 60th Rifles and 47th Regiment assisted in the Grand but Mournful Procession. This Print is respectfully Dedicated. / William Burgess.' With Kent Gunners either side, Sergeant Monger's gun carriage draped with the Union flag stands silent. Two of his fellow sergeants, one holding the coffin covering, patiently await the order to march off. All down the winding hill troops line the roadway. Behind them the mourners, family, colleagues and friends.

The Times for Saturday 11 August 1860 reported the accident at Archcliffe Fort with the comment that the explosion of a gun had killed two and seriously injured several others. Of Sergeant George Monger it was noted that he was a tobacconist of Dover and a nephew of Captain Wollaston, the commander of the Dover Artillery Volunteers. Mr GT Thompson (Lieutenant Thompson) was a solicitor in the town and had been killed from a fragment of the exploding gun. Captain Wollaston is mentioned as having received concussion of the brain and Mr Gilfillan, a tailor, Mr Hadlow, a painter and a youth named Houlden were noted as those that were wounded.

On Saturday 27 April 1861, the *Dover Express* reported that a memorial obelisk to Sergeant Monger had been erected at St Mary's Cemetery. The funeral of Lieutenant Thompson, it was reported, was a private affair, his body being interred in his family's vault at St Andrew's Church in Sheaperdswell.

The Anne SK Brown Military Collection at the Brown University Library, USA hold a copy of this print and note that it was a best seller, the scene showing the cortege at South Front Military Hospital.

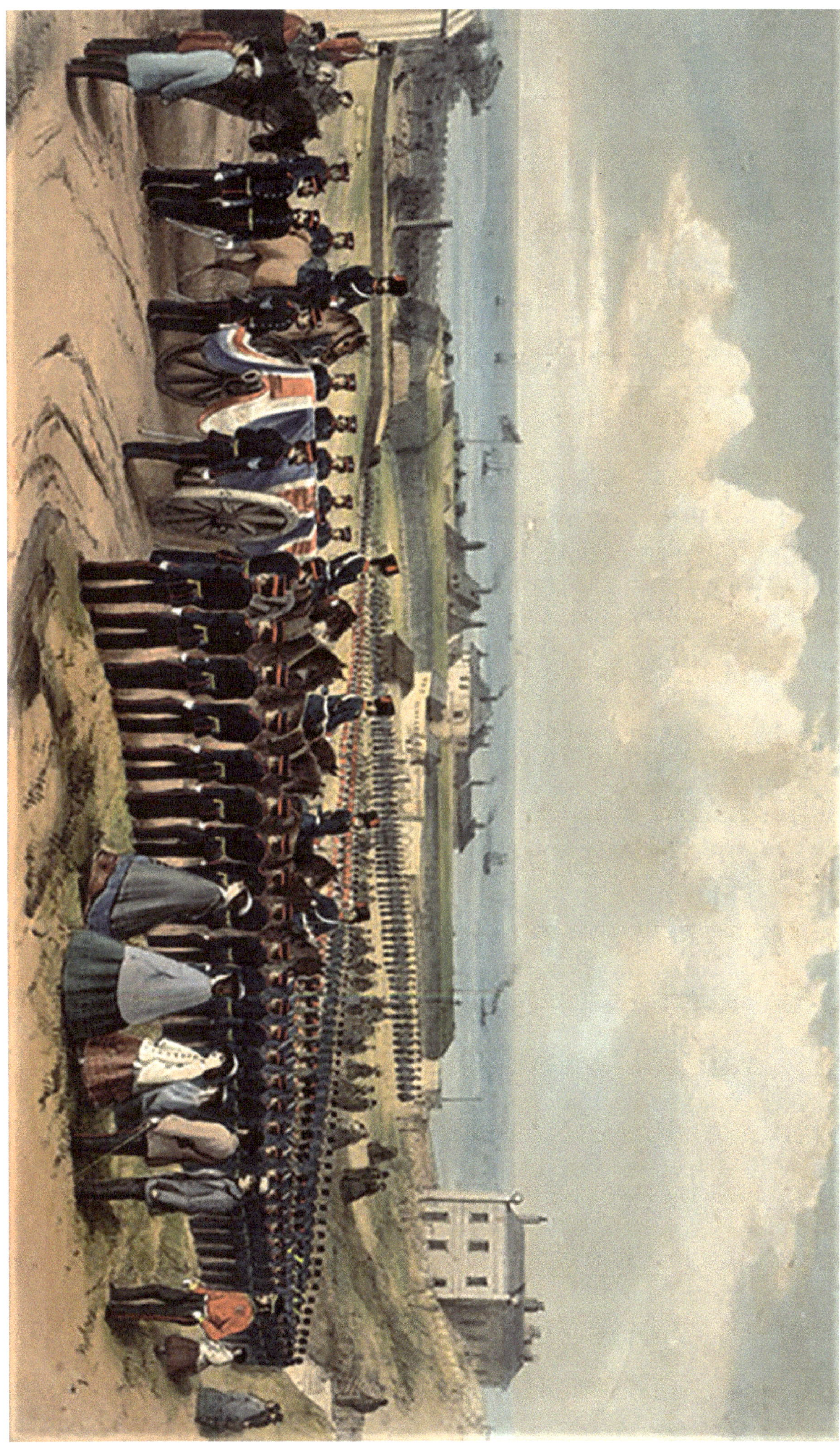

64 – STEP TOGETHER, THE VOLUNTEER'S SONG

Print signed by RJ Hamerton showing a long line of volunteers dressed in grey marching along a country lane. In the distance, surrounded by trees on a hill, a windmill. As the column march in fours with their rifles held at the trail, two mounted officers observe from the slope. A complete, un-cropped copy of this image is held at the Anne SK Brown Military Collection, Brown University Library which shows the title 'Step Together' at the top of the image, and 'The Volunteer's Song' at the bottom. They give the composer as EL Hime, artist as Robert Jacob Hamerton and printer as Standard & Dixon.

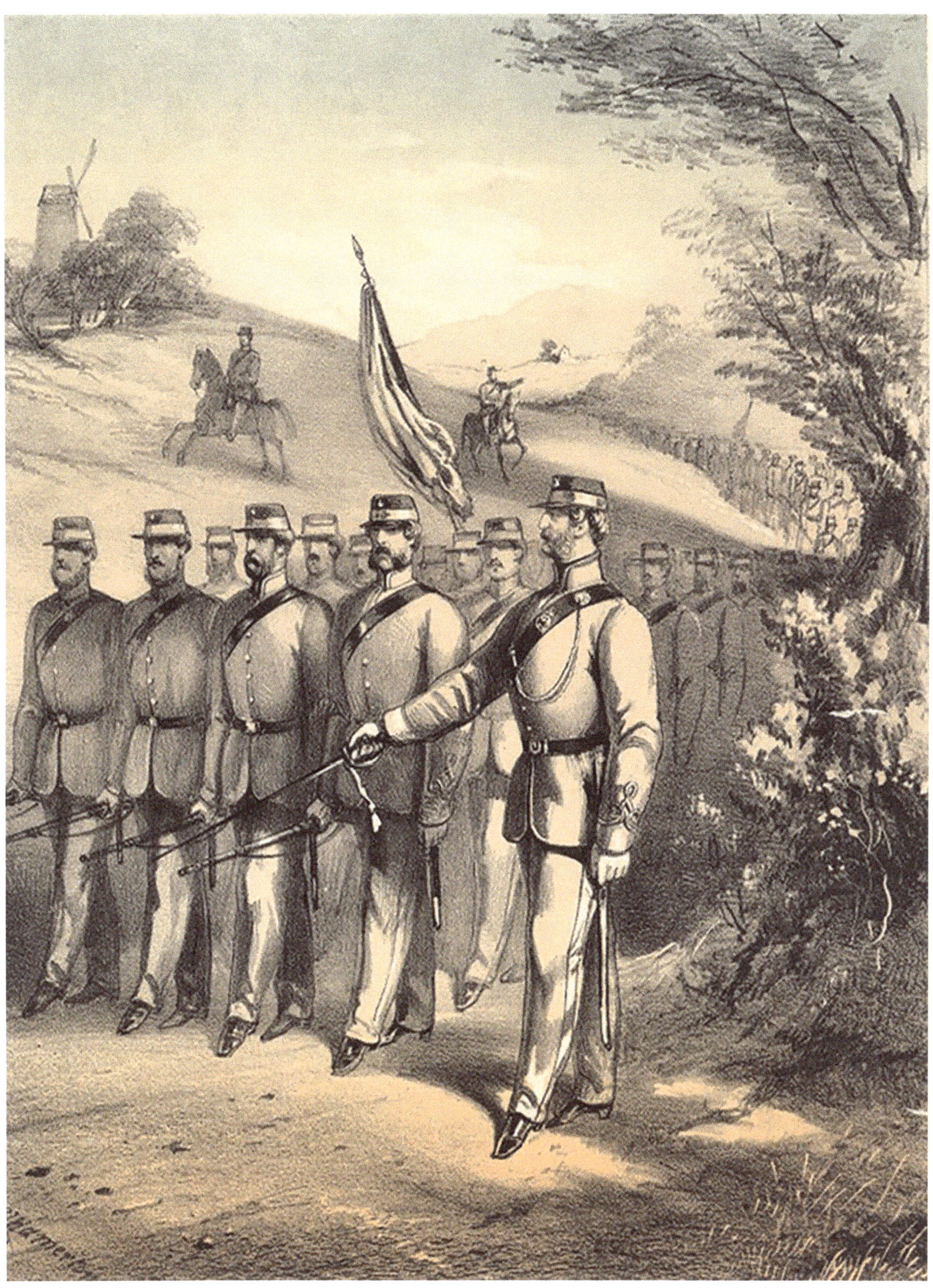

65 – NATIONAL RIFLE ASSOCIATION COMPETITION, WIMBLEDON 2 JULY 1860

Chromolithograph by Thomas Picken after George Housman Thomas showing Queen Victoria firing the first shot at the National Rifle Association's first meeting. Edward Walford writing of the Volunteer Force and Wimbledon in his *Greater London: A Narrative of Its History, Its People, And Its Places*, recorded how, 'The 2nd of July marked an epoch in the progress of the movement. On that day the first meeting of the National Rifle Association was held on Wimbledon Common. The weather was bright and a brilliant assembly had gathered to witness the proceedings. The first shot at the targets was fired by the Queen herself; and Mr Whitworth [Sir Joseph Whitworth, designer of the Whitworth Rifle] had so adjusted one of the rifles as to secure a good score for her Majesty at the 400 yards range.' Accurate was the sighting, the queen hitting the bull's eye and, in accordance with the rules of the NRA, scored three points. George Housman Thomas's image shows how the rifle had been set up on a canopied platform covered in red cloth. Horizontal, the weapon is fixed to a framework of wood and steel rods, two large, hanging, metal spheres acting as stabilisers. Volunteers in various uniforms all around bring their rifles to the present as her majesty, via a long cord and with Mr Whitworth standing close by so as to render assistance if necessary, pulls the trigger. Behind her are Prince Albert and members of the royal family.

'For six successive days' (Edward Walford again) 'the competition for the prizes for the best shooting continued. The number of volunteers who entered for the regulated prizes was 292, while 494 competed for those open to all-comers. The first Queen's Prize of £250, with the gold medal of the Association, was wone by Mr Ross, of the 7th York….' Edward Ross, Junr, a member of the 7th Yorkshire (North Riding) Rifle Volunteer Corps. (*Image courtesy of the Ann SK Brown Military Collection, Brown University Library*)

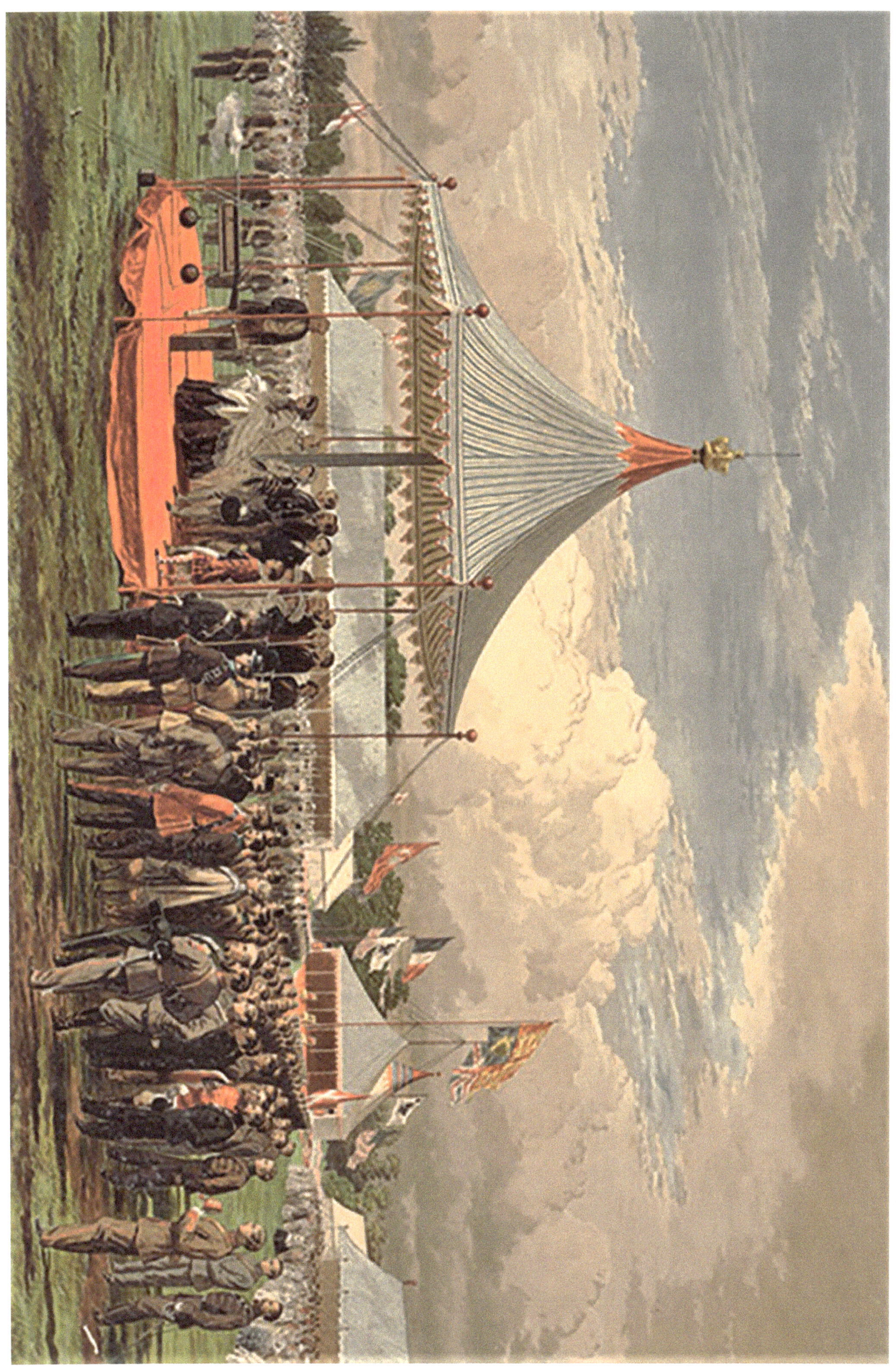

66 – VOLUNTEERS AT A FIRING POINT, WIMBLEDON 1866

Mezzotint by Thomas Lewis Atkinson after a painting by Henry Tanworth Wells and published by Henry Richard Graves of 6 Pall Mall, London on 27 February 1872. As a member of the Scots Guards leans sleepily against the upright pole of a canvas screen, a volunteer is in the process of capping his rifle. Behind him, an official peers through a tripod-mounted telescope towards the target as another, a sergeant, sits ready to record a score. Other volunteers stand by, one kilted and wearing a thistle badge in his glengarry cap, another in a striped shirt and sporting several shooting prize awards on the sleeve of his coat, as aim is taken by a marksman lying on the ground.

A copy of this print is held at the Anne SK Brown Military Collection, Brown University Library and is catalogued with a note to the effect that the image recalled the visit on 19 July 1866 of the Prince of Wales to the National Rifle Association's Wimbledon Prize Meeting. Captain Horatio Ross's company [the 7th Yorkshire North Riding] is mentioned as featuring in the picture, his son Edward (see image above) being the volunteer capping his Whitworth rifle, Captain Heaton, the man lying down and taking aim. Lord Elcho, of the London Scottish Volunteers, is seen on horseback at the back.

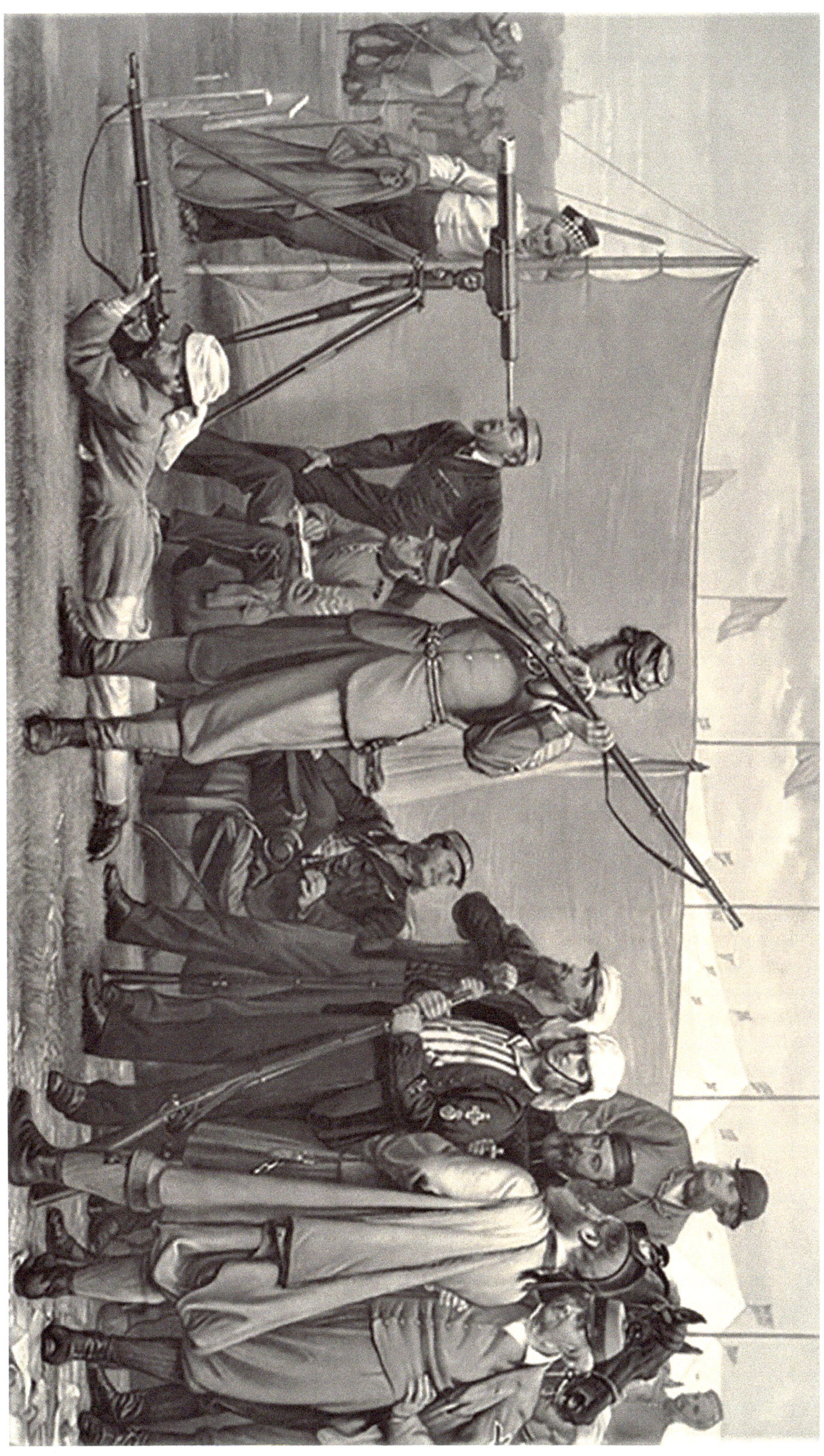

67 – THE GREY TOWER VALSE

Sheet music cover to the 'Grey Tower Valse' composed by Bandmaster H Carter of the Essex Artillery Volunteers. Litho by HC Maguire, printing by AB Court of 46 Poland Street, Soho, London. Volunteers are seen manning two guns on the lawn before an embattled country house. Fourteen gunners are present, one of them a young boy bugler.

Three individual artillery corps were formed in Essex during 1860-61 and these in 1880 were merged as the 1st Corps with headquarters at Stratford. Grey Towers was a mansion standing in eighty-five acres on the Hornchurch Road, Hornchurch, Essex, built in 1876 for Lieutenant-Colonel Henry Holmes, the owner of the Hornchurch Brewery. A deputy lieutenant for Essex, Colonel Holmes served with the 1st Essex AVC. (*Image courtesy of the Ann SK Brown Military Collection, Brown University Library*)

"GREY TOWER" VALSE,

Respectfully Dedicated to, MRS HOLMES, OF HORNCHURCH ESSEX.

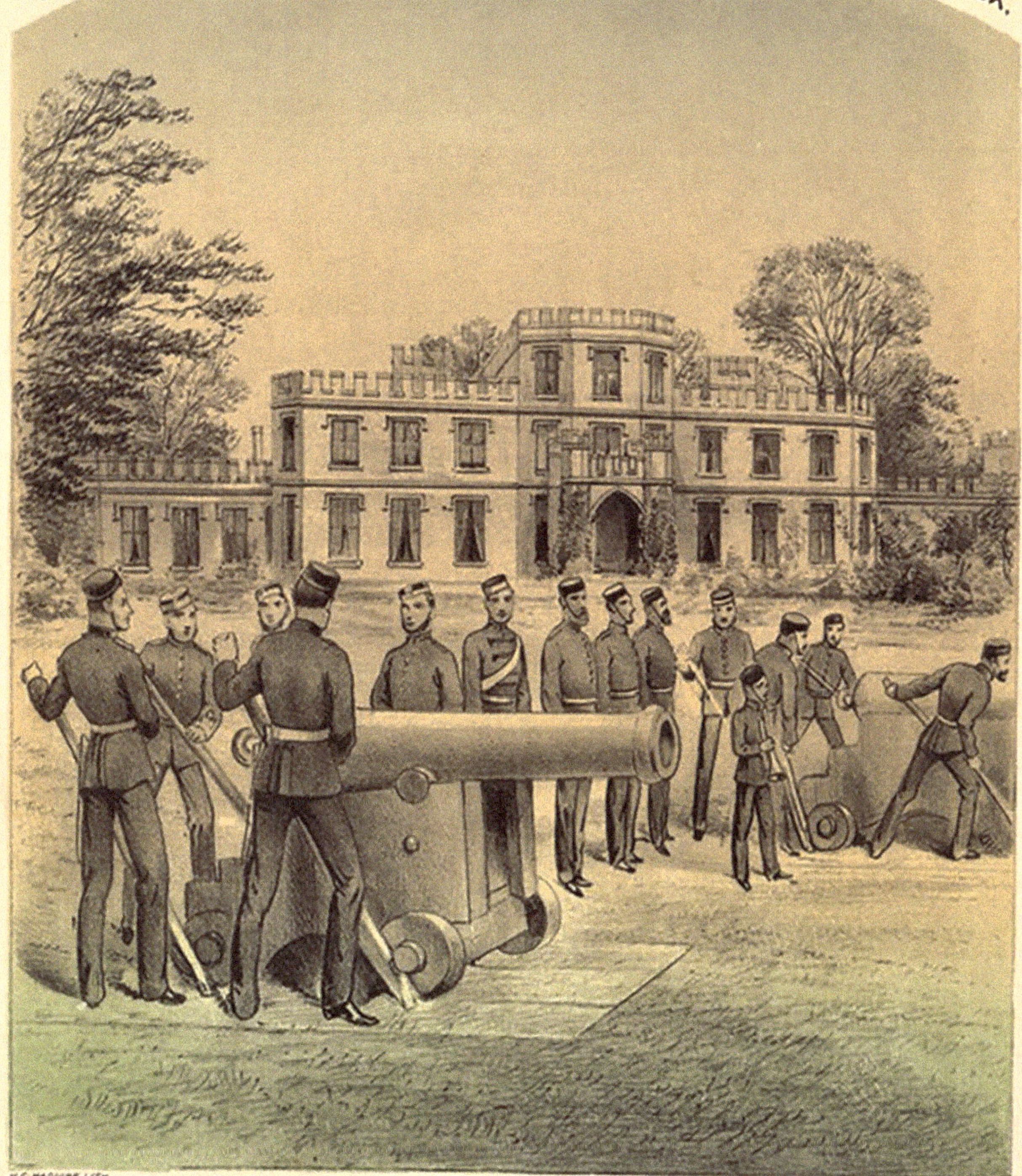

COMPOSED BY

H · CARTER.

(B·M· ESSEX ARTILLERY VOLUNTEERS, (LATE B·M· 1ST D·D· ROYAL ARTILLERY.)

(AUTHOR OF THE, "ARTILLERY VOLUNTEER," SONG, SUNG AT HER MAJESTY'S THEATRE, "THE BRITISH VOLUNTEERS" &C &C

ENT STA HALL.

(AUTHOR'S PROPERTY.)

68 – 1st MIDDLESEX VOLUNTEER ARTILLERY MARCH

Sheet music cover to the 1st Middlesex Volunteer Artillery March by CC Amos and 'Respectfully Dedicated To The Officers And Privates.' Published by CC Amos of 14 Craven Terrace, Hyde Park Gardens, London, litho work by Concanen & Lee, printed by Stannard & Dixon. Three volunteers are featured wearing dark blue uniforms with scarlet collars, cuffs and piping. Three different forms of headdress are in evidence, a fur busby with scarlet bag (left), a blue field cap (centre) and a cocked hat with black feathers (right).

The 1st Middlesex Volunteer Artillery was formed on 16 July 1860, its first headquarters being recorded as No 70 Quadrant, Regent Street. A series of moves later followed with the corps ending up at Leicester Square by 1863. Disbandment came in 1876. (*Image courtesy of the Ann SK Brown Military Collection, Brown University Library*)

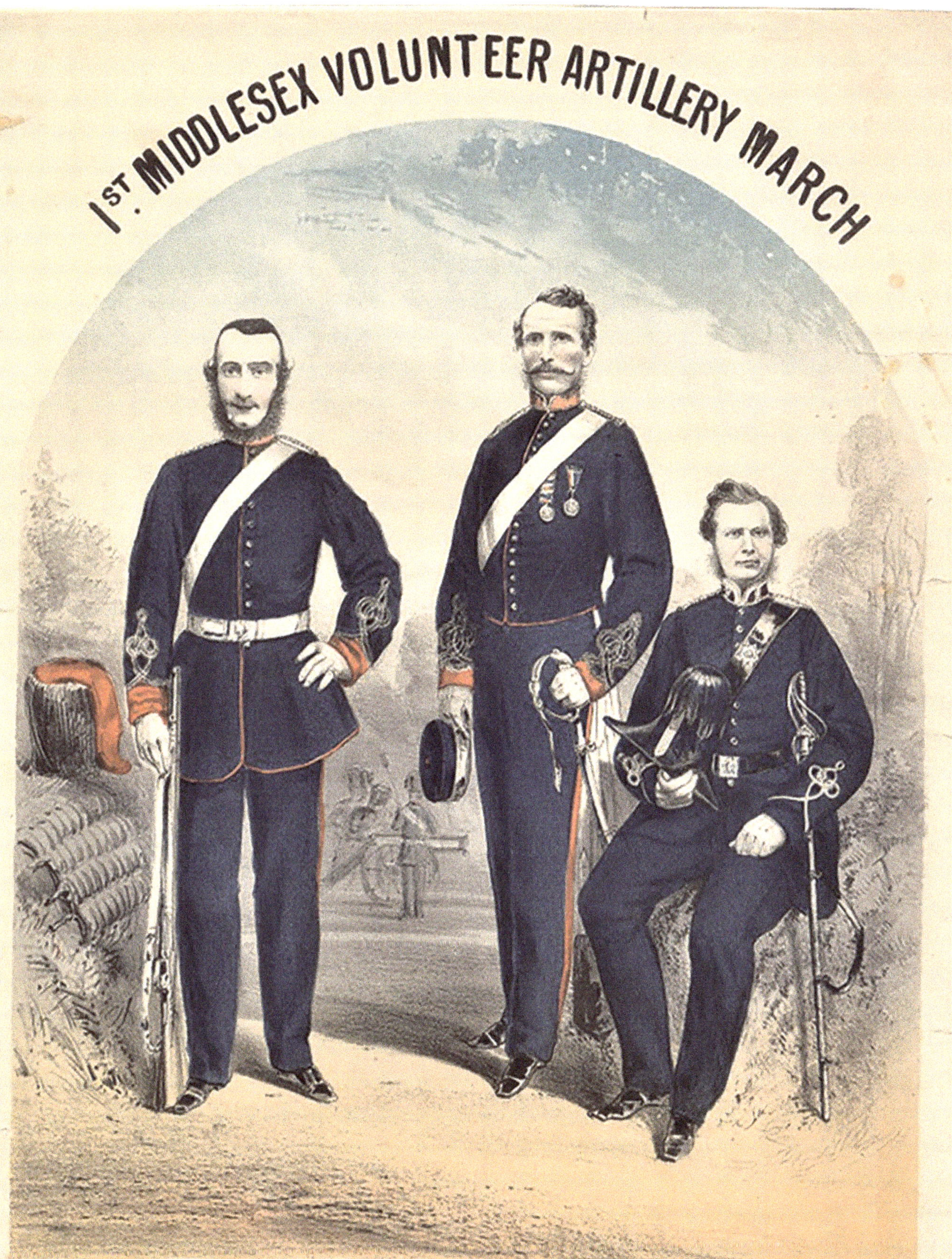

RESPECTFULLY DEDICATED TO THE OFFICERS AND PRIVATES.

BY

C. C. AMOS.

ENT. STA. HALL.

P 3/

c. 1860

PUBLISHED BY C. C. AMOS

14, CRAVEN TERRACE, HYDE PARK GARDENS, W.

69 – 1st RENFREWSHIRE AND DUMBARTON ROYAL GARRISON ARTILLERY (VOLUNTEERS)

Detail from Plate IV of *Records of the Scottish Volunteer Force, 1859-1908* written and illustrated by Lieutenant-General Sir James Moncrieff Grierson, published in 1909 by William Blackwood & Sons. Two volunteers are featured, a battery sergeant major of 1880 (left) and a company sergeant major for 1907 (right).

In 1863 an administrative brigade was formed with headquarters at Greenock which included the 1st, 2nd and 3rd Renfrewshire Artillery Volunteer Corps together with those from neighbouring Dumbartonshire which were also numbered as 1st to 3rd. The 1st Renfrewshire had been formed at Greenock on 20 January 1860 and in 1864 absorbed the 2nd and 3rd Corps, also at Greenock. In 1880 the brigade was consolidated in as 1st Renfrewshire and Dumbartonshire, the several batteries then being organised as follows: Nos 1 to 4 at Greenock (late 1st Renfrewshire), No 5 at Helensburgh (late 1st Dumbartonshire) and Nos 6 and 7 at Dumbarton (late 3rd Dumbartonshire).

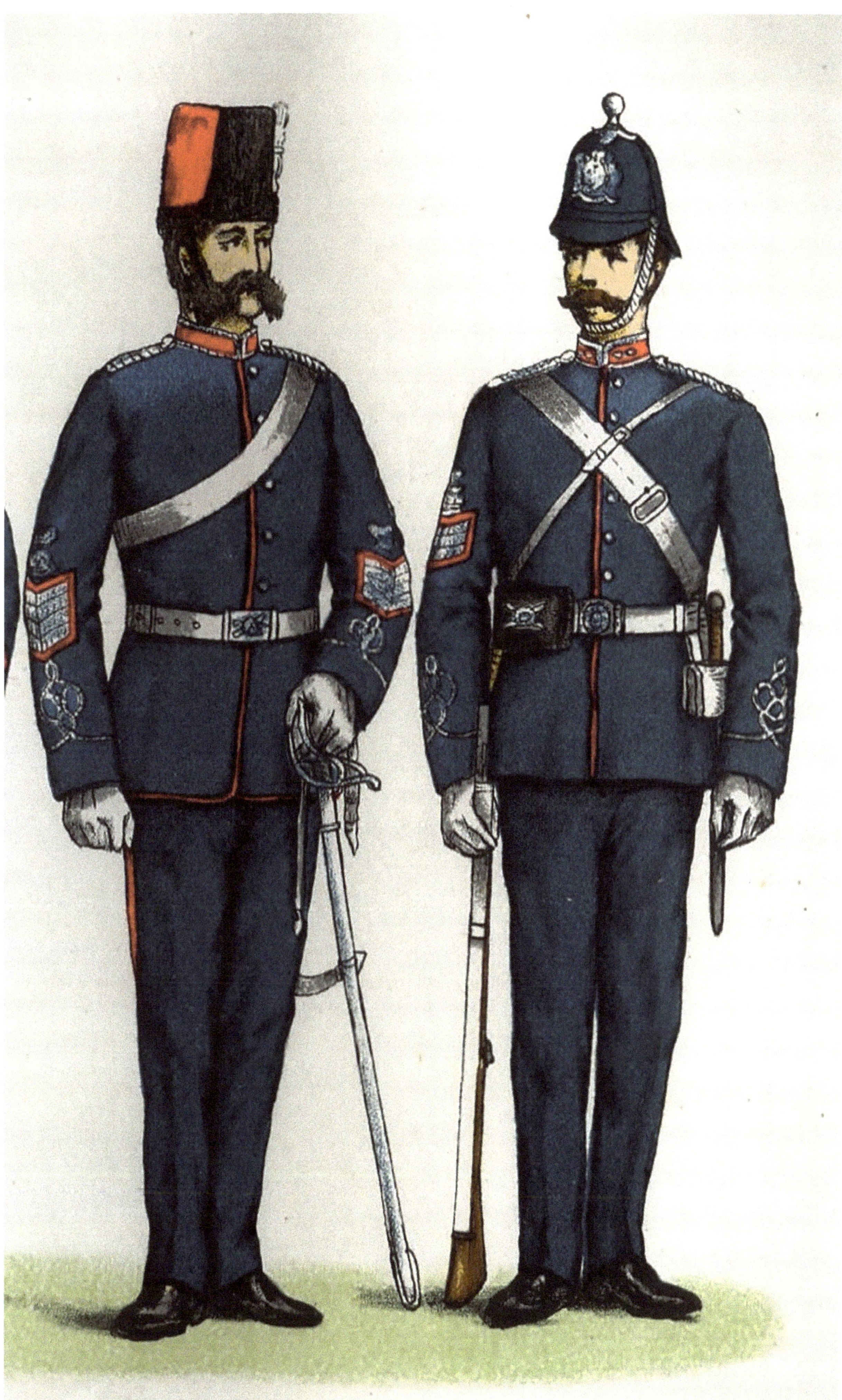

70 – 5TH VOLUNTEER BATTALION SCOTTISH RIFLES

Plate XXIII from *Records of the Scottish Volunteer Force, 1859-1908* written and illustrated by Lieutenant-General Sir James Moncrieff Grierson, published in 1909 by William Blackwood & Sons. The three figures are, from left to right, a private of the 4th Administrative Battalion Lanarkshire Rifle Volunteers of 1863 to 1871, a private of the same battalion from 1871 to 1879, and a private of the 29th (later 7th) Lanarkshire Rifle Volunteer Corps wearing the uniform of 1879 to 1897.

The 4th Administrative Battalion was formed with headquarters at Airdrie on 14 May 1862 and to it were added the 29th, 32nd, 43rd, 48th, 95th, 97th, 98th, 99th, 100th, 101st and 104th Lanarkshire Rifle Volunteers Corps. The first commanding officer of the battalion was former 2nd Dragoons officer, Major WW Hozier. On 19 September 1873 the battalion was consolidated as the new 29th Corps which comprised twelve companies: 'A' Coatbridge (late 29th Corps), 'B' Airdrie (late 32nd Corps and No 1 Company of 48th), 'C' Shotts (late 43rd Corps), 'D' Airdrie (late No 2 Company of 48th Corps), 'E' Baillieston (late 95th Corps), 'F' Coatbridge (late 97th Corps), 'G' Greengairs (late 98th Corps), 'H' Clarkston (late 99th Corps), 'I' Calderbank (late 100th Corps), 'K' Newarthill (late 101st Corps), 'L' Bellshill (late 104th Corps), 'M' Harthill and Benhar (late 100th Corps).

In 1875 'E' and 'F' Companies were amalgamated 'E' at Coatbridge and a new 'F' formed at Chryston. Two years later the corps was reduced to eight companies and reorganised as follows: 'A' Coatbridge, 'B' Airdrie, 'C' Shotts (formed by 'C' and 'M' Companies), 'D' Airdrie (formed by 'D' and 'L' Companies), 'E' Coatbridge, 'F' Cheyston, 'G' Caldecruix (formed by 'G' and 'H' Companies), 'H' Newarthill (formed by 'I' and 'K' Companies).

The 29th Corps was renumbered 7th in 1880 and designated as 5th Volunteer Battalion Cameronians (Scottish Rifles) in 1887. With effect from 1 April 1897, however, the battalion was disbanded as a result of severe criticism regarding discipline by the officer commanding the 26th Regimental District.

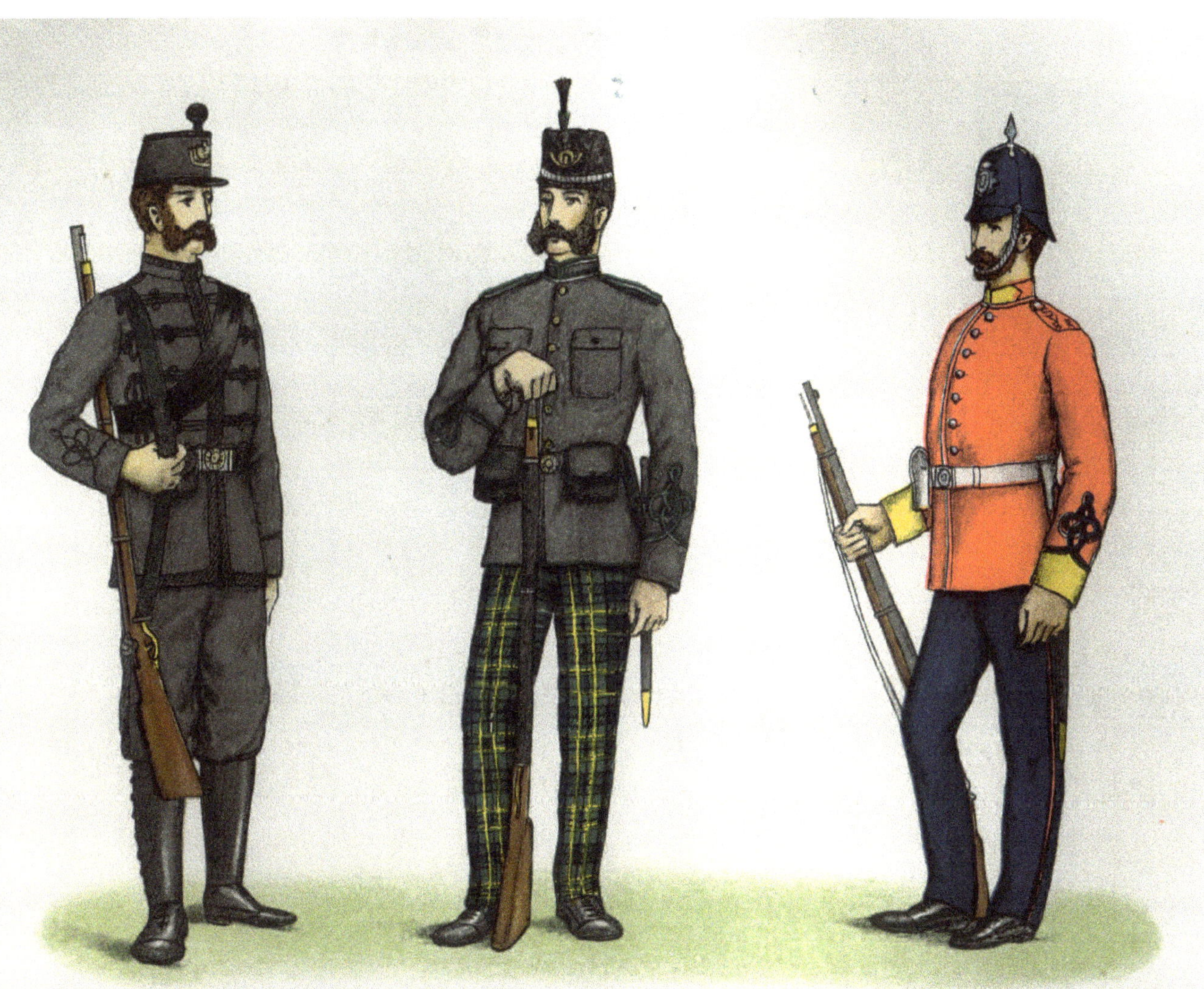

Private, 4th Ad. Bn. Lk. R.V. 1863–1871

Private, 4th A.B. (29th) L.R.V. 1871–1879

Private, 29th (7th) L.R.V. and 5th V.B.S.R. 1879–1897

5th VOL. BN. SCOTTISH RIFLES

71 – 1st DUMBARTONSHIRE VOLUNTEER RIFLE CORPS

Plate XLIV from *Records of the Scottish Volunteer Force, 1859-1908* written and illustrated by Lieutenant-General Sir James Moncrieff Grierson, published in 1909 by William Blackwood & Sons. From left to right the figures are: a private of the 6th Dumbartonshire Rifle Volunteer Corps in 1860, a private of the same corps for 1861 to 1864, a sergeant of the 1st Administrative Battalion of Dumbartonshire Rifle Volunteers wearing the green uniform of 1864 to 1874, a private of 1874 to 1882, lieutenant for 1882 to 1887 and a colour sergeant in review order, 1887 to 1908.

All rifle corps raised within the county of Dumbartonshire joined the 1st Admin Battalion which was consolidated as the new 1st Corps in 1880. They were numbered 1st to 14th and were as follows:

1st—One company formed at Row with Alex H Denistoun as captain, Colin D Wilson, lieutenant and James Honeyman, ensign. All three held commissions dated 18 February 1860. Absorbed the 8th Corps at Gareloch in June 1865, headquarters moving to Helensburgh, two miles away, in January 1873. Became 'A' Company of the new 1st Corps in 1880.

2nd—One company formed at East Kilpatrick with Captain Archibald Campbell Colquhoun, Lieutenant John Leckie Ewing and Ensign Hugh Kirkwood commissioned on 8 February 1860. Headquarters moved to Maryhill in 1868, the strength increasing by a half-company at the same time. Became 'H' Company of the new 1st Corps in 1880.

3rd—One company formed at Bonhill with Captain Mathew Gray, Lieutenant Thomas Logan Stillie and Ensign Edward McIntyre commissioned on 8 February 1860. Became 'D' Company of the new 1st Corps in 1880.

4th—One company formed at Jamestown with Captain Archibald Orb Ewing and Ensign Thomas Roxburgh commissioned on 8 February 1860. Became 'E' Company of the new 1st Corps in 1880.

5th—One company formed at Alexandria with Captain Mathew Clark commissioned on 8 February 1860. Became 'F' Company of the new 1st Corps in 1880.

6th—One company formed at Dumbarton with John Macausland as captain, William Paterson, lieutenant and William Graham, ensign. All three officers held commissions dated 8 February 1860. Increased to one-and-a-half companies in 1878 and became 'C' Company of the new 1st Corps in 1880.

7th—The services of one company were accepted at Cardross on 11 November 1859, the officers' commissions: Captain Tucker Geils, Lieutenant John William Burnes and Ensign David MacBrayne, being dated 15 March 1860. Became 'B' Company of the new 1st Corps in 1880.

8th—One sub-division formed at Gareloch with Lieutenant John Cabbell and Ensign Robert Bennett Browne commissioned on 16 February 1860. Increased to a full company in 1863. General Grierson in Records of the Scottish Volunteers states that the 8th was absorbed into the 1st Corps at Row on 24 June 1865. The corps, however, remained in the Army List with all three of its officers until 1869.

9th—One sub-division formed at Luss with Lieutenant Montagu J Martin and Alex Macniven being commissioned on 8 February 1860. Increased to a full company on 28 August 1868 and became 'M' Company of the new 1st Corps in 1880. The village of Luss is on the west side of Loch Lomond.

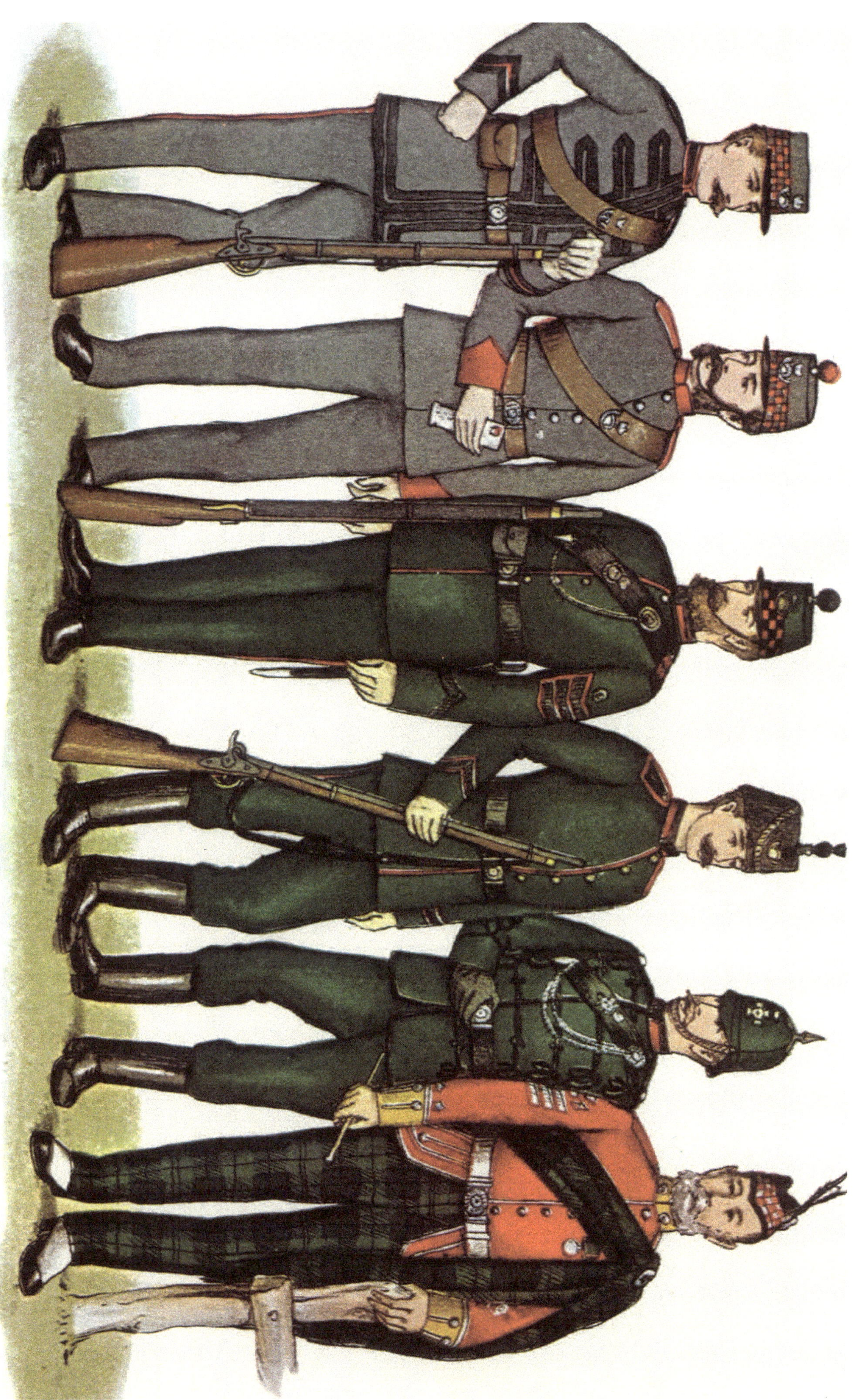

10th—One company formed at Kirkintilloch with John M Gartshore as captain, Alex Brown Armour, lieutenant and Thomas Brown, ensign. All three officers held commissions dated 5 March 1860. Increased to one-and-a-half companies in 1874 and became 'K' Company of the new 1st Corps in 1880.

11th—One company formed at Cumbernauld with James Mackenzie as captain, Thomas Watson, lieutenant and David Coutts, ensign. All three held commissions dated 13 June 1860. Became 'L' Company of the new 1st Corps in 1880.

12th—One sub-division formed at Tarbert with a detachment at Arrochar on 7 March 1861—the original officers being Lieutenant Thomas Shedden and Ensign James McMurrich. The corps was disbanded in 1869.

13th—The services of one company were accepted at Milngavie on 9 August 1867, its original officers: Captain Hugh Kirkwood, Lieutenant Alex Ross, Ensign John Granger, Surgeon Peter F Robertson, MD and Chaplain, the Rev Robert Bell were all commissioned on 23 August. Became 'I' Company of the new 1st Corps in 1880.

14th—The services of one company at Clydebank were accepted on 18 May 1875, its first officers: Captain James R Thomson and Sub Lieutenant Robert Carswell, being commissioned on 23 June 1875. Became 'G' Company of the new 1st Corps in 1880.

The 1st Admin Battalion was formed with headquarters at Balloch on 7 May 1860 and consolidated as the new 1st Corps in 1880. Headquarters were placed at Helensburgh and there were twelve companies: 'A' Helensburgh (late 1st Corps), 'B' Cardross (late 7th Corps), 'C' Dumbarton (6th Corps), 'D' Bonhill (3rd Corps), 'E' Jamestown (4th Corps), 'F' Alexandria (5th Corps), 'G' Clydebank (14th Corps), 'H' Maryhill (2nd Corps), 'I' Milngavie (13th Corps), 'K' Kirkintilloch (10th Corps), 'L' Cumbernauld (11th Corps), 'M' Luss (9th Corps).

Became a Volunteer battalion of the Argyll and Sutherland Highlanders (without change of title) in 1881. 'M' Company at Luss was disbanded in January 1882 but replaced the following month at Renton. The disbandment of the Luss Company had been as a result of the direct defiance by the corps to change its uniform to that then in use by the whole battalion (see 9th Corps). 'L' Company was absorbed into 'K' as a detachment in 1884 and at the same time a new 'L' was formed at Yorker. A Mounted Infantry Company lettered 'O' was added at Maryhill in 1900, then in the same year 'Q' (Cyclist) was raised at Dumbarton. Some ninety-eight members of the battalion were sent out to join the Regulars of 1st Battalion Argyll and Sutherland Highlanders during the war in South Africa. Of those who lost their lives, the names of Sergeant J C Morrison, Corporal W L L Fitzwilliams, Lance Corporal T Stevenson, Privates M Donnelly, R M Duncan, W Kelly and D W Moore appear on the war memorial outside the Municipal Buildings in Garshake Road, Dumbarton.

To enlarge upon the disbandment of 'M' Company in January 1882, it would seem that for some time the commanding officer of the new 1st Dumbartonshire RVC, Henry Currie, was far from satisfied with the conduct of the Luss Volunteers. As a kilted company wearing blue bonnets, it was the colonel's opinion that they spoilt the appearance on parade of the rest of the battalion who were dressed in helmets and green uniforms. On 25 August 1881, a Royal Review at Edinburgh attended by Queen Victoria, was to include the 1st Dumbarton. Colonel Curie, who did not wish 'M' Company to attend, issued orders directing that it was 'to stay at home' and subsequently the battalion left for Edinburgh without Luss. After taking up their positions in the parade, members of the Dumbarton RVC were astonished to see 'M' Company not only there, but marching with another battalion.

72 – OFFICER, ROYAL ENGINEERS VOLUNTEERS, 1901

Original watercolour, thought to be the work of Richard Simkin, showing an officer in review order. The tunic is of scarlet cloth with collar and cuffs of Garter blue velvet. The collar is edged with silver lace and has a grenade device each side. A shoulder belt of Russia leather, two inches wide and with silver lines, is worn, the waist belt the same but with two straight silver lines. The blue home service helmet bears the royal arms in silver. (*Image courtesy of the Anne SK Brown Military Collection, Brown University Library*)

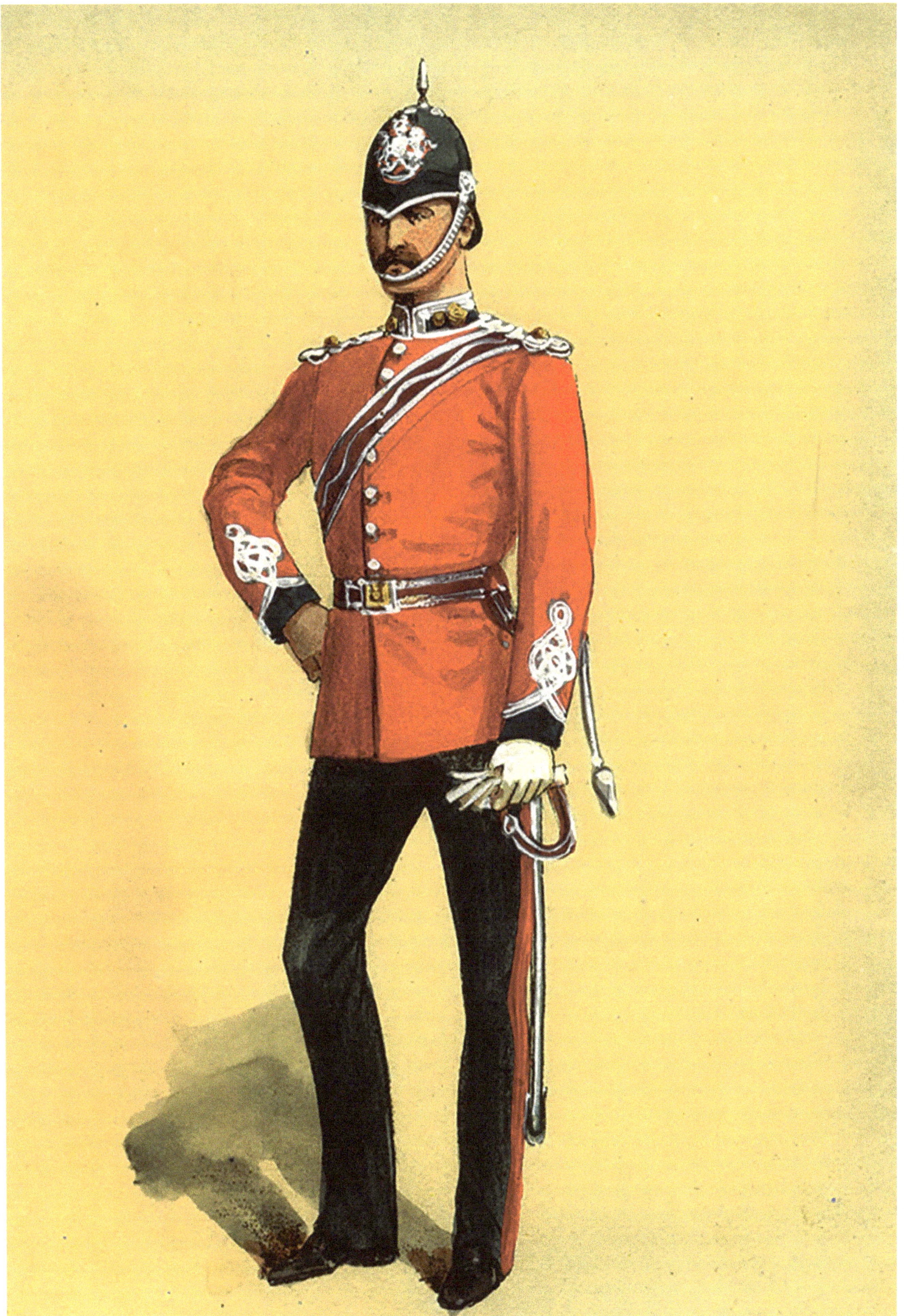

73 – 22ND MIDDLESEX RIFLE VOLUNTEER CORPS

Original watercolour signed and dated 1885 by Harry Payne. A single figure dressed in green dark green jacket and trousers. The collar is scarlet, and piping of the same colour provides a edging down the front of the coat, on the cuffs below a lighter green Austrian knot, around the shoulder straps which are embroidered with the designation '22 Mx', and as a backing to chevrons and a proficiency star on the upper right arm. The green home service helmet has bronze fittings and a Maltese cross plate.

The 22nd Middlesex Rifle Volunteer Corps was formed from members of the legal profession with the number 40th on 30 April 1860. The corps comprised eight companies at Gray's Inn, London and was included in the 3rd Admin Battalion of Middlesex Rifle Volunteers until 1861 when made independent. In that year Lieutenant Colonel Alfred PFC Somerset, late of the 13th Regiment of Foot, took command, Central London Rifle Rangers was added to title and the 35th Middlesex RVC at Enfield was absorbed. Re-numbering as 22nd was in 1880. The corps became a volunteer battalion (without change in title) of the Royal Fusiliers in 1881, and transferred to the King's Royal Rifle Corps in the following year. Mayall College Cadet Corps at Herne Hill was affiliated in 1891 but removed from the Army List in 1899.

Volunteers from the corps saw active service in South Africa during the Boer War. Lieutenant W Brian L Alt, who had been first commissioned into the 22nd on 2 June 1894—his father, W J Alt, had commanded the corps since1881—was killed at Diamond Hill on 12 June 1900 while serving with the City Imperial Volunteers. He would be the only officer of the CIV to lose his life. Also, from the 22nd Middlesex RVC was Charles Gwyn Trivet Bromfield who died from wounds received in action near Boshof on 16 February 1902. From the ranks, he had risen to captain in the 87th Company, Imperial Yeomanry. The 22nd became the 12th (County of London) Battalion of the London Regiment upon transfer to the Territorial Force in 1908. (*Image courtesy of the Ann SK Brown Military Collection, Brown University Library*)

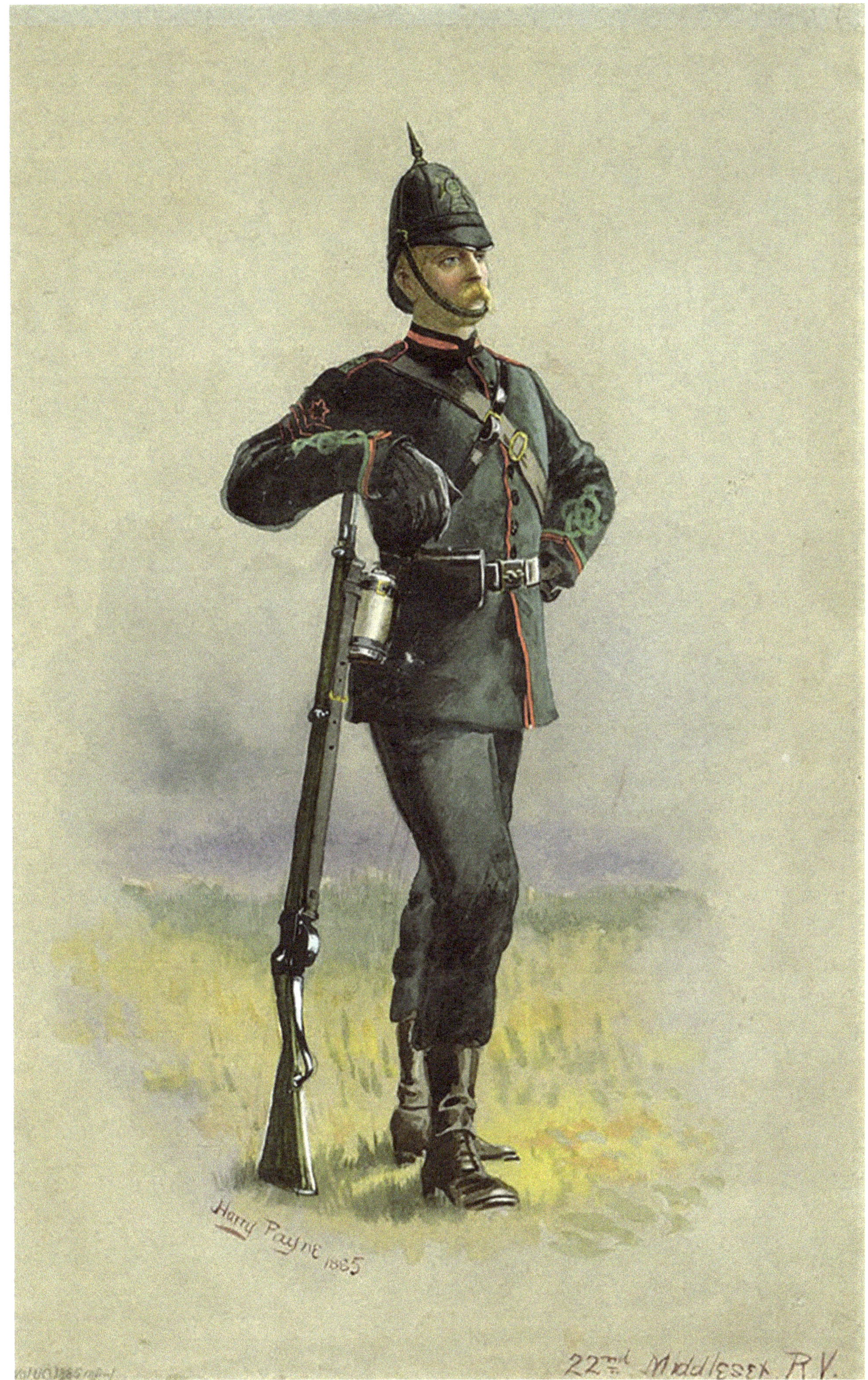
Harry Payne 1885
22nd Middlesex R.V.

74 – OUR BRITISH VOLUNTEERS

Chromolithographic plate after Alfred William Cooper published as a supplement to the *Boy's Own Paper*'. Drawn especially for the publication, artist Alfred William Cooper was a serving member of the 2nd Middlesex (South Middlesex) Rifle Volunteer Corps. The image provides a good example of the various uniform colours in use by members of the Volunteer Movement—scarlet, green and various shades of grey.

Working from left to right we can see wearing grey and a black patent leather pouch-belt with silver fittings, a member of the Civil Service Rifles (12th Middlesex RVC). Next to him, and with his rifle at his side, one of the London Irish (16th Middlesex RVC) who is in conversation with a kilted member of the London Scottish (7th Middlesex RVC), a rifleman of the Queen's Westminsters (13th Middlesex RVC) who has a red band and pom-pom on his grey cap, in green one of the Paddington Rifles (18th Middlesex RVC) and in scarlet, a member of the 3rd London RVC. Wearing a bearskin cap and standing at the back of the group, a member of the Honourable Artillery Company and in a home service helmet and scarlet jacket, a volunteer engineer. A sergeant of the 2nd (South) Middlesex wearing light grey with scarlet facings stands by the side of a mounted officer from the London Rifle Brigade (1st London RVC). Those seated are from the 2nd (South) Middlesex, Tower Hamlets Rifle Volunteers and 20th Middlesex (Artists' Rifles) RVC. (*Image courtesy of the Ann SK Brown Military Collection, Brown University Library*)

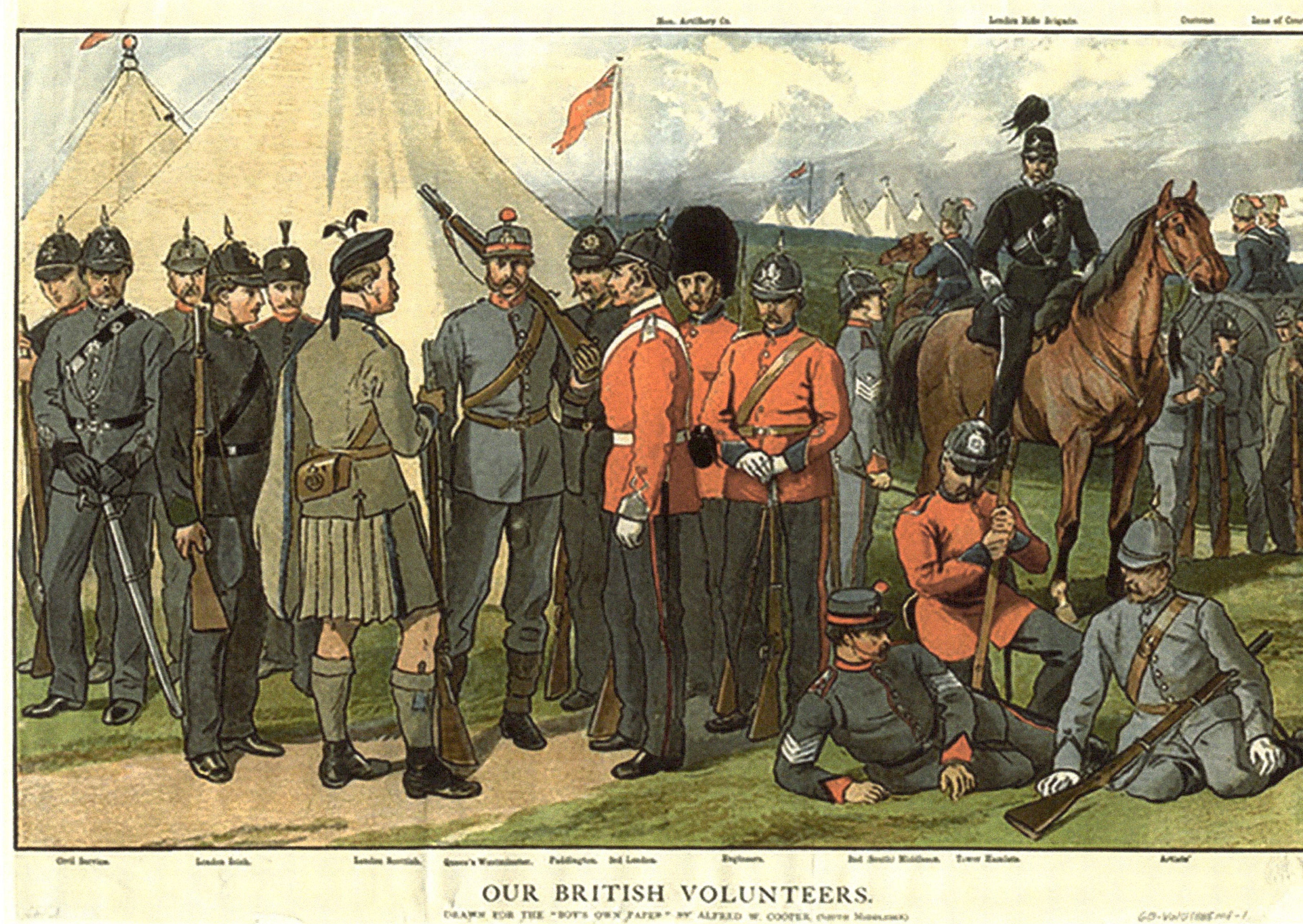

OUR BRITISH VOLUNTEERS.

DRAWN FOR THE "BOY'S OWN PAPER" BY ALFRED W. COOPER (South Middlesex)

75 – TOMMY ATKINS

Sheet music cover of Brandon Thomas's composition 'Tommy Atkins', artwork by Frank Dadd who features one of the Artists Rifles in his grey uniform. A rolled greatcoat can be seen slung across the body and the artist's 'FD' initials in the bottom right hand corner of the image. This particular copy is from the Anne SK Brown Military Collection who also hold a letter from Brandon Thomas dated London 1887 dedicating the song to a fellow comrade in the Artists' Rifles, one Private EV Salaman of 'F' Company. The full title of the regiment at the time was 20th Middlesex Rifle Volunteer Corps (Artists), its headquarters being in Duke's Road, Euston, London. As the name suggests, this part-time regiment was made up of painters, musicians, actors and others connected with the arts. (*Image courtesy of the Anne SK Brown Military Collection, Brown University Library*)

To My Comrade, E. V. Salaman.

"TOMMY ATKINS"

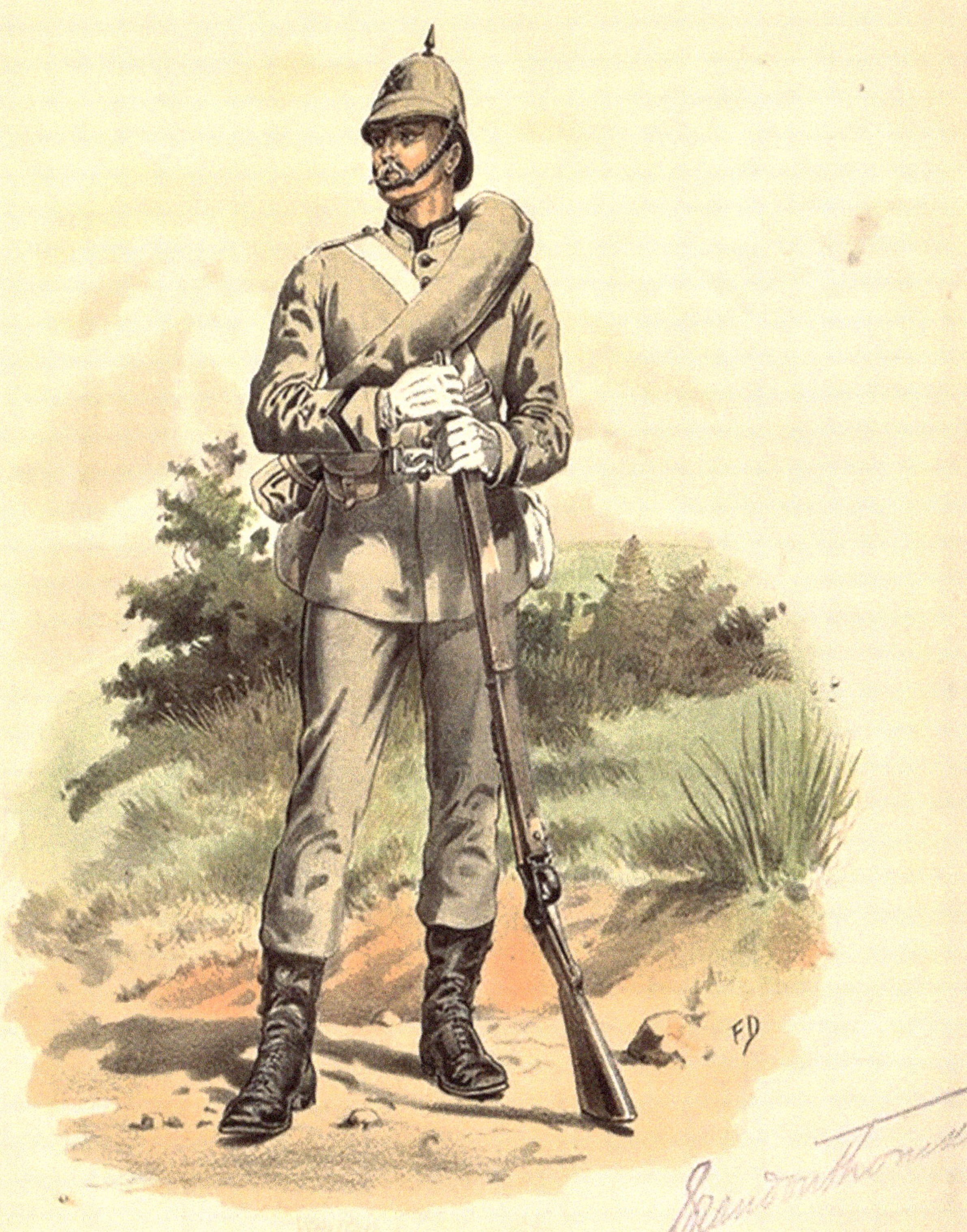

Written & Composed by

BRANDON THOMAS.

(Artist's Corps, 20th Middlx.)

Ent. Sta. Hall. Pr 4/-

LONDON:
J. BATH, 23, BERNERS STREET, W.

76 – 4TH VOLUNTEER BATTALION ROYAL SCOTS

Postcard publisher by W & AK Johnston Ltd. The 4th Volunteer Battalion of the Royal Scots had its origins in a company of the 1st Edinburgh Rifle Volunteer Corps that consisted entirely of total abstainers. It had been founded in 1859 by John Hope, a prominent member of the British Temperance League. George McCrae, seen here wearing the Volunteer Decoration with its green ribbon, had taken command on 28 January 1905.

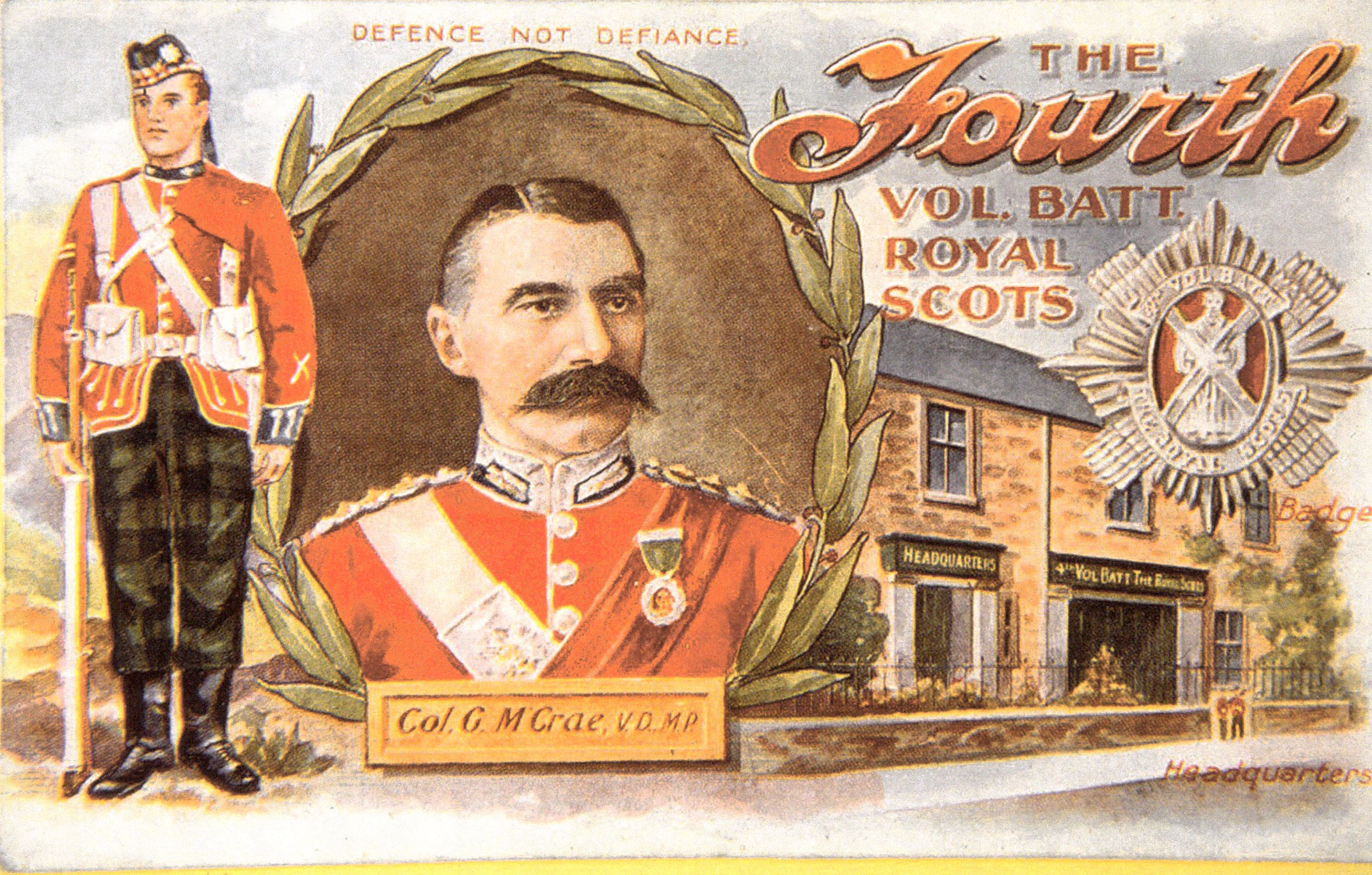
DEFENCE NOT DEFIANCE.
THE Fourth
VOL. BATT.
ROYAL
SCOTS
Col. G. McCrae, V.D. M.P.
HEADQUARTERS
4th VOL BATT THE ROYAL SCOTS
Badge
Headquarters

77 – 1st Middlesex Rifle Volunteer Corps (Victoria Rifles)

Chromolith colour plate after GD Giles from *Her Majesty's Army* by Walter Richards and published by JS Virtue & Co Ltd of 294 City Road and 26 Ivy Lane, London during the 1890s. The image shows members of the signal section.

Upon the general disbandment of volunteers in 1814, the Duke of Cumberland's Sharpshooter, which had been formed in 1803, was permitted to continue service—although not formally recognised as a military body, but as a rifle club. In 1835 permission was granted to style the organisation as the Royal Victoria Rifle Club and in 1853 sanction to form a volunteer corps was given. As the Victoria Volunteer Rifle Corps, whose first officers' commissions were dated 4 January 1853, the club subsequently, in 1859, became the 1st Middlesex RVC. The additional title 'Victoria' was added by March 1860.

Headquarters were in Kilburn, North-West London but a move was made to Marlborough Place, off Hamilton Terrace, St John's Wood in 1867. The corps had become a volunteer battalion (ranked as 4th) of the King's Royal Rifle Corps, but without change in title, in 1881. Headquarters moved to 56 Davies Street, Westminster in 1892, and in the same year an amalgamation took place on 1 June with the 6th Middlesex (St George's) RVC. The new title adopted being 1st Middlesex (Victoria and St George's). Transfer to the Territorial Force in 1908 saw the 1st Middlesex amalgamated with the 19th Middlesex to form the 9th Battalion London Regiment. A cadet corps with headquarters in Marlborough Place was formed towards the end of 1866, but this was later disbanded and last seen in the Army List for January 1898.

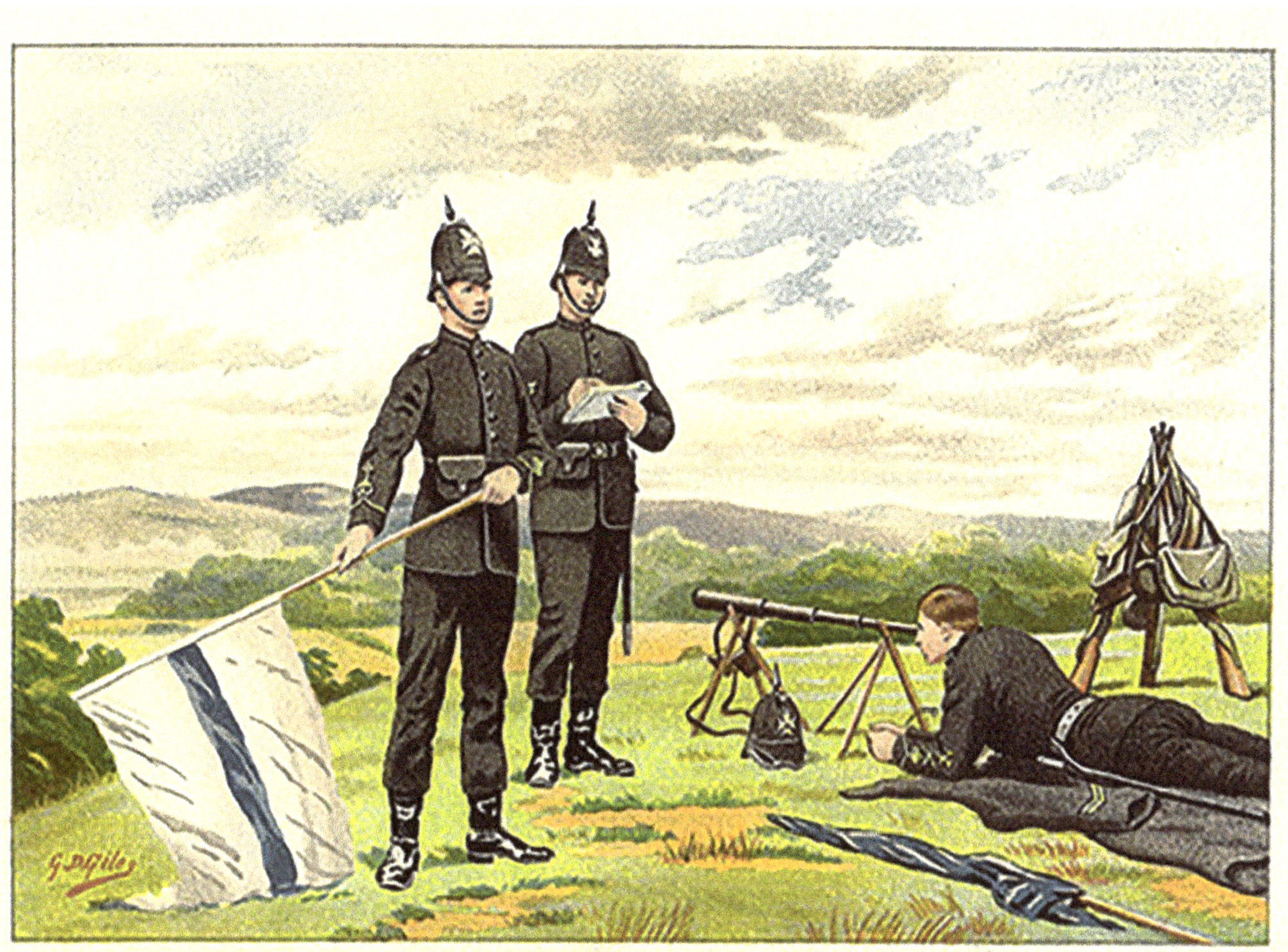

THE 1st MIDDLESEX (VICTORIA RIFLES)

VOLUNTEERS.

(4th Volunteer Battalion King's Royal Rifle Corps.)

78 – THE AWKWARD SQUAD

Sheet music cover to 'The Awkward Squad, Or the Experience Of A Volunteer Rifleman' by Henry Walker and published by Metzler & Co of 35, 37 & 38 Great Marlborough Street. The litho work was done by Thomas Packer, printing by Stannard & Dixon. With a tented camp in the background, a group of civilians and two cackling geese enjoy the spectacle of seven volunteer riflemen lining up before a stout NCO. Tall, short, fat and strangers to military discipline, the 'awkward squad' look exactly that. Composer Henry Walker, a volunteer himself, dedicates his work to his comrades. (*Image courtesy of the Anne SK Brown Military Collection, Brown University Library*)

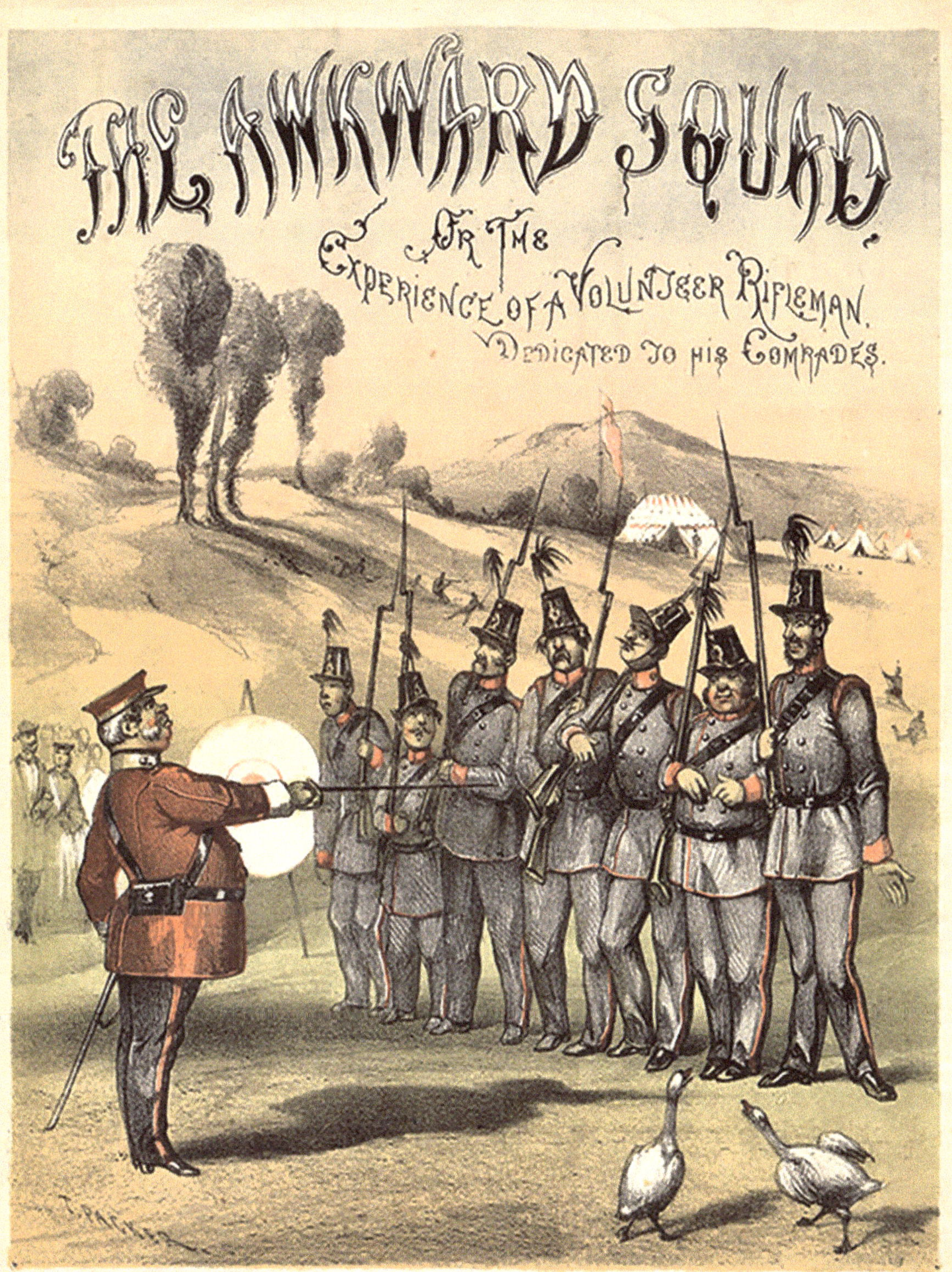

T. PACKER, LITH. STANNARD & DIXON

WRITTEN AND ARRANGED BY

HENRY WALKER.

ENT. STA. HALL. Pr. 2/6

LONDON,
METZLER & Co. 35, 37 & 38, Gt. MARLBOROUGH ST. W.

79 – 2nd Shropshire Rifle Volunteer Corps

Illustration of the 2nd Shropshire Rifle Volunteer Corps after RJ Marrion from an article by Ray Westlake published in 'Military Modelling' magazine, 1989. Bob Marrion shows an officer (left) and private (right).

A 2nd Administration Battalion of Shropshire Rifle Volunteers was formed with headquarters at Shrewsbury in July 1860 and to it were added the 2nd, 3rd, 7th, 8th, 12th, 13th, 15th and 18th Corps. The battalion was consolidated in 1880 as the new 2nd Corps with seven companies: 'A' Market Drayton (late 2nd Corps), 'B' Whitchurch (late 3rd Corps), 'C' Wellington (late 7th Corps), 'D' Hodnet (late 8th Corps), 'E' Wem (late 12th Corps), 'F' Oswestry (late 15th Corps), 'G' Newport (late 18th Corps).

Corps headquarters were transferred to Newport shortly after consolidation. 'H' Company was added at Ellesmere in 1885 and in 1887, under General Order 181 of December, the 2nd Shropshire RVC became 2nd Volunteer Battalion King's (Shropshire Light Infantry).

Below, Bob Marrion's illustration of 2nd Shropshire Rifle Volunteer Corps c.1896. Officer (left) and other rank.

80 – 13th Middlesex Rifle Volunteer Corps

One of three chromolith plates by Kelother of London after Herbert R Benham published with the *Volunteer Service Magazine* between May 1892 and May 1894. Three figures running, a corporal and private followed by an officer, who wear light grey uniforms with scarlet collars and cuffs. The grey home service helmets have Maltese cross-type plates, the two leading men wearing brown leather belts and ammunition pouches. The officer has a rifle-style jacket with five rows of cord across the chest, and a pouch-belt of brown leather to which is fixed a silver whistle and chain set.

The post-1880 13th Middlesex Rifle Volunteer Corps was originally numbered as 22nd Middlesex (Queen's) at Pimlico, having been formed there in January 1860 from several companies raised earlier. A standing order of the time stated that 'On 13 January 1860, the Queen's Rifle Volunteers amalgamated with the several companies raised in the parishes of St. John's, St. Margaret's, St Mary's Strand, St Paul's Covent Garden, St James, St Martin's in the Fields, St Anne's John Street, St Clement Danes and with the King's College.' Also included in the corps was a number of men who had enrolled into a corps formed at Messrs J Broadwood & Sons Ltd of Horseferry Road, Westminster. The first officers' commissions were dated 25 February 1860.

The corps comprised fifteen companies divided into two battalions under the command of Lieutenant-Colonel Commandant the Earl Grosvenor. Headquarters were given as Westminster from March 1860. The corps was re-numbered as 13th in 1880 and became a volunteer battalion (without change in title) of the King's Royal Rifle Corps in 1881. By 1900 the establishment had reached sixteen companies which were organised and named as follows: 'A', 'B', 'C', 'D' Pimlico Division, 'E', 'F' St John's Division, 'G' St Margaret's Division, 'H' St James's Division, 'I', 'K' St Martin's Division, 'L' Schoolbread's Company, 'M' St Clement Dane's Division, 'O' Royal Welsh, 'R' Greater Westminster, 'S' Mounted Infantry, 'T' Cyclists.

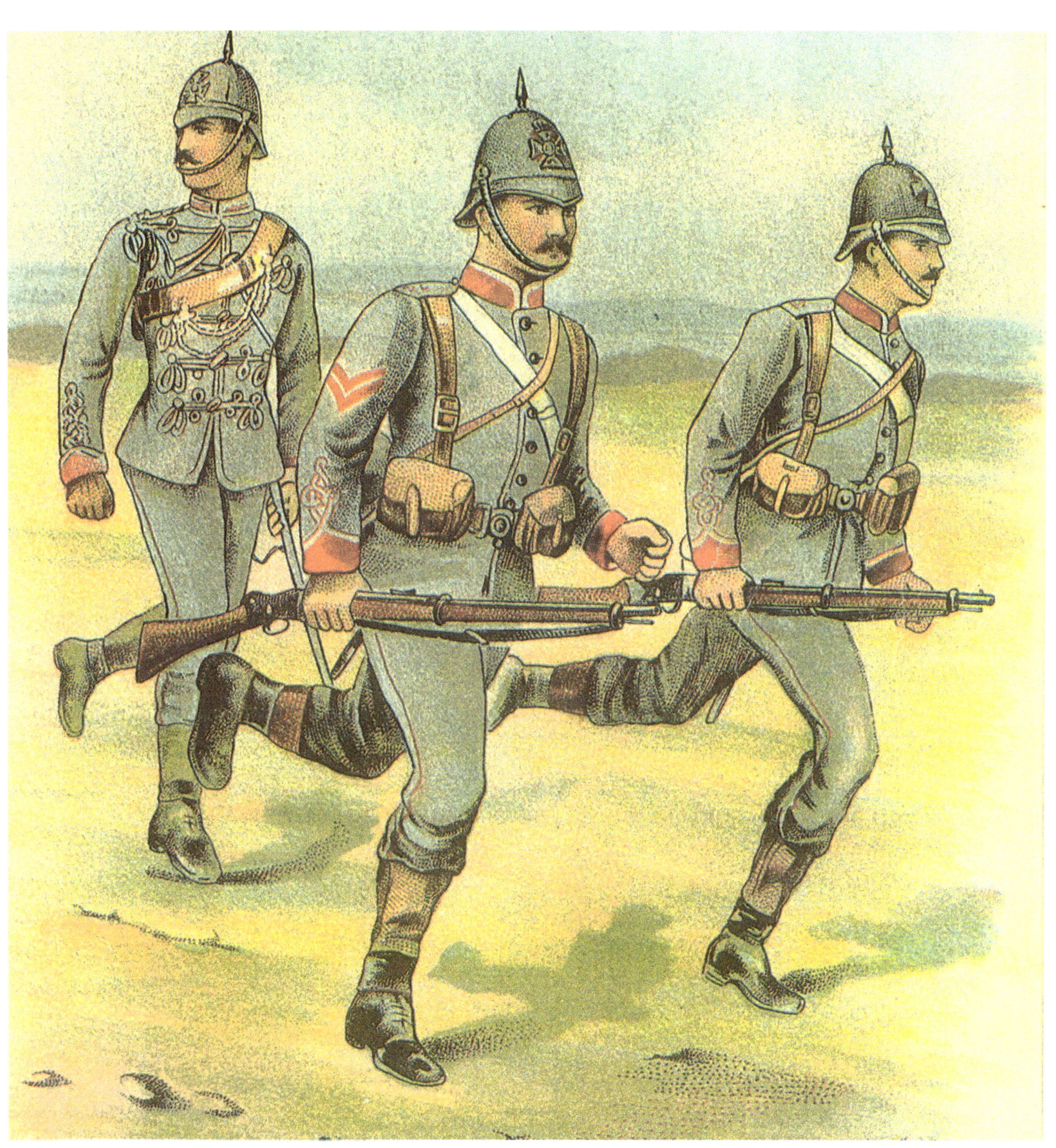

81 – 1st VOLUNTEER BATTALION ROYAL WARWICKSHIRE REGIMENT

Colour plate after Frank Dadd facing page 334 of Colonel Charles J Hart's book, The History of the 1st Volunteer Battalion The Royal Warwickshire Regiment and its Predecessors, published by the Midland Counties Herald Ltd, Birmingham, 1906. The image has the caption 'Uniforms of the Battalion, 1906' and shows three figures. Dressed as a rifle regiment, the uniform of the battalion is dark green with scarlet collars, cuff edgings. The same colour is used for the lines running down the front of the jackets, down the seams of the trousers and for the shoulder titles, 1 over VB over WARWICK. The green helmet has a scarlet backing in the centre of a Maltese Cross plate.

Formed in Birmingham on 4 November 1859, the 1st Warwickshire Rifle Volunteer Corps comprised twelve companies recruited from various sources. There was one formed by workers employed in the newspaper industry, one made up of gun makers, another of Scots resident in the city. In 1883 1st Warwickshire RVC was re-designated as the 1st Volunteer Battalion Royal Warwickshire Regiment. Four new companies were added in 1891, the battalion then being divided into two: 'A' to 'H' Companies (1st Battalion) and 'I' to 'Q' (2nd Battalion). A Cyclist Section was formed in 1894, this being increased to a full company in 1900. At Birmingham University in the same year, 'U' Company was formed from staff and students and this, in 1908, became part of the Senior Division Officers Training Corps. In the same year the 1st Volunteer Battalion transferred to the Territorial Force as 5th and 6th Battalions Royal Warwickshire Regiment.

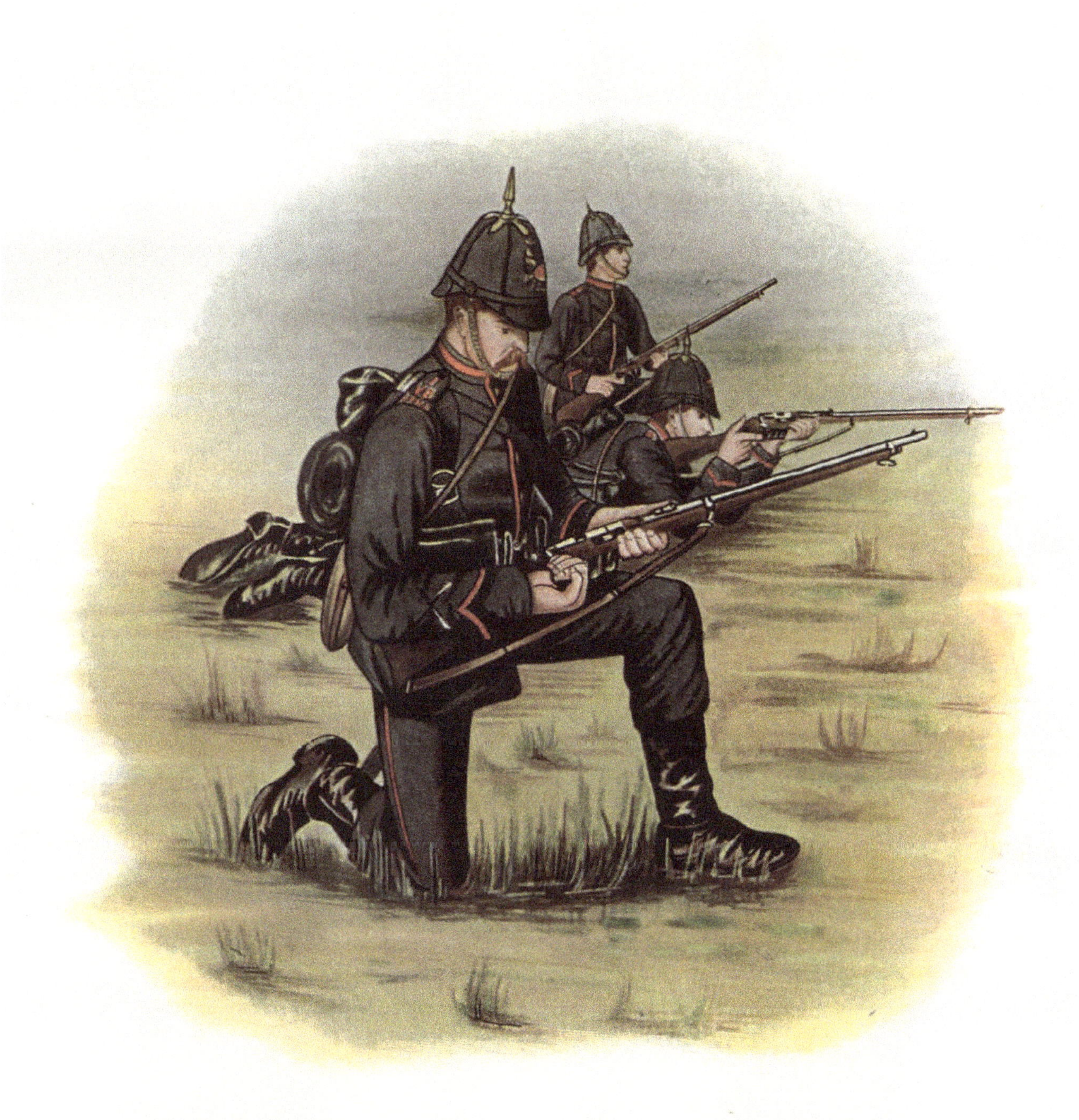

82 – 3rd Volunteer Battalion Royal Fusiliers

Colour illustration after RJ Marrion from an article written by Ray Westlake, published in the 'Military Modelling' magazine, September 1985. Two figures wearing scarlet jackets with dark blue facings and white metal grenade collar badges. Clearly seen on the shoulder strap of the main character is the white embroidered title of 3 / V / grenade / RF. A similar identification appears on the back-pack of the other. The fur caps have white metal grenade badges.

Formed on 13 December 1859, the 20th Middlesex Rifle Volunteer Corps of three companies had its headquarters in Euston Square, London and was mainly formed from men employed by the London and North Western Railway Company. Thomas Edward Bigge, who had previously served with the 23rd Royal Welsh Fusiliers, was appointed captain commandant in command. The corps was included in the 4th Admin Battalion of Middlesex Rifle Volunteers until May 1861 and in 1880 was re-numbered as 11th. The battalion joined the King's Royal Rifle Corps (without change in title) as one of its volunteer battalions in 1881, transferring to the Middlesex Regiment in 1882 and then the Royal Fusiliers as its 3rd Volunteer Battalion in 1890. Additional personnel were sanctioned in 1900/01 brought the establishment up from eight to thirteen companies. After the war in South Africa, however, a reduction was made to eleven. The battalion occupied several headquarters in the Euston area, 5 Albany Street, Regent's Park then at Edward Street off Hampstead Road. Transfer to the Territorial Force in 1908 was as the 3rd (City of London) Battalion The London Regiment (Royal Fusiliers).

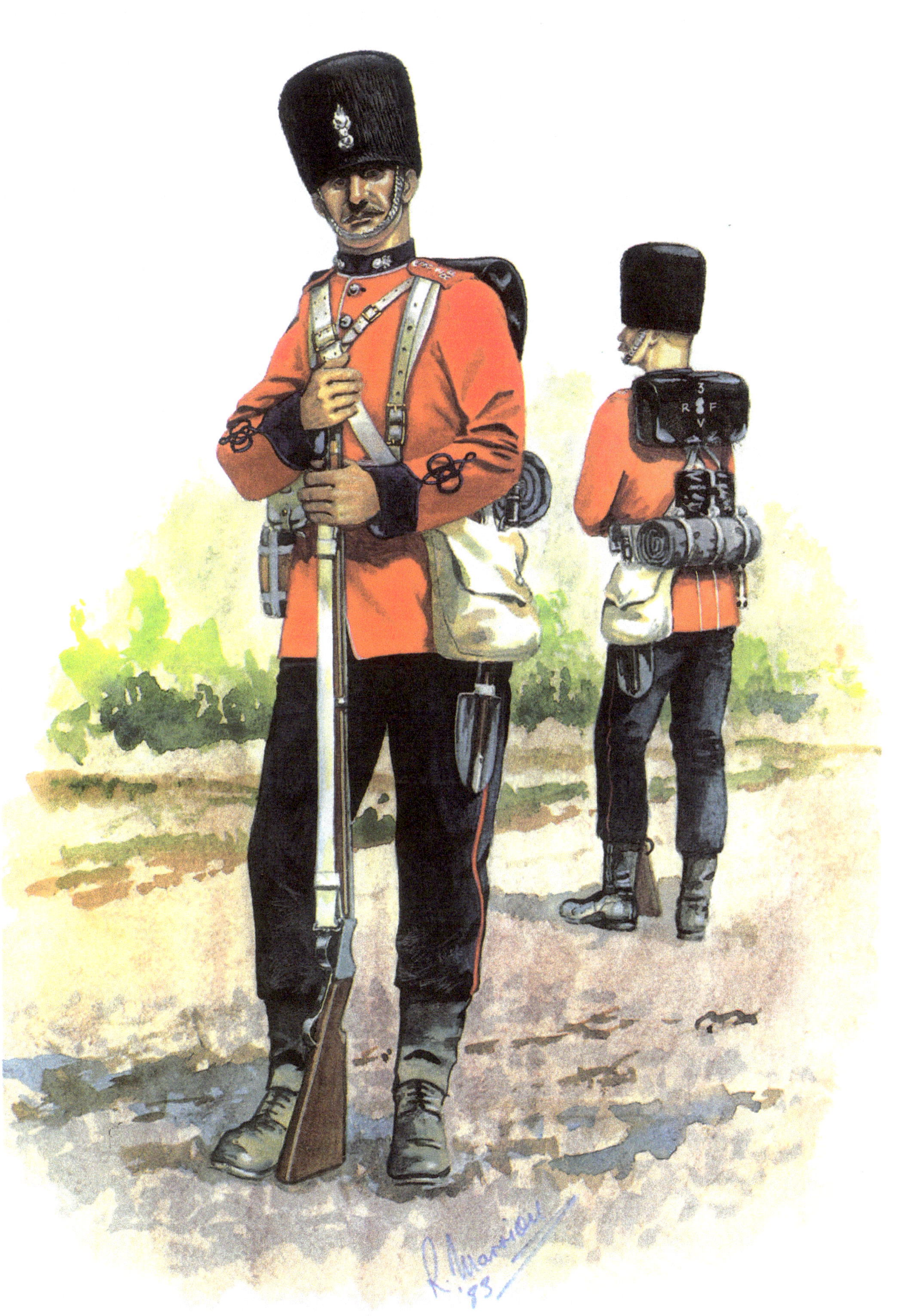
3
R F
V
R. Marrion '93

83 – MIDDLESEX RIFLE VOLUNTEERS

Colour illustration after RJ Marrion from an article written by Ray Westlake entitled 'Middlesex Rifle Volunteers', published in the 'Military Modelling' magazine for February 1989. Three figures of the 1859-60 period, from left to right: 14th Corps, 13th Corps and 3rd Corps.

3rd Middlesex Rifle Volunteer Corps—ET Evans in his book *Records of the Third Middlesex Rifle Volunteers*, records how in about June 1859 three residents of Hampstead (Messrs Jay, Bennett and another) met a number of Highgate residents at the Spaniards Inn to consider the formation of a volunteer corps; but through lack of interest, nothing more was done until Monday 4 July when another meeting took place at the residence of J Gurney Hoare, Esq of The Hill, Hampstead Heath. Subsequently the 3rd Middlesex RVC was formed with a strength of sixty, the first drills taking place at the Holly Bush Assembly Rooms and the Infant School in Well Road. The first officers, John R MacInnes, Basil Field and George Holford, were gazetted on 6 December 1859. In May 1860 rifle practice began at Child's Hill. During 1860 the corps used the Christ Church School for drill, Evans mentioning a 'Kilburn' contingent that used the St Mary's School in that area for a short time. Permission was obtained to increase the establishment to two companies in September 1860.

The corps joined the 2nd Admin Battalion of Middlesex Rifle Volunteers on 28 November 1860 and in 1862 permission was received to include 'Hampstead' in the title. New headquarters in Well Walk were taken over on Tuesday 16 December 1862, the building being a former chapel and before that, the old Hampstead pump-room. These premises, and the house next door, were used until notice to quit was received at the end of 1881. Not having the required enrolled strength, the corps was reduced to one company and a sub-division in July 1864. A room was taken for drill purposes at Hendon for volunteers recruited there in July 1866, but lack of interest in the area saw the detachment soon disbanded. The Hampstead Athletic Club, which met at Well Walk, was formed from within the corps in 1878. In March 1880, the 2nd Admin Battalion was consolidated as 3rd Middlesex RVC, the 3rd Corps becoming its 'A' and 'B' Companies.

13th Middlesex Rifle Volunteer Corps —Formed as a result of a meeting held at Crouch Hall, Crouch End on the evening of Friday 10 June 1859. An application to form a corps was subsequently submitted, notification that its services had been accepted as 13th Middlesex RVC being received on 2 November 1859. Joseph H Warner was appointed as captain, J Bird as lieutenant and John Martineau Fletcher as ensign. An establishment was fixed at one company and headquarters were place in Hornsey. The 13th joined the 2nd Admin Battalion of Middlesex Rifle Volunteers on 22 November 1860. A range belonging to the 12th Middlesex RVC at Highwood Hill and another at Hornsey Wood House were used, then premises at Tottenham were taken in 1862.

Writer ET Evans noted the death from small-pox in 1865 of Sergeant Henry St John Walton, a window in his memory being erected in Hornsey Church. Thirty recruits were enrolled at Southgate in 1866 but plans to set up a company or sub-division at Wood Green were dropped in 1869. At a general meeting of the corps held on 26 April 1870 it was announced that a lease had been taken out on premises in Crouch End for use as headquarters. Evans records a general fall-off in numbers, the year 1872 seeing a reduction from seventy to sixty-four, of which the majority were resident in Southgate. Upon the consolidation of 2nd Admin Battalion in 1880, the 13th became 'D' Company of the new 3rd Corps.

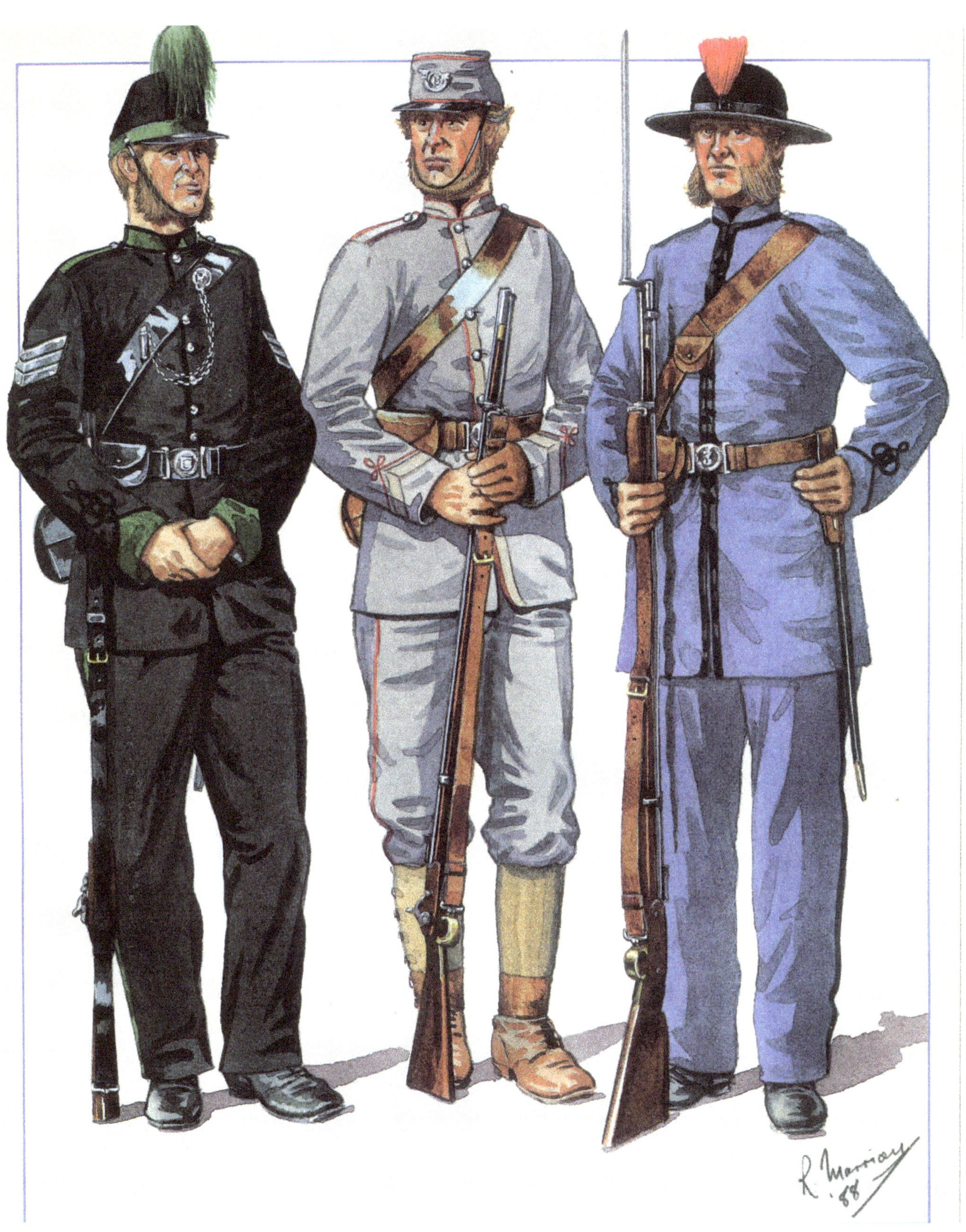
R. Marrion '88

14th Middlesex Rifle Volunteer Corps—ET Evans records that the origins of the 14th Corps lay in a private meeting held to discuss the possibilities of forming a volunteer rifle corps at Highgate and its vicinity at the home of William H Bodkin (afterwards Sir William Bodkin) on 24 May 1859. A subsequent meeting was held at the Swain's Lane cricket field on 21 June 1859. First drills later took place at Swain's Lane. The services of the Highgate Volunteers were accepted in the autumn of 1859, the War Office allotting the title 14th Middlesex RVC with an establishment of one company. Officers' commissions were dated 2 November 1859. Headquarters were established at Southwood Lane, Highgate in a building belonging to the governors of Highgate School. An additional company was authorised on 16 February 1860—Captain Commandant Josiah Wilkinson in command—and a third in June 1860 (although the latter was never formed). Rifle practice was now taking place at Hornsey Wood House and drills, not only in Highgate, but in Gray's Inn Hall or Gardens, and frequently at Albany Street Barracks.

The corps became part of 2nd Admin Battalion on 28 November 1860. Evans notes how in 1860 efforts were made to form companies at Kentish Town and Finchley without success. There were, however, always many members of the 14th that were resident in those areas. A cadet corps was formed and affiliated to the corps at Christ College, Finchley in 1864, its commanding officer being appointed on 5 December—but this was disbanded towards the end of 1867. Corps headquarters, at the end of 1870, were moved to Hornsey, but were back again at Highgate in 1879. The new location, Northfield Hall, was taken over on 6 January. Establishment was reduced to one company on 23 September 1874, but a new second company was authorised before the end of 1876, its first officer not, however, being commissioned until 10 January 1878. The consolidation of volunteer admin battalions in 1880 saw the 14th as 'E' and 'F' Companies of the new 3rd Corps in 1880.

84 – 20TH MIDDLESEX RIFLE VOLUNTEER CORPS (ARTISTS)

Chromolith colour plate after GD Giles from Her Majesty's Army by Walter Richards and published by JS Virtue & Co Ltd of 294 City Road and 26 Ivy Lane, London during the 1890s. The image shows two members of the 20th Middlesex Rifle Volunteers by a railway line, one firing, the other loading.

The 20th Middlesex RVC was formed as three companies with headquarters at Burlington House, London on 25 May 1860 with the painter Henry W Phillips as captain commandant. Numbered originally as 38th, the corps was recruited from painters, sculptors, musicians, architects, actors and other members of artistic occupations. A private in the corps was Queen's Medallist and Engraver to the Signet JW Wyon who was responsible for designing the Artists Rifles badge, an apt device which included the heads of Mars, the god of war, and Minerva, the goddess of the arts. Headquarters moved to the Arts Club, Hanover Square in 1869, the word 'Artist's being included in the title from 1877. The corps was re-numbered as 20th in 1880.

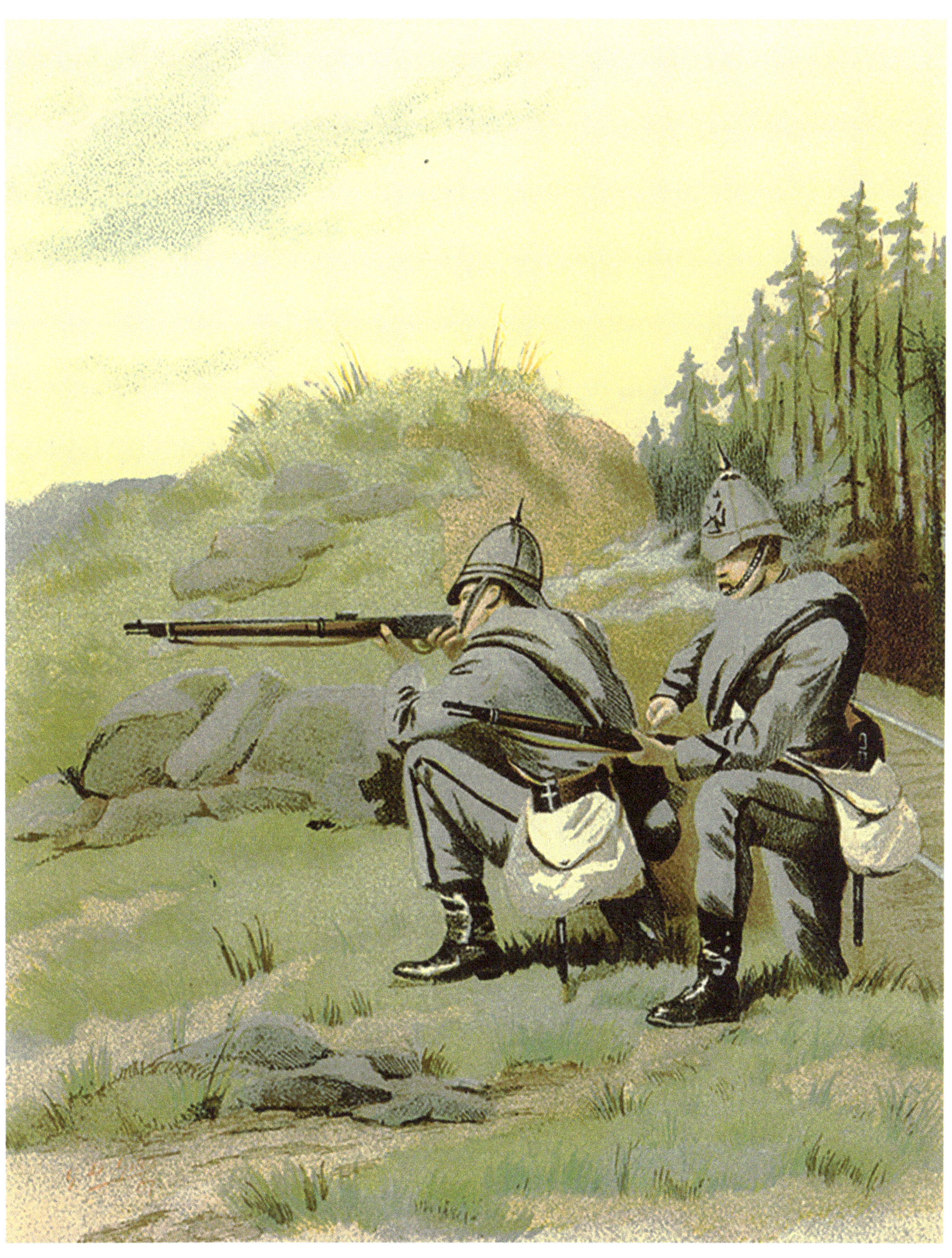

85 – THE LONDON SCOTTISH

Chromolith colour plate after GD Giles from *Her Majesty's Army* by Walter Richards and published by JS Virtue & Co Ltd of 294 City Road and 26 Ivy Lane, London during the 1890s. The image shows a sergeant and the date 1888.

Although still known as the 7th Middlesex Rifle Volunteer Corps, the London Scottish were at the time of the painting serving as one of the volunteer battalions attached to the Rifle Brigade. Some 218 Volunteers from the corps saw active service in South Africa, the first contingent under Lieutenant BC Green joining the City Imperial Volunteers in December 1899. Four men were mentioned in despatches, two receiving the Distinguished Conduct Medal. Another detachment served with the 2nd Battalion Gordon Highlanders.

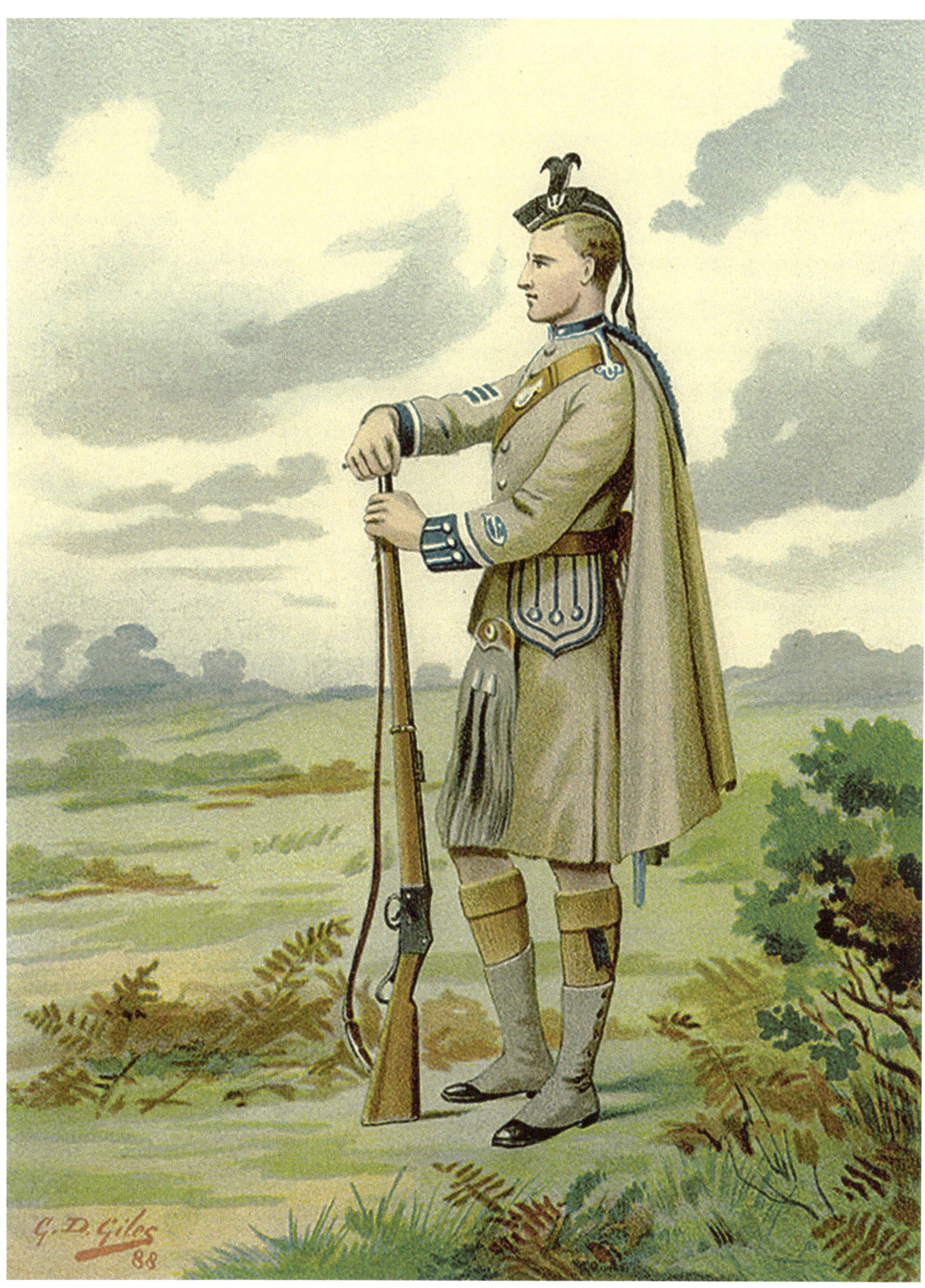
G. D. Giles
88

86 – 5TH VOLUNTEER BATTALION GORDON HIGHLANDERS

Detail from Plate XXXVI of Records of the Scottish Volunteer Force, 1859-1908, written and illustrated by Lieutenant-General Sir James Moncrieff Grierson and published in 1909 by William Blackwood & Sons. On the left a private of the 1st Administrative Battalion of Kincardineshire Rifle Volunteers wearing the uniform of 1864 to 1876, and on the right wearing a green doublet, a private for 1876 to 1908.

All rifle corps formed within the county of Kincardineshire joined the 1st Admin Battalion which after consolidation in 1880 provided a new 1st Corps. The several corps were:

1st —Formed as one company at Fetteresso on 10 January 1860 with T Fraser Duff as captain, J Black, lieutenant and John Milne, ensign. Headquarters moved to Stonehaven in 1867 and the corps was disbanded in October 1870.

2nd—Formed as one company at Banchory on 28 January 1860 with Patrick Davidson as captain, William Black Fergusson, lieutenant and John Gordon, ensign. Became 'A' Company of the new 1st Corps in 1880.

3rd—Formed as a sub-division at Laurencekirk in February 1860 with Alfred H W Farrell in command. Increased to a full company on 23 May 1860 and absorbed into the 5th Corps in 1873.

4th—Formed as a sub-division at Fettercairn on 13 March 1860 with William McInvoy as lieutenant and David Durie, ensign. Absorbed into the 5th Corps in 1871.

5th—Formed as one company at Auchinblae on 9 June 1860 with James C Burnett as captain, Alexander Taylor, lieutenant and George Smart, ensign. Absorbed the 4th Corps to the south-west at Fettercairn in 1871 and 3rd Corps at Laurencekirk on the Stonehaven road in 1873. Headquarters moved to Laurencekirk in 1878 and became 'B' Company of the new 1st Corps in 1880.

6th—Formed as one company at Netherley on 7 May 1860 with Horatio Ross as captain, Robert Walker, lieutenant and George J Walker, ensign. Headquarters moved to Portlethen, on the coast to the north-east, in May 1869 and became 'C' Company of the new 1st Corps in 1880.

7th—Formed as one company at Durris on 13 February 1861 with James Thompson Mackenzie as captain, David Morrice, lieutenant and Robert Salmon, ensign. Became 'D' Company of the new 1st Corps in 1880.

8th—Formed at Maryculter and Peterculter on 21 October 1869 and became 'E' Company of the new 1st Corps in 1880.

The 1st Admin Battalion was formed with headquarters at Stonehaven on 14 May 1861 with William McInroy, late of the 91st and 69th Regiments of Foot, taking command. Headquarters transferred to Banchory on 23 February 1876 and in the same year the 8th, 14th, 21st and 23rd Aberdeenshire RVC were also included. By the end of 1876 'Deeside Highland' formed part of the battalion title. When the battalion was consolidated in 1880 the title then assumed was 1st Kincardineshire and Aberdeenshire (Deeside Highland) RVC. There were ten companies: 'A' Banchory (late 2nd Kincardine), 'B' Laurencekirk (late 5th Kincardine), 'C' Portlethen (late 6th Kincardine), 'D' Durris (late 7th Kincardine), 'E' Maryculter (late 8th Kincardine), 'F' Echt (late 8th Aberdeen), 'G' Tarland (late 14th Aberdeen), 'H' Aboyne (late No 1 Company, 21st Aberdeen), 'I' Ballater (late No 2 Company, 21st Aberdeen), 'K' Torphins (late 23rd Aberdeen).

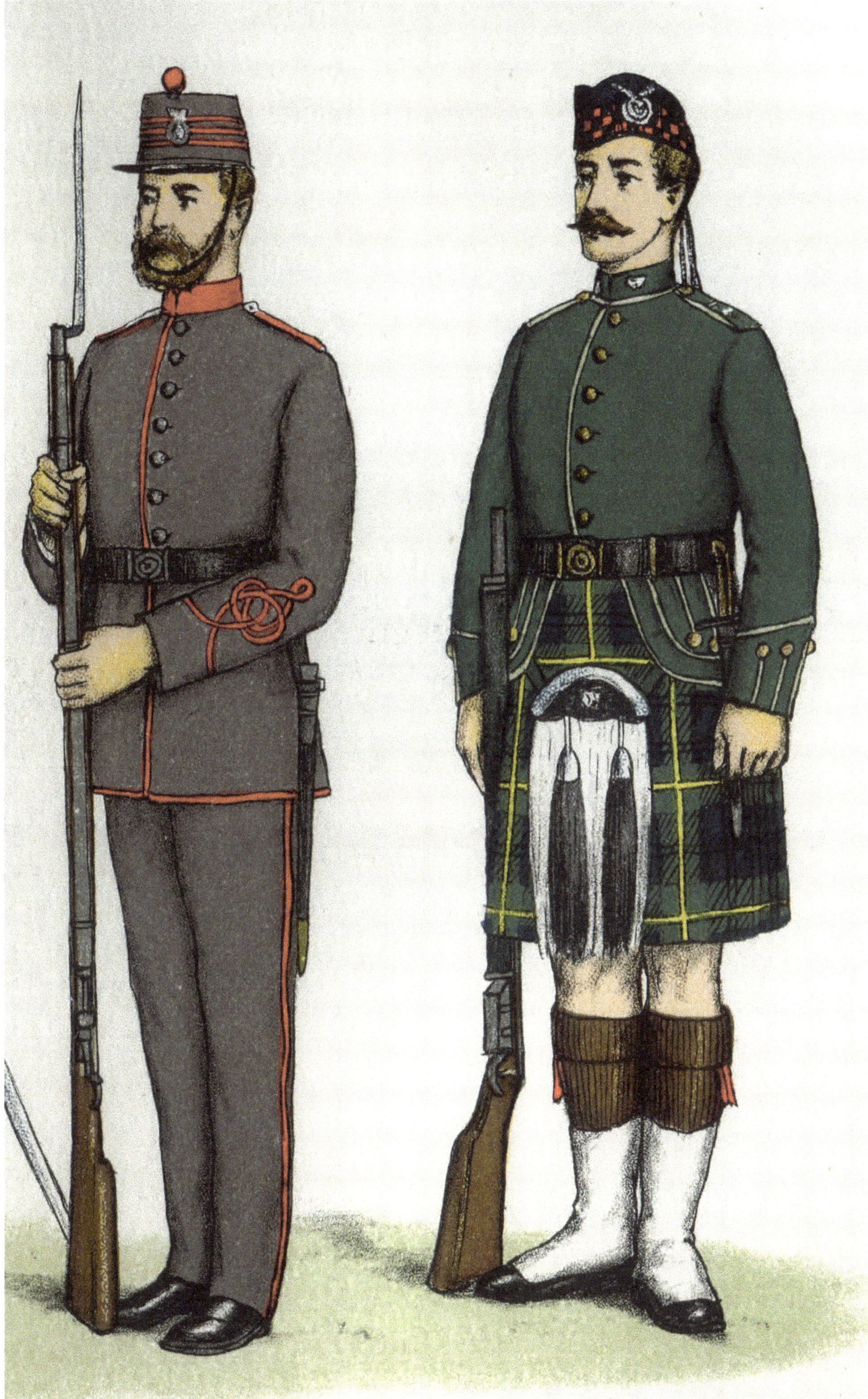

In 1883 a series of company mergers and changes in location began when on 28 November 'K' Company was amalgamated with 'A' and a new 'K' formed at Stonehaven. 'G' and 'H' were merged in May 1885, battalion headquarters moved to Aberdeen in May 1886 and in 1887 and 1891 respectively 'E' Company moved to Peterculter and 'F' to Skene. The corps was re-designated 5th (Deeside Highland) Volunteer Battalion Gordon Highlanders on 17 January 1884 and headquarters moved back to Banchory in July 1894.

Some seventy-eight members from the battalion saw active service in South Africa, one man being wounded at Komati Poort on 30 September 1900 and two at Rooikopjes on 24th July. Private P Stuart was killed on 8 September at Lydenburg.

87 – VOLUNTEER CORPS OF LONDON

Original watercolour signed by Richard Simkin. Against a backdrop of St Paul's Cathedral, the artist provides examples of the uniforms worn by the several volunteer corps from London. To the right of the gun, a member of the City Imperial Volunteers which should date the image as post 1900. Behind him in scarlet and buff facings is one of the 3rd London Rifle Volunteers. Easily identified in his fur cap with grenade badge is a member of one of the volunteer battalions associated with the Royal Fusiliers and of course kneeling in the front rank in Elcho grey and blue facings is a member of the London Scottish. Tending the gun are several gunners and mounted two from the Imperial Yeomanry. Standing and kneeling, the volunteers are seen in their scarlets, greys and greens. Simkin has also included examples of earlier volunteer corps in the figure standing on the extreme left, and the mounted cavalryman wearing a scarlet jacket and black fur-crested helmet. (*Image courtesy of the Anne SK Brown Military Collection, Brown University Library*)

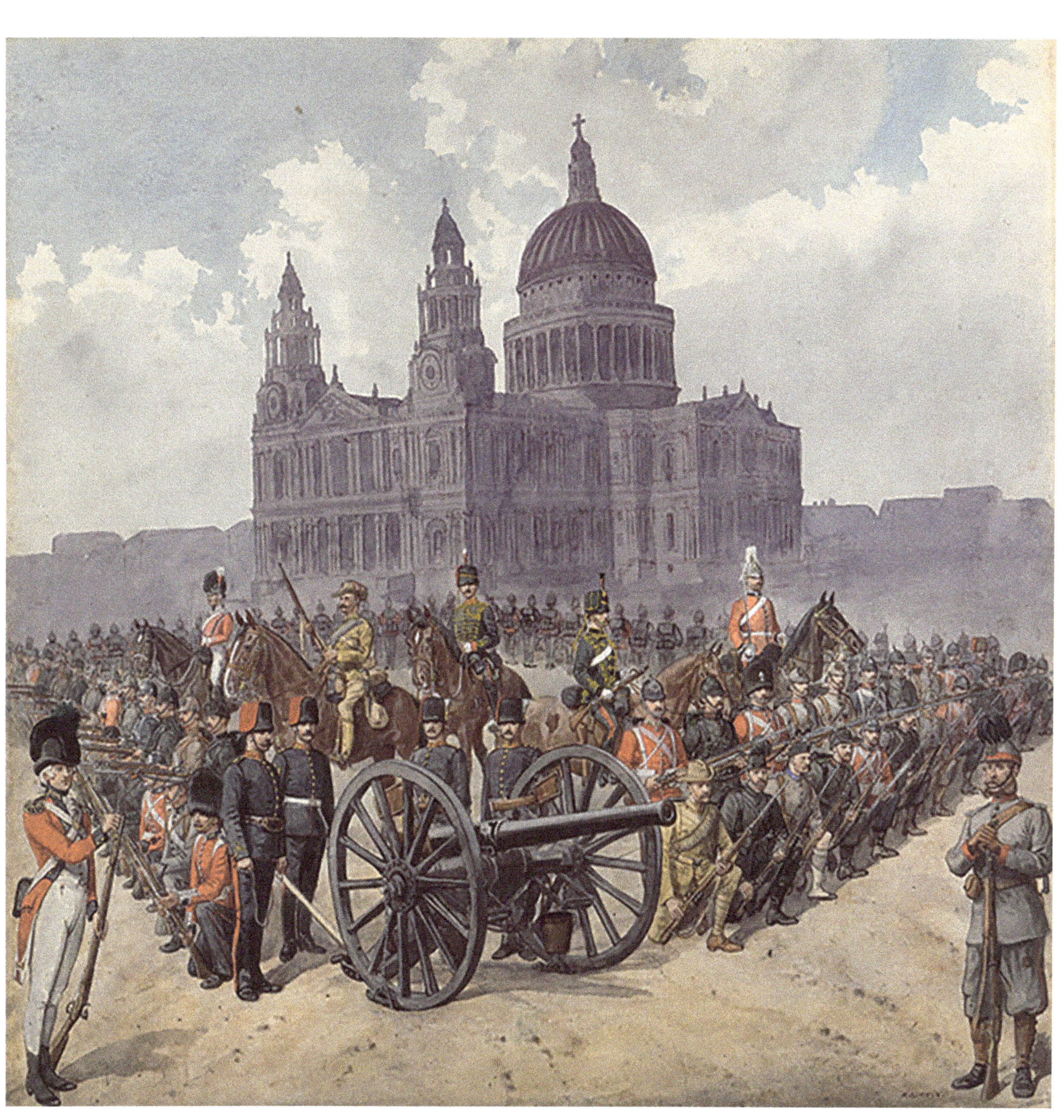

88 – 4TH VOLUNTEER BATTALION GORDON HIGHLANDERS

Plate XXXVIII from *Records of the Scottish Volunteer Force, 1859-1908*, written and illustrated by Lieutenant-General Sir James Moncrieff Grierson and published in 1909 by William Blackwood & Sons. The figures are from left to right: a private of the 10th Aberdeenshire Rifle Volunteer Corps (1860), private 11th Aberdeenshire RVC (1860), corporal 7th Aberdeenshire RVC (1860), private 1st Administrative Battalion of Aberdeenshire Rifle Volunteers (1864-1869), sergeant 1st Admin Battalion (1869-1887), private (1887-1903) and sergeant (1903-1908).

The 1st Administrative Battalion of Aberdeenshire Rifle Volunteers was formed with headquarters at Inverurie in May 1860 and to it were added the 3rd (Cluny), 4th (Alford), 7th (Huntly), 8th (Echt), 10th (Inverurie) and 11th (Kildrummy) Aberdeenshire Corps. The battalion was consolidated as 4th Aberdeenshire RVC, then in re-designated as 4th Volunteer Battalion Gordon Highlanders in 1884.

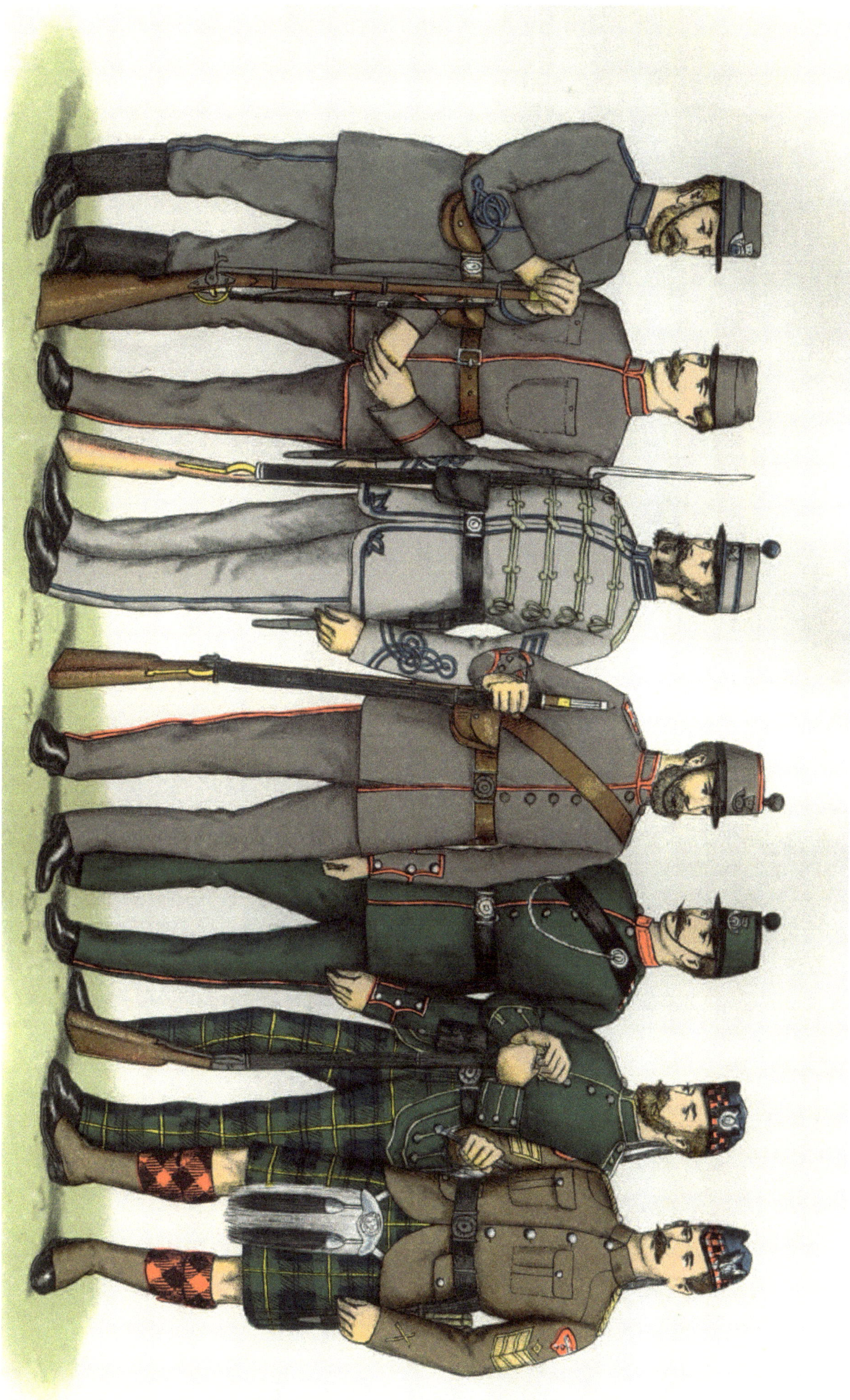

89 – 3rd VOLUNTEER BATTALION GORDON HIGHLANDERS

Plate XXXVII from *Records of the Scottish Volunteer Force, 1859-1908*, written and illustrated by Lieutenant-General Sir James Moncrieff Grierson and published in 1909 by William Blackwood & Sons. The figures from left to right are: ensign 5th Aberdeenshire Rifle Volunteer Corps (1860), lieutenant 9th Aberdeenshire RVC (1860), lieutenant 17th Aberdeenshire RVC (1860), captain 20th Aberdeenshire RVC (1860), captain 3rd Administrative Battalion of Aberdeenshire Rifle Volunteers (1863-1868), captain 3rd Admin Battalion (1872-1883) and corporal 3rd Volunteer Battalion (1903-1908).

The 3rd Administrative Battalion was formed with headquarters at Peterhead in January 1862 including the following Aberdeenshire corps: 5th (New Deer), 9th (Peterhead), 17th (Old Deer) and 20th (Longside). The battalion was consolidated as 3rd Aberdeenshire RVC in 1880, the re-designated as 3rd (The Buchan) Volunteer Battalion Gordon Highlanders in 1884.

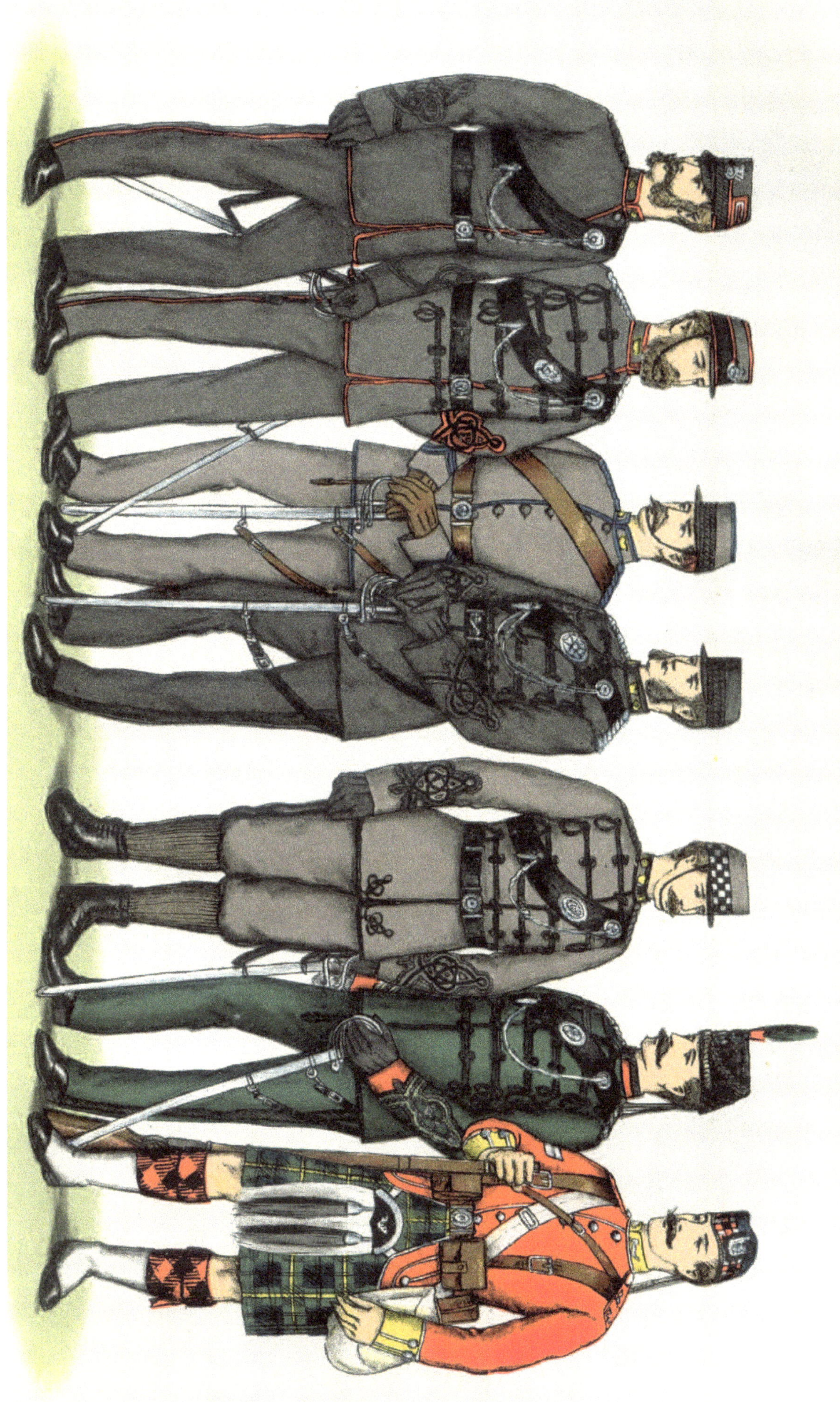

90 – 1st (CITY OF DUNDEE) VOLUNTEER BATTALION BLACK WATCH

Plate XXIV from *Records of the Scottish Volunteer Force, 1859-1908*, written and illustrated by Lieutenant-General Sir James Moncrieff Grierson and published in 1909 by William Blackwood & Sons. The four figures are, from left to right: captain 1st Forfarshire Rifle Volunteer Corps (1860), lieutenant 1st Forfarshire RVC (1862-1877), private 1st Forfarshire RVC (1877-1880) and private 1st Volunteer Battalion (1904-1908).

The services of the 1st Forfarshire Rifle Volunteer Corps at Dundee were accepted in November 1859. Re-designation as 1st (Dundee) Volunteer Battalion was in 1887, 'City of Dundee' being substituted for 'Dundee' in February 1889.

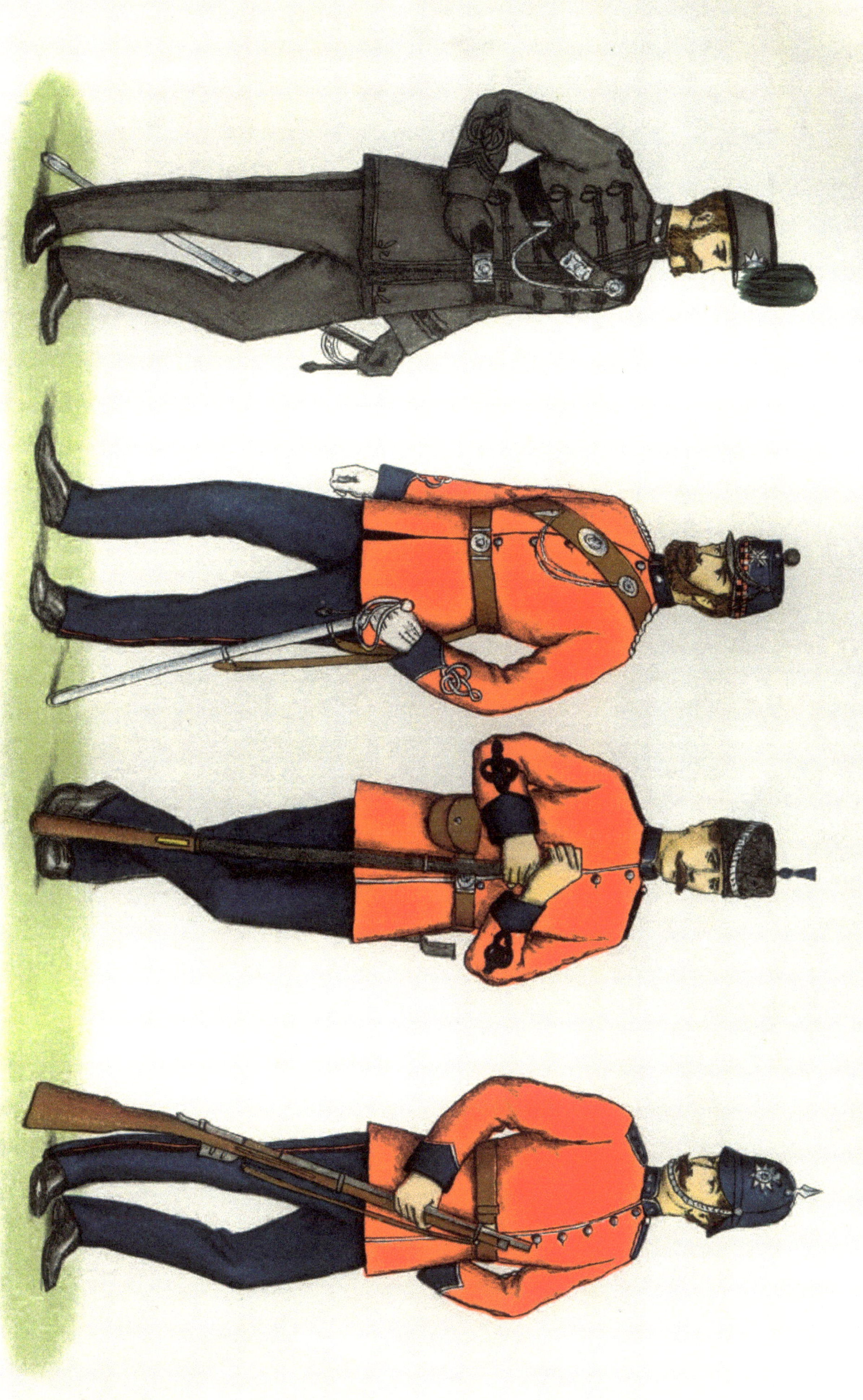

91 – 6TH (FIFESHIRE) VOLUNTEER BATTALION BLACK WATCH

Plate XXVII from *Records of the Scottish Volunteer Force, 1859-1908*, written and illustrated by Lieutenant-General Sir James Moncrieff Grierson and published in 1909 by William Blackwood & Sons. The three figures are from left to right: private 5th Fifeshire Rifle Volunteer Corps (1860-1863), corporal 1st Administrative Battalion of Fifeshire Rifle Volunteers (1863-1875) and sergeant 1st Fifeshire RVC, later 6th Volunteer Battalion (1880-1908).

The 1st Administrative Battalion of Fifeshire Rifle Volunteers was formed with headquarters at St Andrew's in September 1860 and to it were added the following Fifeshire Corps: 1st (Dunfermline), 2nd (Cupar), 3rd (Kilconquhar), 4th (Colinsburgh), 5th (St Andrews), 6th (Strathleven), 7th (Kirkcaldy), 8th (Auchterderran) and 9th (Newburgh). The battalion was consolidated as 1st Corps in 1880, then re-designated as 6th (Fifeshire) Volunteer Battalion in 1887.

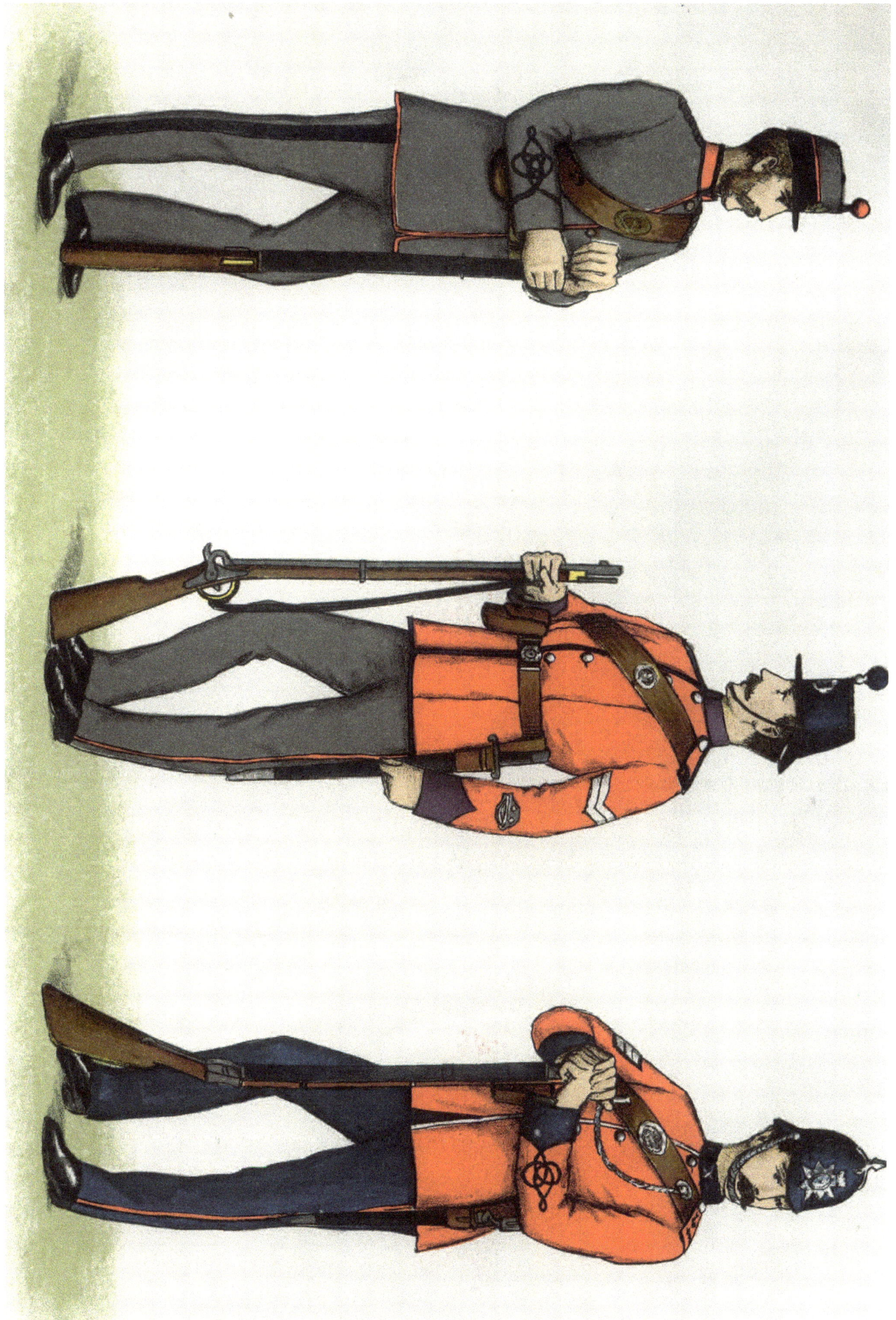

92 – 7TH MIDDLESEX (LONDON SCOTTISH) VOLUNTEER RIFLE CORPS

Plate XLVI from *Records of the Scottish Volunteer Force, 1859-1908*, written and illustrated by Lieutenant-General Sir James Moncrieff Grierson and published in 1909 by William Blackwood & Sons. The four figures from left to right are: private (1860), private, kilted company (1860), lieutenant (1907) and private 1907).

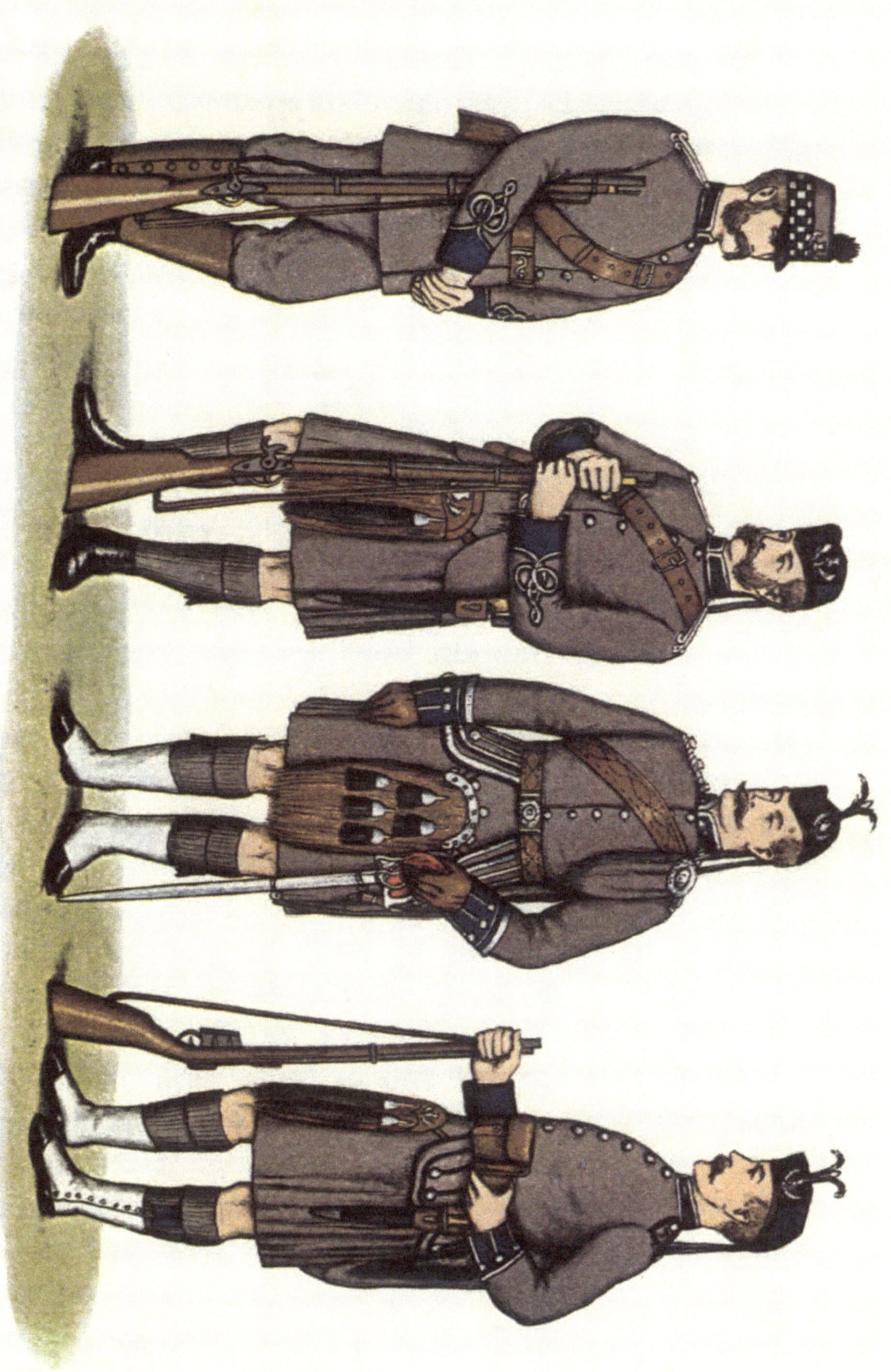

93 – ARMY SERVICE CORPS (VOLUNTEERS) AND ROYAL ARMY MEDICAL CORPS (VOLUNTEERS)

Plate XLVII from *Records of the Scottish Volunteer Force, 1859-1908*, written and illustrated by Lieutenant-General Sir James Moncrieff Grierson and published in 1909 by William Blackwood & Sons. Two figures, both dated 1907.

Volunteer Army Service Corps companies date from 1902 and were allotted one to each volunteer infantry brigade. First formed as the Volunteer Medical Staff Corps, the tile RAMC (Volunteers) was assumed in 1902.

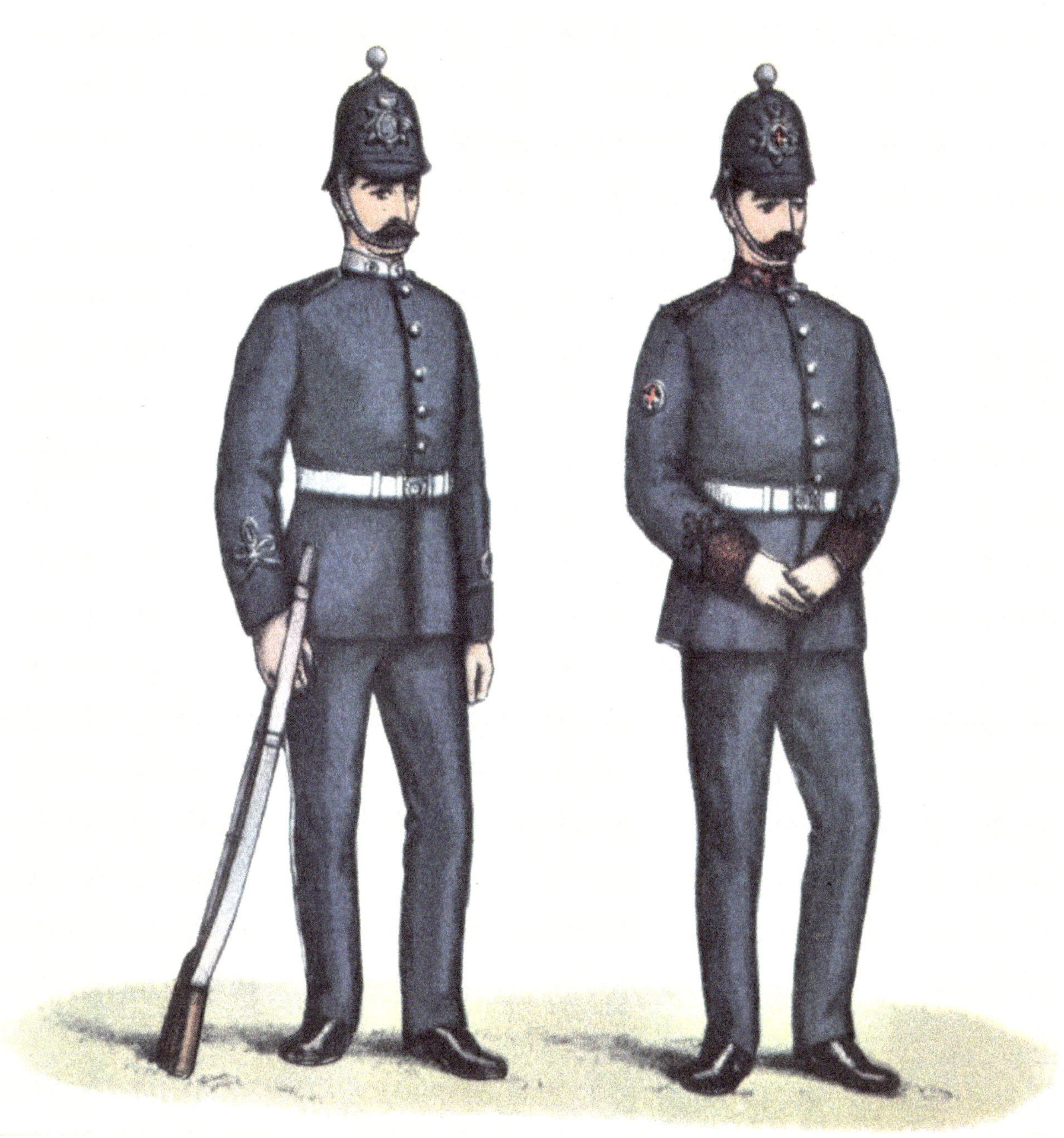

94 – 7th (Clackmannan and Kinross) Volunteer Battalion Argyll and Sutherland Highlanders

Plate XLV from *Records of the Scottish Volunteer Force, 1859-1908*, written and illustrated by Lieutenant-General Sir James Moncrieff Grierson and published in 1909 by William Blackwood & Sons. Four figures from left to right: private 1st Clackmannanshire Rifle Volunteer Corps (1860), private 1st Administrative Battalion of Clackmannanshire Rifle Volunteers (1867-1874), captain 1st Admin Battalion, later 1st Corps (1874-1888) and field officer 7th Volunteer Battalion.

Two corps, 1st at Alloa and 2nd at Tillicoultry, were formed in Clackmannanshire in 1860, both being later included in the county's 1st Administrative Battalion. To this in 1868 was added the 14th Stirlingshire RVC and in 1873 the 1st Kinross RVC. The battalion was consolidated as the 1st Clackmannan and Kinross RVC in 1880 the re-designated 7th (Clackmannan and Kinross) Volunteer Battalion Argyll and Sutherland Highlanders in 1887.

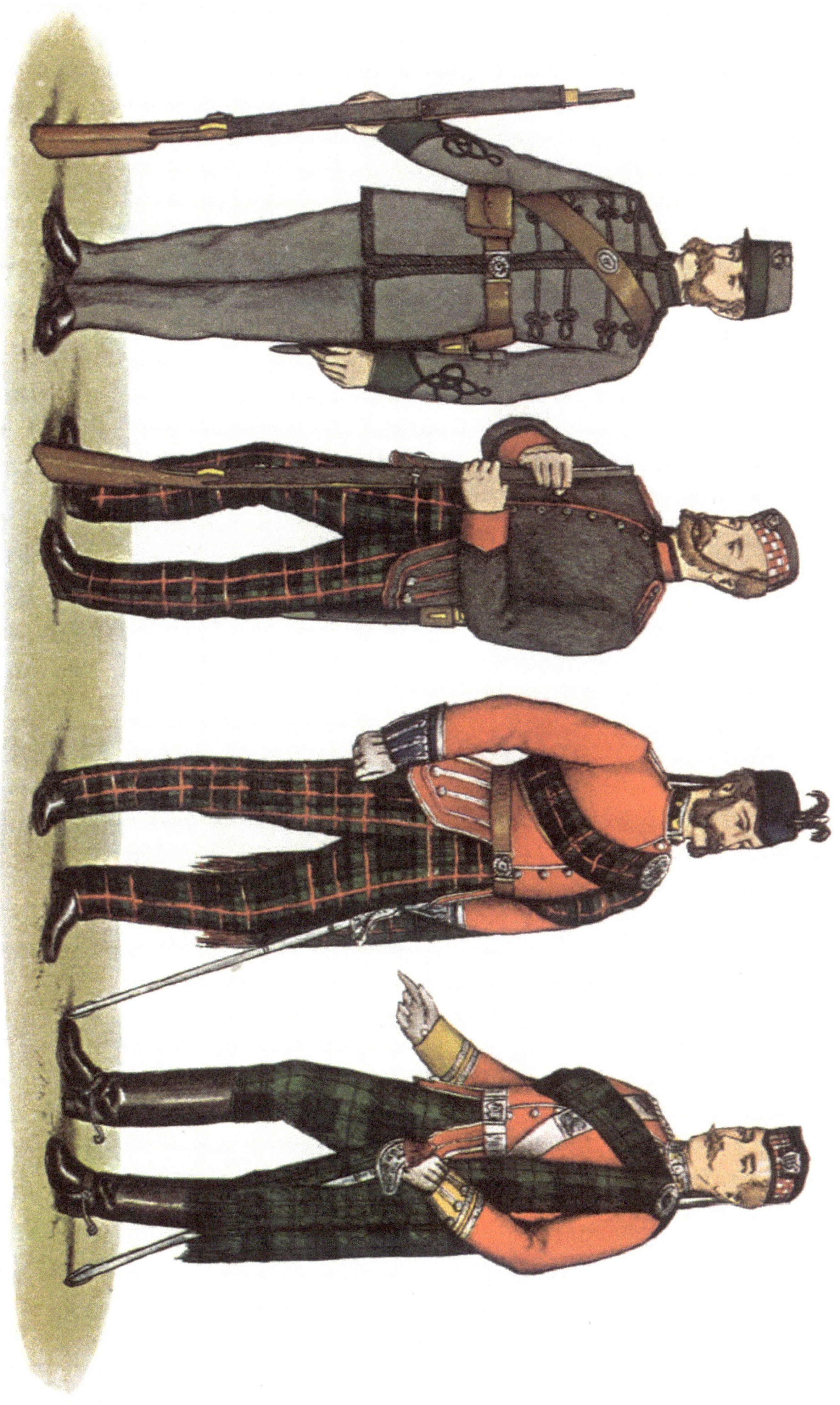

95 – 1st LANARKSHIRE ROYAL ENGINEERS (VOLUNTEERS)

Plate VIII from *Records of the Scottish Volunteer Force, 1859-1908*, written and illustrated by Lieutenant-General Sir James Moncrieff Grierson and published in 1909 by William Blackwood & Sons. Five figures from left to right: captain 1st Lanarkshire Engineer Volunteer Corps (1860), 97th Lanarkshire Rifle Volunteer Corps (1862), lieutenant 2nd Lanarkshire EVC 1860), sapper (1881) and sapper (1907).

The 1st Lanarkshire Engineer Volunteer Corps was formed in May 1863 by the amalgamation of the 1st, 2nd and 3rd Lanarkshire EVC and the 97th Lanarkshire Rifle Volunteer Corps. The 97th had provided four of the six companies its members, all of them of exceptional physique, giving it the nickname of The Guards. The six companies were increased to eight in 1883 and in 1885 a 9th (Submarine Mining) Company was formed. A second devoted to the same duties was raised in 1888 but in that same year this and the 9th were removed to form the Clyde Division Submarine Miners. A new 9th made up of railway workers was soon formed, but this was disbanded after less than a year's service. Springburn, in the north of Glasgow, however, provided another 9th. In 1894 headquarters were moved from Glasgow to Kelvinside, and in 1900 three new companies were raised.

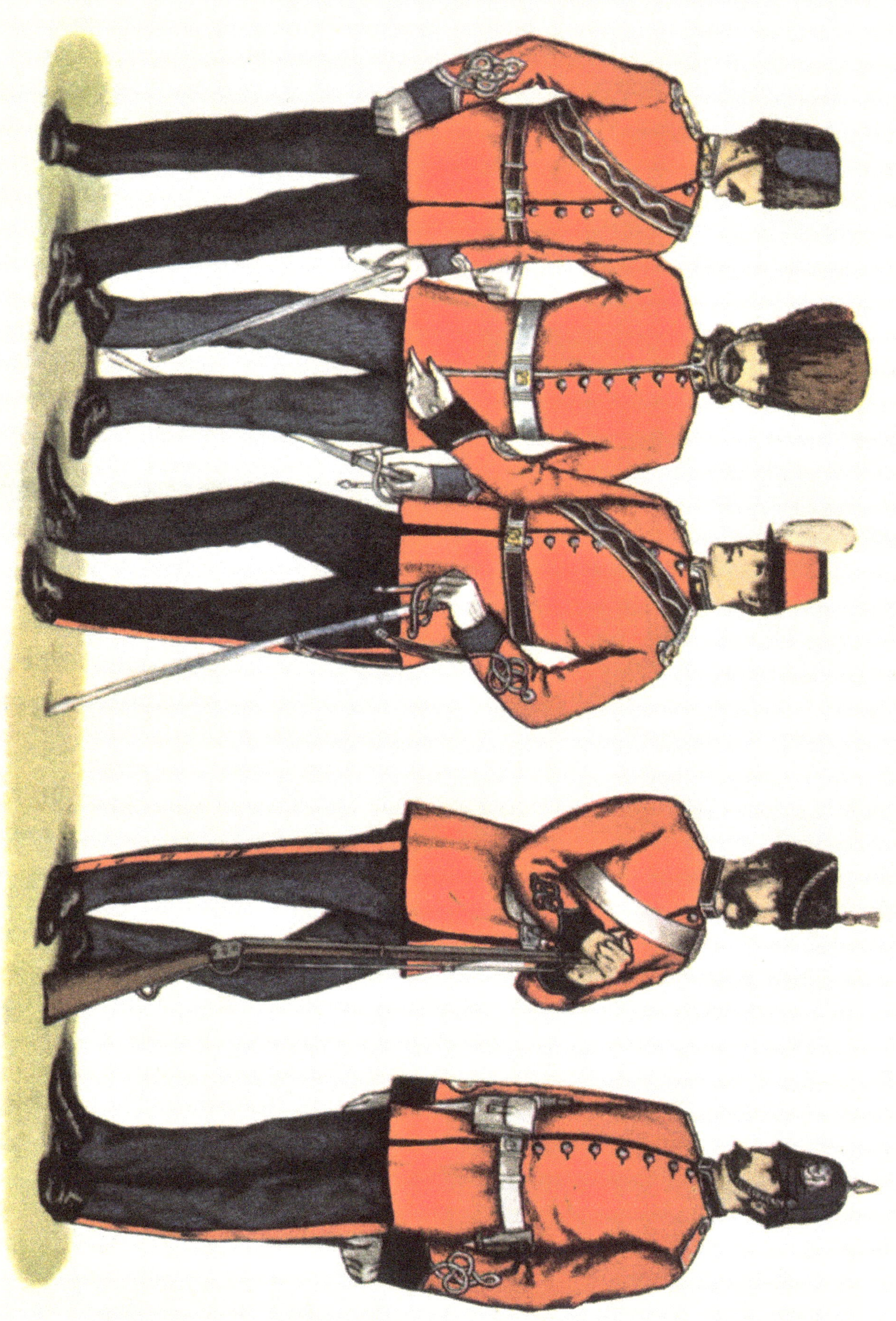

96 – BUGLER, 4TH ROXBURGHSHIRE RIFLE VOLUNTEER CORPS

Engraving from the *Illustrated London News*. The services of the 4th Roxburghshire Rifle Volunteer Corps at Hawick were accepted on 11 June 1860, the uniform being slate grey with red collars and black braid. Kilmarnock bonnets with a red pom-pom were worn, the belts, brown.

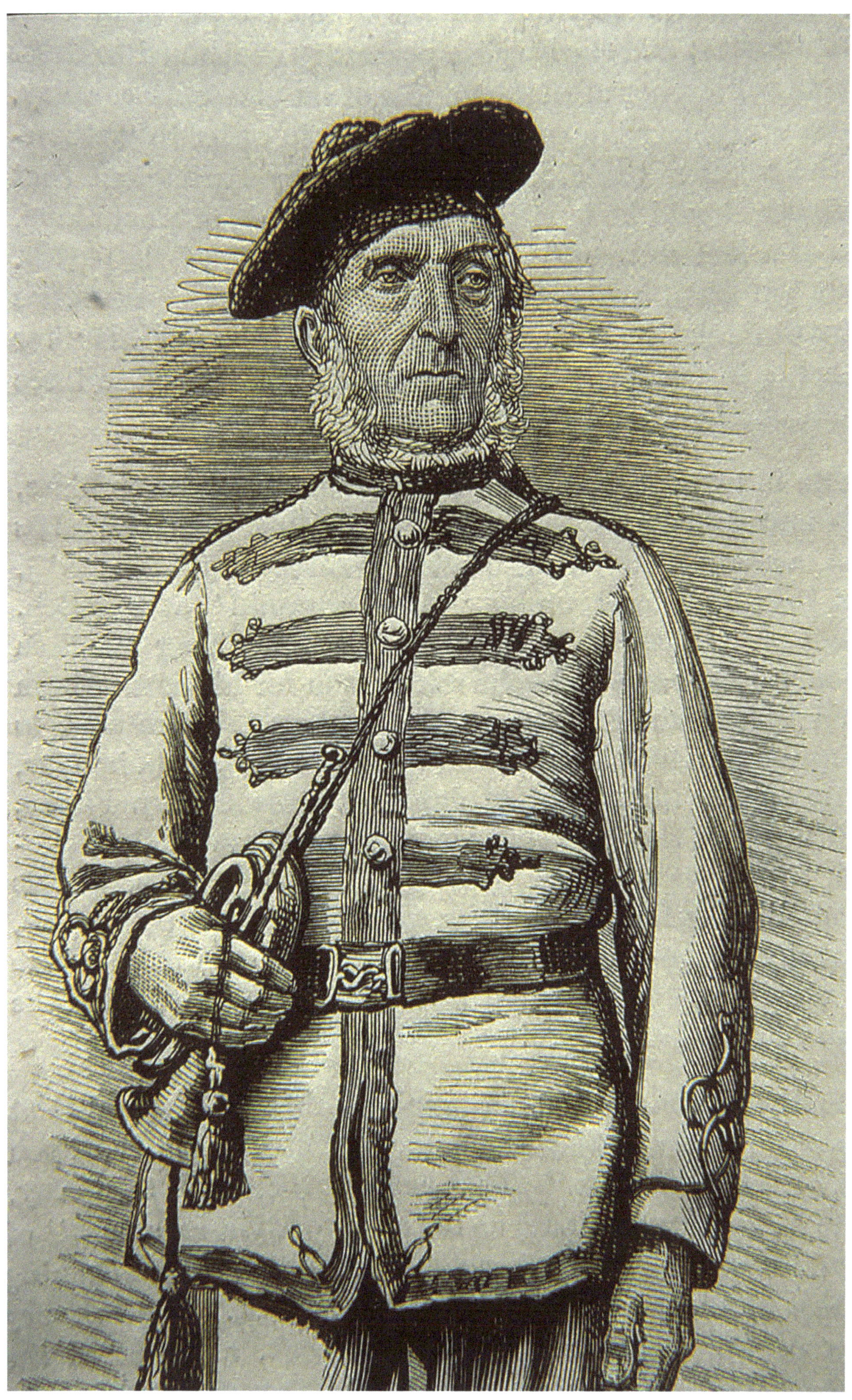

97 – THE QUEEN'S RIFLE VOLUNTEER BRIGADE

Plate X from *Records of the Scottish Volunteer Force, 1859-1908*, written and illustrated by Lieutenant-General Sir James Moncrieff Grierson and published in 1909 by William Blackwood & Sons. Six figures from left to right: private (1859), private 2nd Highland Company (1862), private (1864), corporal (1881), sergeant om marching order (1901) and lieutenant-colonel (1907).

From the very beginning it was decided to group all companies of rifle Volunteers raised within the City of Edinburgh into one regiment to be known as the 1st City of Edinburgh RVC. Lieutenant-Colonel Commandant the Rt Hon James Lord Moncreiff, whose commission was dated 31 August 1859, took command, and by the end of 1860 the regiment consisted of twenty-two companies divided into two battalions. All companies were numbered, and in addition held sub-titles which served to indicate the trade or profession of its members: No 1 (Advocates), formed 31 August 1859, No 2 (1st Citizens), formed 31 August 1859, No 3 (Writers to the Signet), formed 31 August 1859, No 4 (Edinburgh University), formed 31 August 1859, No 5 (Solicitors before the Supreme Court), formed 31 August 1859, No 6 (Accountants), formed 31 August 1859, No 7 (Bankers), formed 31 August 1859, No 8 (1st Artisans), formed 31 August 1859, No 9 (2nd Artisans), formed 31 August 1859, No 10 (Civil Service), formed 7 October 1859, No 11 (3rd Artisans), formed 7 December 1859, No 12 (Freemasons), formed 7 December 1859, No 13 (4th Artisans), formed 7 December 1859, No 14 (2nd Citizens), formed 8 December 1859, No 15 (1st Merchants), formed 21 December 1859, No 16 (Total Abstainers), formed 29 February 1860, No 17 (2nd Merchants), formed 11 May 1860, No 18 (High Constables), formed 25 May 1860, No 19 (5th Artisans), formed 8 November 1860, 1st (Highland), formed 31 August 1859, 2nd (Highland), formed 18 May 1860, 3rd (Highland), formed 23 July 1860.

Additional information regarding the several companies appears in Lieutenant General Sir James Moncrieff Grierson's book *Records of the Scottish Volunteer Force 1859-1908*: It appears that the 1st to 6th Companies were all self-supporting companies, ie, the members paid for their own uniforms, equipment and arms, and paid a fixed amount annually towards general expenses. In the case of No 7 (Bankers) Company, formed from clerks and other employees, the several banks concerned contributed towards costs, while the men of the Artisan companies paid for their uniforms by instalments—the expenses of the companies being defrayed by public subscription. Interest in the Freemasons Company (No 12) soon fell off and had, by 1861, almost ceased to exist. A Miss Catherine Sinclair, however, came forward with funds and as a result No 12 was reorganised and recruited mainly from the Water of Leith District. While on the subject of Freemasonry, it is of interest to note that Rifle Lodge No 405 was formed from within the brigade on 7 May 1860. Messrs Cowen & Co, and Messrs C Lawson & Sons paid the expenses of forty members from No 15 (1st Merchants). Tailoring firms provided members of their staff and expenses for No 19 (5th Artisans), but after 1873 this company was recruited from all trades. The Highland companies came from members of the Highland Society of Edinburgh.

The title 1st Queen's City of Edinburgh Rifle Volunteer Brigade was conferred in 1865, and on 23 February 1867 the 1st Corps absorbed the 2nd at Messrs W D Young's Ironworks, Fountainbridge, at the west end of the city, as its 4th, 5th and 6th (Highland) Companies. Formed on 27 December 1867 was the 7th (Highland) Company, recruits for this being, in the main, natives of Caithness now living in Edinburgh. Nos 1 and 3 Companies were disbanded in 1868.

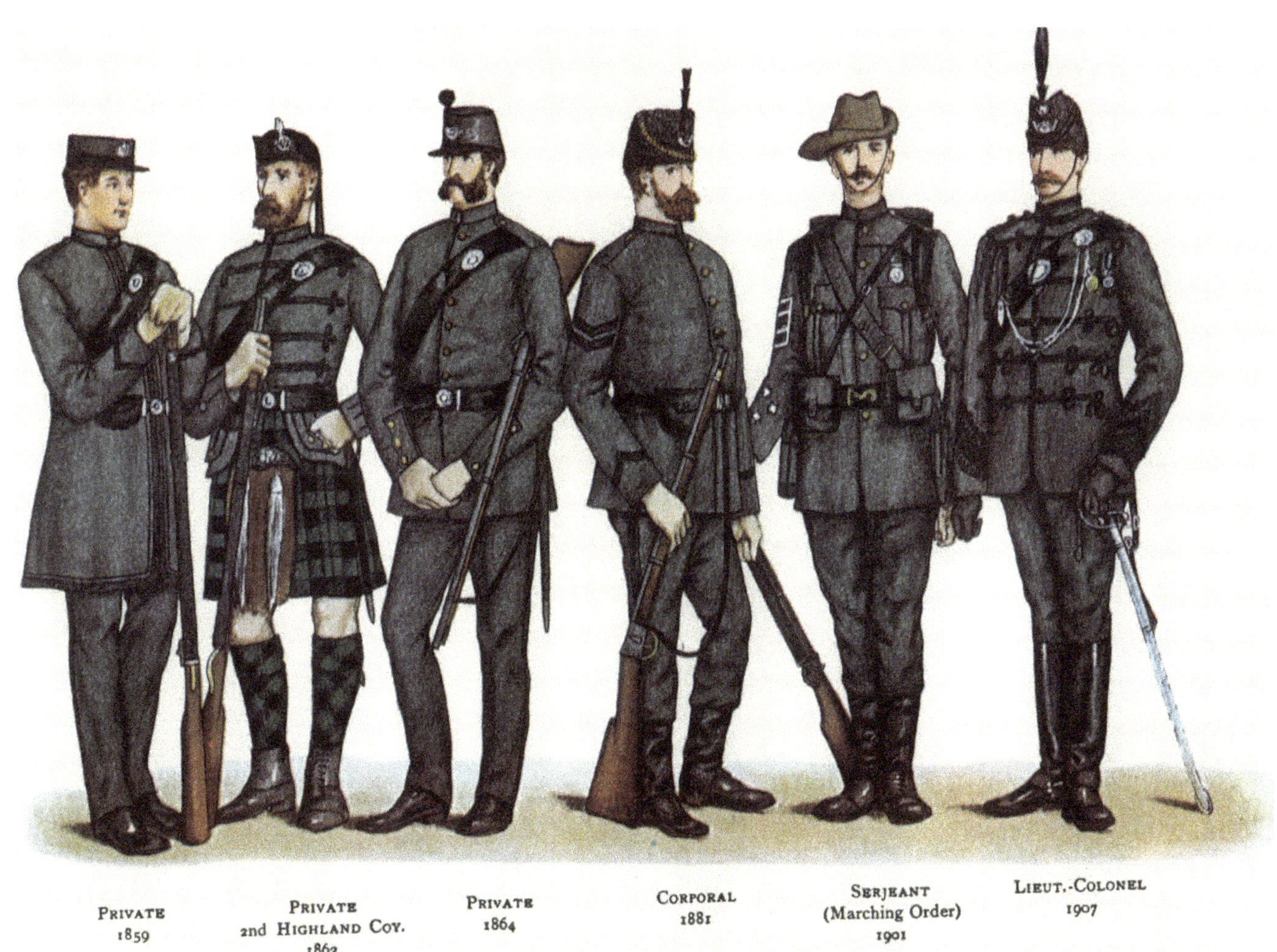

QUEEN'S RIFLE VOLUNTEER BRIGADE, THE ROYAL SCOTS.

A No 20 Company was added on 19 March 1869, and at the same time the regiment was divided into two battalions: 1st Battalion comprising Nos 2, 4, 5, 6, 7, 10, 18 and 1st to 7th Highland Companies, the 2nd Battalion made up of Nos 8, 9, 11, 12, 13, 14, 15, 16, 17, 19 and 20. Three years later, in 1872, premises in Forrest Road, Edinburgh were taken over as headquarters.

The brigade provided two Volunteer battalions of the Royal Scots in 1881 and was designated the Queen's Rifle Volunteer Brigade Royal Scots in 1888. Further company reorganisation at the same time saw the brigade divided, this time into three battalions and with the companies lettered: 1st Battalion: 'A' (late No 2), 'B' (late No 5), 'C' (late No 6), 'D' (late No 7), 'E' (late No 10), 'F' (late No 18), 'G' (late 1st Highland), 'H' (late 2nd Highland), 'I' (late 3rd Highland). 2nd Battalion: 'A' (late No 8), 'B' (late No 9), 'C' (late No 11), 'D' (late No 12), 'E' (late No 13), 'F' (late No 14), 'G' (late No 15), 'H' (late No 16). 3rd Battalion: 'A' (late No 4), 'B' (late No 17), 'C' (late No 19), 'D' (late No 20), 'E' (late 4th Highland), 'F' (late 5th Highland), 'G' (late 6th Highland), 'H' (late 7th Highland).

A new company ('I') was added to the 3rd Battalion four miles south-west of Edinburgh at Colinton and a Cyclist Company attached to brigade headquarters in 1900. In the same year the Mounted Infantry detachment formed in 1886 was increased from one to three sections. A complete new kilted battalion of eight companies, designated as The Highland Battalion, was formed in 1900, but this was detached to form the 9th (Highlanders) Volunteer Battalion of the Royal Scots in the following year (see below). A cadet corps was formed and attached to the brigade by Merchiston Castle School in 1886, followed by another at George Watson's Boys' College in 1905.

98 – 1st ARGYLLSHIRE ARTILLERY VOLUNTEER CORPS

Sketch after George Rice specially produced for *The Volunteer Artillery 1859-1908* by Norman Lichfield and Ray Westlake, published by the authors in 1982. The image shows an officer's waistbelt clasp c1860. See below.

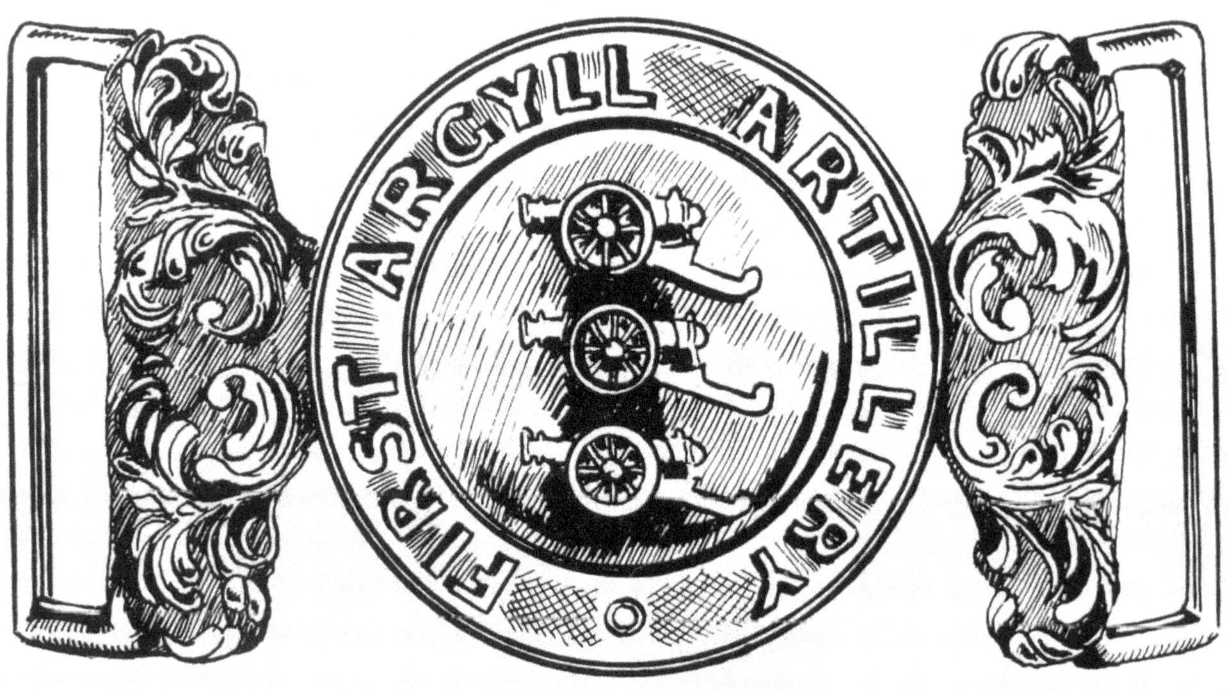
FIRST ARGYLL ARTILLERY

99 – 1st ARGYLLSHIRE ARTILLERY VOLUNTEER CORPS

Sketch after George Rice specially produced for *The Volunteer Artillery 1859-1908* by Norman Lichfield and Ray Westlake, published by the authors in 1982. The image shows an officer's pouch-belt plate of 1860 to 1880.

The 1st Admin Brigade of Argyllshire Artillery Volunteers was consolidated in 1880 as the 1st Argyll and Bute AVC of twelve and a half batteries: Nos 1 and 2 Easdale (late 1st Corps), No 3 Oban (late 3rd Corps), Nos 4 and 5 Campbeltown (late 6th Corps), No 6 Port Ellen (late 7th Corps), No 7 Castle Toward (late 8th Corps), No 8 Rothesay (late 1st Bute), No 9 Millport (late 2nd Bute), No 10 Lochgilphead (late 10th Corps), No 11 Tarbert (late 11th Corps), No 12 Inveraray (late 12th Corps). Headquarters were at Lochgilphead and the half battery was provided by the 9th Corps at Tobermory.

In 1887 the Inveraray Battery was disbanded and in its place a new No 12 was raised at Rothesay. In the following year headquarters of No 8 Battery were moved to Dunoon and those of the corps to Tarbert in 1906.

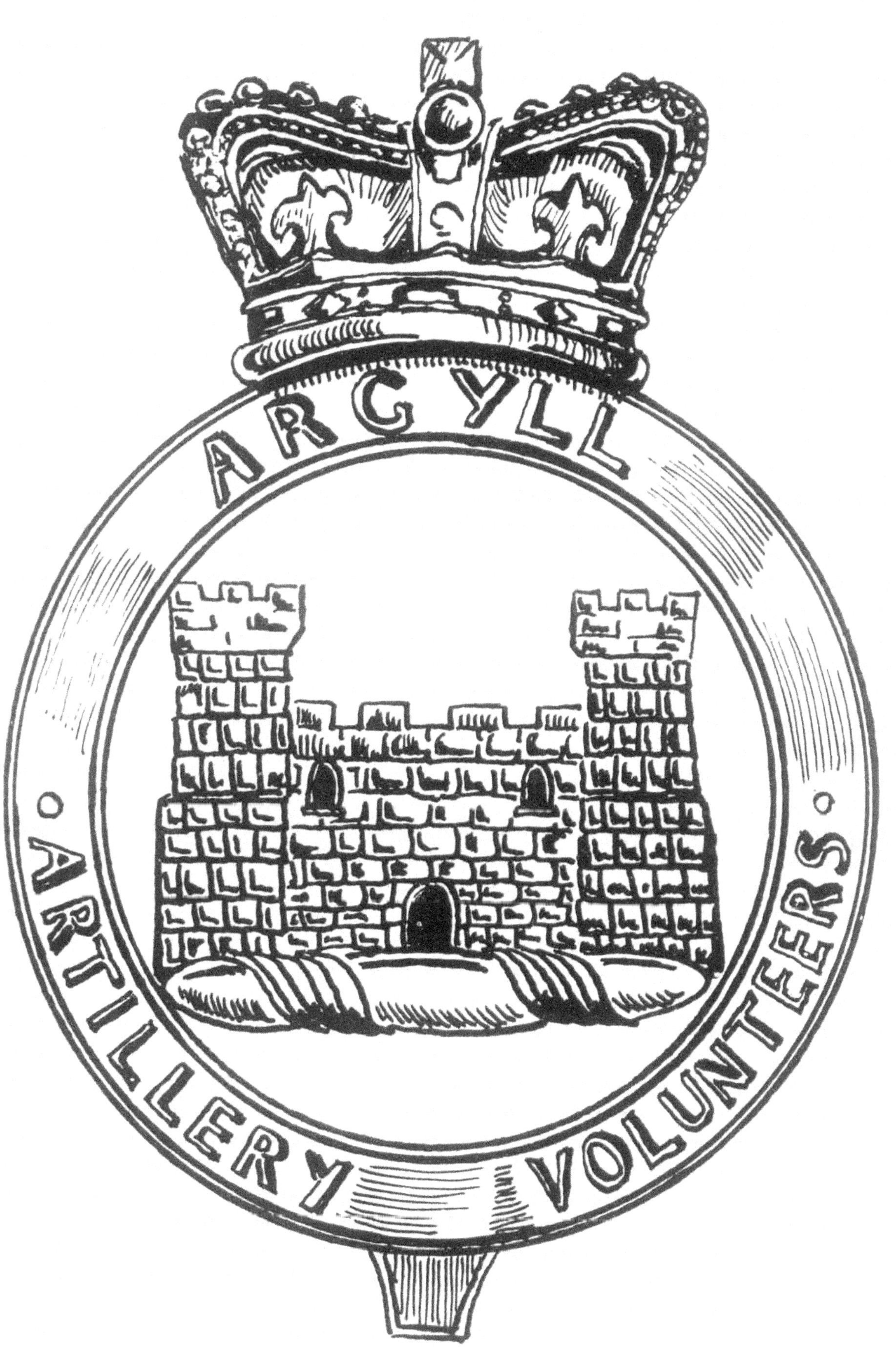
ARGYLL
ARTILLERY VOLUNTEERS

100 – 1st YORKSHIRE (EAST RIDING) ARTILLERY VOLUNTEERS

Sketch after George Rice specially produced for *The Volunteer Artillery 1859-1908* by Norman Lichfield and Ray Westlake, published by the authors in 1982. The image shows an officer's waist-belt plate c1860.

Formed at Bridlington on 9 December 1859 with the designation 1st, this corps later disappeared from the Army List and instead was shown as 6th. Headquarters of the 6th were also at Bridlington and one of its officers was previously listed with the 1st Corps.

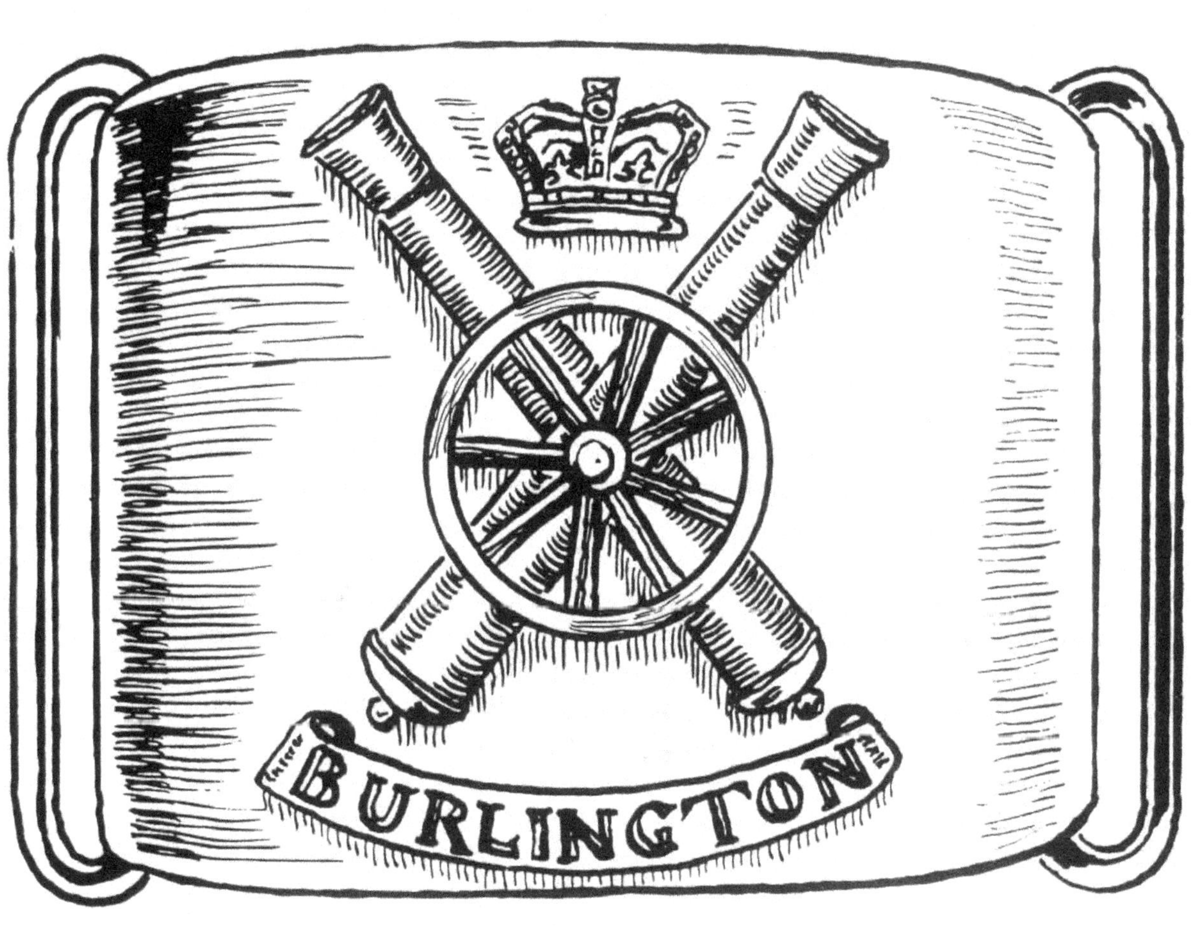
BURLINGTON

101 – THE FIRING EXERCISE

Illustration from Our Battalion by L Raven-Hill, published by *Punch* of 10 Bouverie Street, London in 1902. The image was published with the following text below: 'The Firing Exercise. Our own thoughtful Subaltern has carefully studied the new firing positions, and has also read that "methods must be improvised for utilizing the fire of two or even more ranks," and, by the above arrangement, he hopes to fulfil both conditions.'

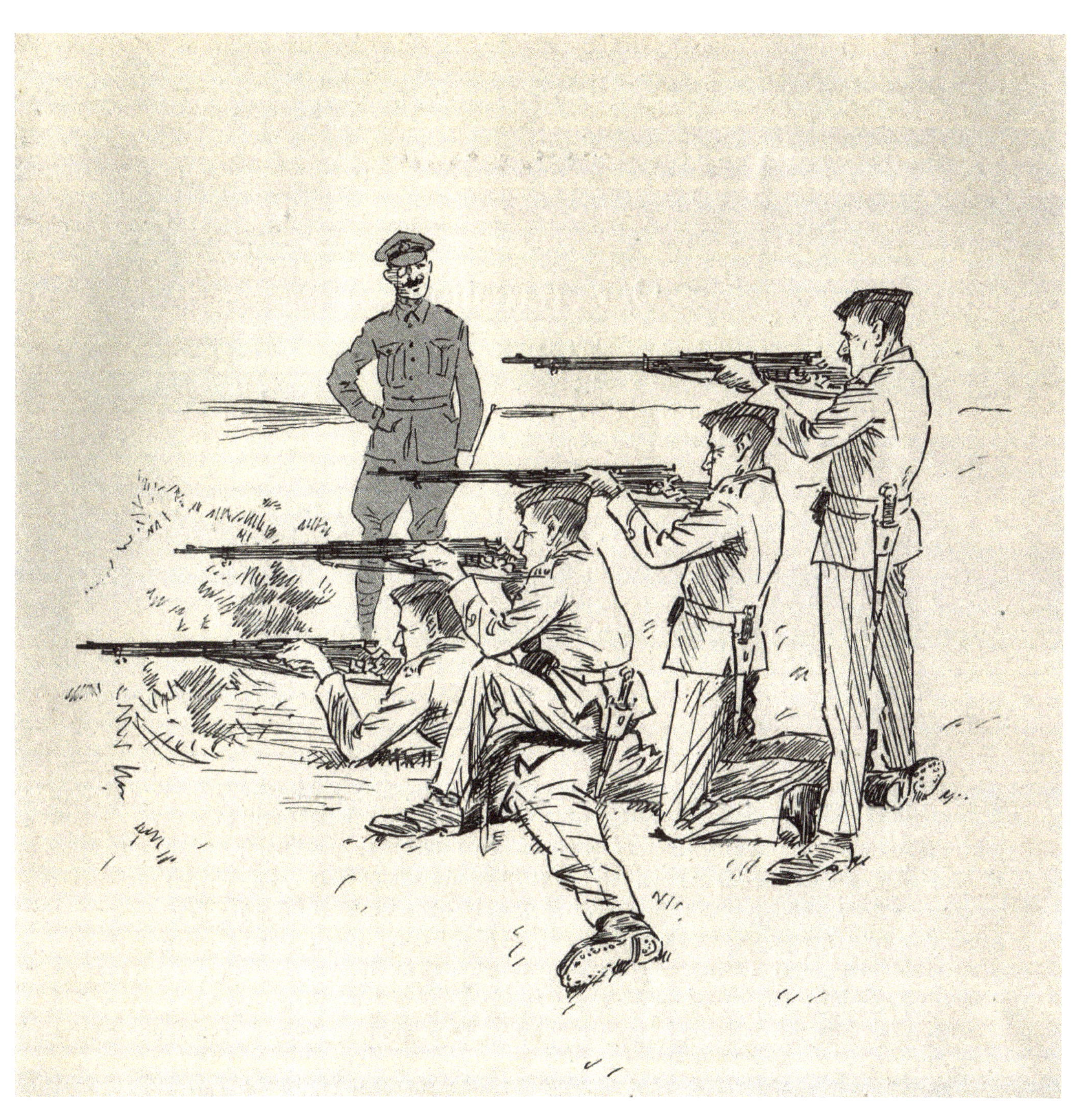

102 – OUR BATTALION

Cover illustration from *Our Battalion* by L Raven-Hill, published by *Punch* of 10 Bouverie Street, London in 1902.

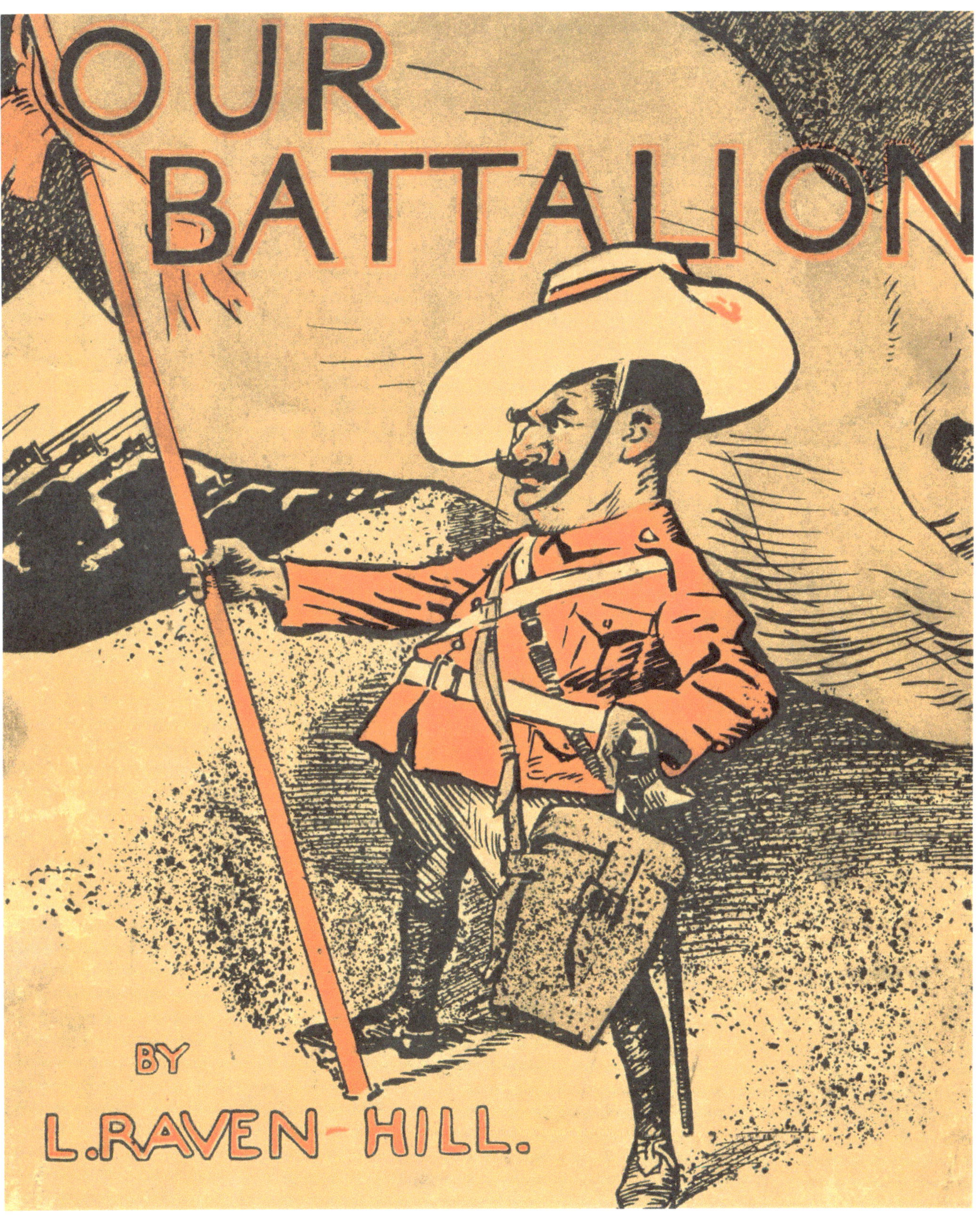
OUR
BATTALION
BY
L. RAVEN-HILL.

REFERENCES

Beckett, Ian F W. *Riflemen Form*. Ogilby Trust, Aldershot, 1982.

Grierson, Major General Sir James. *Records of the Scottish Volunteer Force*. Blackwood & Sons, 1909

Litchfield, Norman and Ray Westlake. *The Volunteer Artillery 1859-1908*. Sherwood Press, 1982

Owen, Bryn. *The History of the Welsh Militia and Volunteer Corps—Anglesey and Carnarvon*. Palace Books, Caernarfon, 1989.

Richards, Walter. *His Majesty's Territorial Army*. Virtue & Co. 1910/11.

Westlake, Ray. *Tracing The Rifle Volunteers*. Pen & Sword, 2010.

Westlake, Ray. *Royal Engineers (Volunteers) 1859-1908*. Sherwood Press, 1983.

Bulletin of the Military Historical Society, various issues 1948 to date.

Journal of the Society for Army Historical Research, various issues.

London Gazette 1859-1908.

Monthly Army List 1859-1908.

Territorial Year Book 1909.

Volunteer Service Gazette. Various issues.

Volunteer Service Magazine. Six Vols. May 1892 to June 1898.

Illustrated London News. Numerous issues 1859-1890.

Local newspapers.

Regimental histories, magazines and journals—more than 250 consulted.

BELLANGÉS'S SOLDIERS OF THE FRENCH REPUBLIC AND THE EMPIRE 1795-1814

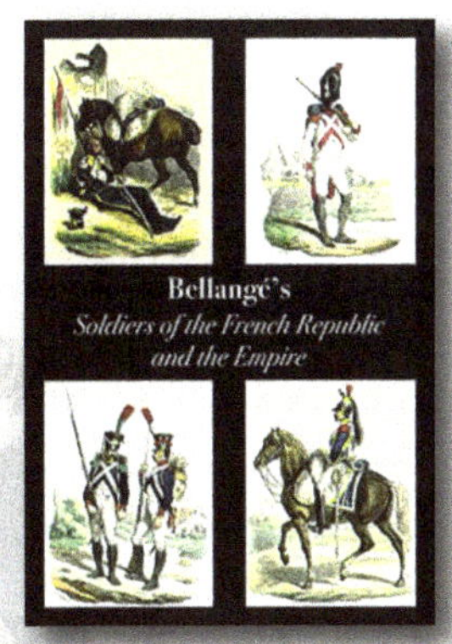

Taken from the first German translation of 'Histoire de l'empereur Napoleon' (1840), that was enlarged for this edition with six new illustrations.

Bellangés's fifty detailed and brightly coloured uniform plates present the soldiers of the different regiments of the French Republic and the Empire in their respective costumes.

9781783318414

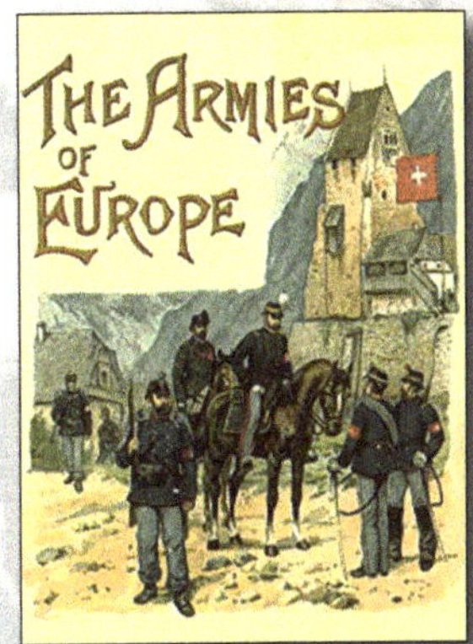

Richard Knötel's ARMIES OF EUROPE ILLUSTRATED (1890)

Classic descriptions complete with colour plates and vignettes by the renowned military artist and pioneer of the study of military uniform Richard Knötel, covering the armies of: The British Empire – The German Army – Austria-Hungary – Italy – France – Russia – Denmark, Sweden and Norway – Spain and Portugal – Switzerland – Holland and Belgium – Turkey and the States of the Balkan Peninsula.

9781783311750

CHARLES HAMILTON SMITH'S COSTUME OF THE ARMY OF THE BRITISH EMPIRE – ACCORDING TO THE 1814 REGULATIONS

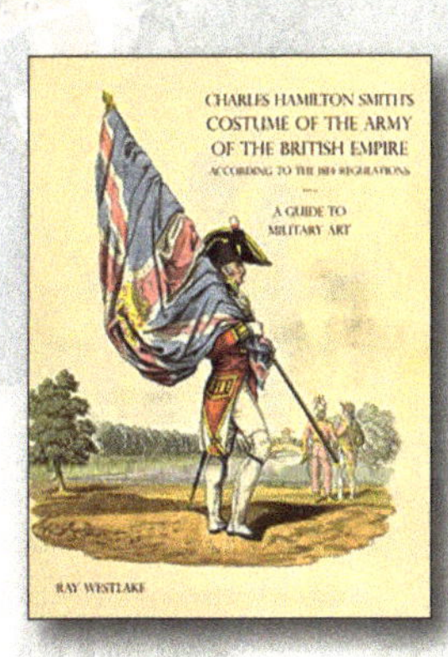

This is a full reissuing of the 60 hand-coloured aquatint plates by I.C. Stadler, after drawings by Smith, originally produced in 1815 for the oldest commercial art gallery in the world, Colnaghi and Co. Paul Colnaghi became the official print-seller to the Prince Regent, and he was asked to organise the Royal Collection, receiving a Royal Warrant when the Prince Regent became George IV. Uniquely, many of Smith's uncoloured original drawings are also included in this edition.

9781783319916

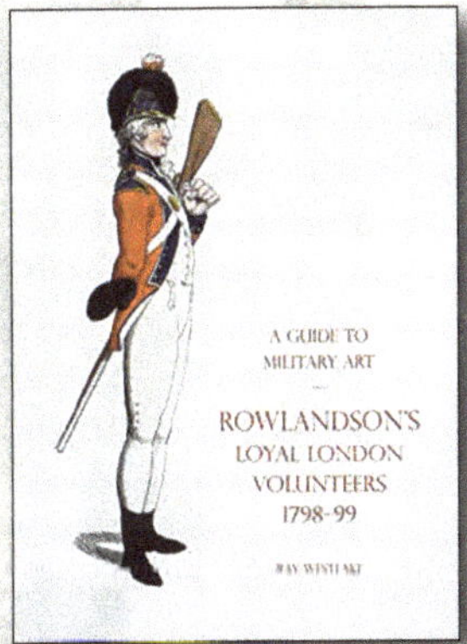

ROWLANDSON'S LOYAL LONDON VOLUNTEERS

The most original set of English military plates from the Napoleonic period – The Loyal Volunteers of London & Environs, Infantry & Cavalry, in their respective uniforms. Representing the whole of the Manual, Platoon & Funeral Exercise in 89 plates. Designed and etched by T. Rowlandson and originally published in London during 1798-99 by Ackermann. Reproduced here from high from an original volume is a full set of Rowlandson's 87 plates, together with an additional two that were to be included in some (even scarcer) bound volumes by the publisher. To accompany each plate, Ackermann prepared a page of letterpress which included details of when the corps had been formed, its uniform and names of officers. That text has been reproduced in full, together with additional notes prepared by Ray Westlake.

9781783318889

www.naval-military-press.com

MAJOR LOVETT'S MILITARY DRESS AND FIELD UNIFORMS OF THE RAJ

During the Years Leading up to the Great War

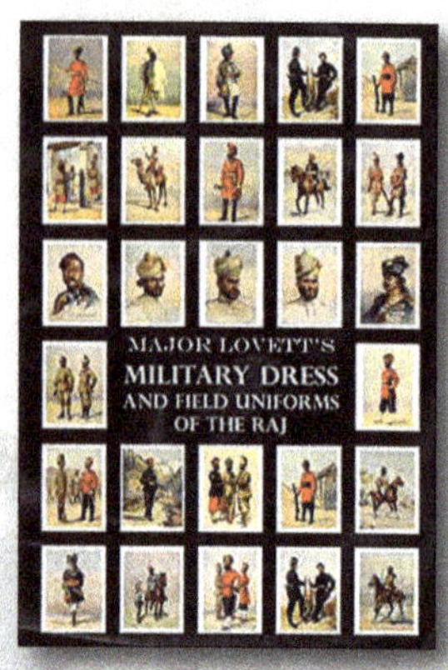

Classic representation of the British Indian Army at the height of the English Age of Empire, in 72 superb uniform plates. This is an invaluable work for anyone interested in the Indian armies and their military uniforms.

9781474536363

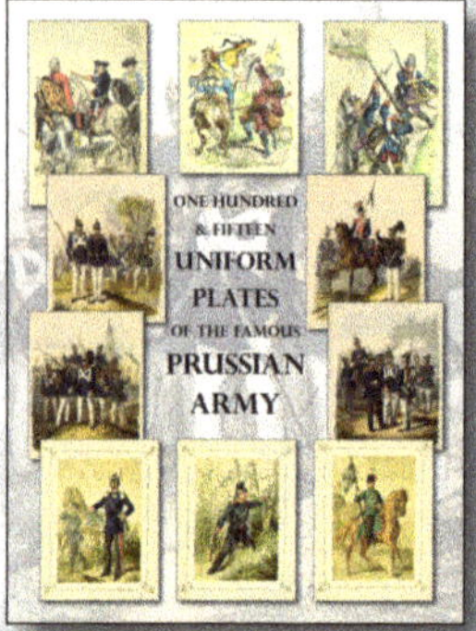

ONE HUNDRED AND FIFTEEN UNIFORM PLATES OF THE FAMOUS PRUSSIAN ARMY UNDER FREDERICK THE GREAT, FREDERICK WILLIAM IV AND PRINCE REGENT WILHELM: OMNIBUS EDITION

This is a compilation omnibus edition of three colourful 19th century military costume plate editions, detailing the Pre-Unification Prussian Army 1751-1855 in accurately hand-coloured facsimile images. Lively commentary from expert Ray Westlake on each plate enhances their historical usefulness.

9781474537551

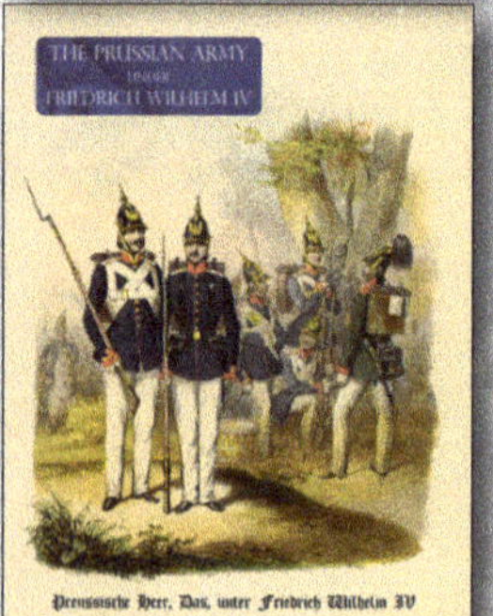

PRUSSIAN ARMY (UNIFORM) UNDER FREDRICH WIHELM IV

PREUSSISCHE HEER, DAS, UNTER FRIEDRICH WILHELM IV

An excellent visual presentation of the Prussian Army and their uniforms under the Kaiser Friedrich Wilhelm IV. Series of 36 facsimile numbered contemporary hand-coloured lithographs. This is a colourful series of military costume plates with over 200 military figures in their 'natural surroundings': camping, in battle, on horseback, on the march, etc.

9781474537582

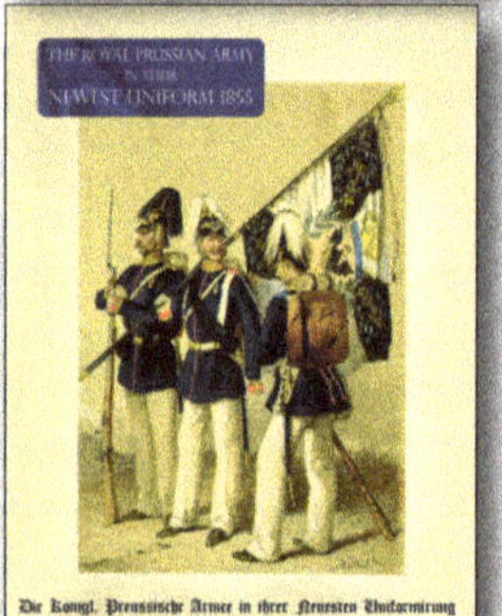

ROYAL PRUSSIAN ARMY IN THEIR NEWEST UNIFORM 1855

DIE KÖNIGL. PREUSSISCHE ARMEE IN IHRER NEUESTEN UNIFORMIRUNG

The beautiful plates depict the various uniforms of the Prussian Army as defined by the 1855 regiment. The work comprises 48 facsimile hand-coloured tinted lithographic plates of military uniforms, each mounted within a lithographed border incorporating the crowned initials of the Prussian king. A small title strip is at the bottom of each leaf, identifying the plate. Mitscher & Röstell, 1859.

9781474537582

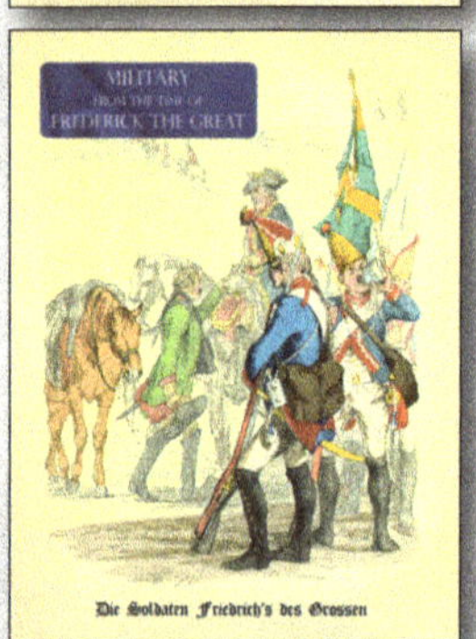

MILITARY (UNIFORM) FROM THE TIME OF FREDERICK THE GREAT

DIE SOLDATEN FRIEDRICH'S DES GROSSEN

Thirty excellent and accurately coloured plates of the uniforms of different Prussian regiments under Frederick the Great by wood engraver Eduard Kretzschmar (1807-1858) and illustrator Adolf von Menzel (1815-1905).

9781474537575

REPRESENTATION OF THE UNIFORMS OF THE IMPERIAL ARMY OF ALL RUSSIA 1790-98

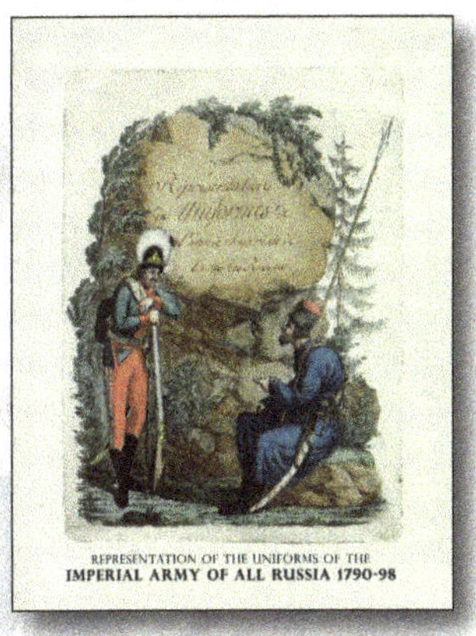

Christian Gottfried Heinrich Geissler, draughtsman and etcher, produced this fine and important series of Russian military costumes when he spent the years 1790 to 1798 serving as the expedition artist with the Prussian zoologist and botanist Peter Simon Pallas, on his travels in the Caucasus and southern Russia.

9781474538275

A GUIDE TO MILITARY ART – THE YEOMANRY AND VOLUNTEERS OF 1794-1808

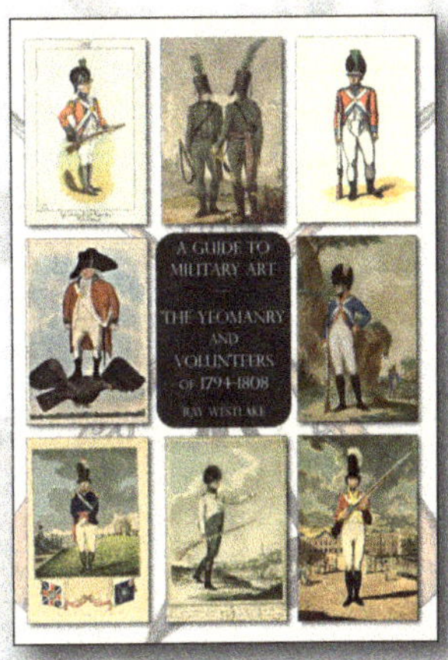

The Volunteer Corps and their mounted component the Yeomanry Cavalry were a voluntary part-time organisation for the purpose of home defence in the event of invasion, during the French Revolutionary and Napoleonic Wars.

The Corps typically drew its members from the propertied classes. Officers were usually members of the gentry and the enlisted ranks tended to be from the lower middle classes. The failed Expédition d'Irlande of 1796 and invasion at Fishguard caused the expansion of the corps, including the formation of workplace units in which the enlisted ranks were filled by the workmen and the officers were drawn from the clerks and foremen. Such units, made up of working-class men, became more common in the late 1790s and early 1800s due to the increased fear of invasion.

9781474538305

A GUIDE TO MILITARY ART – THE VOLUNTEER, 1859-1908

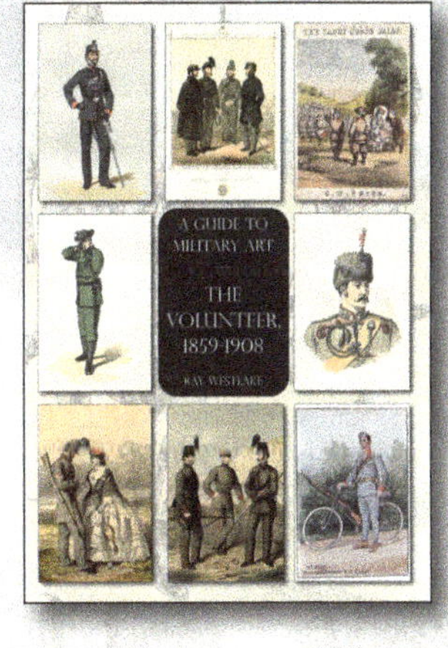

102 manly colour plates taken from various contemporary sources, illustrating the many and varied uniforms of The British Volunteer Force 1859-1908. This part-time military force which came into being to meet the mid-nineteenth century fear of French invasion. It survived and grew for fifty years until in 1908 it was renamed and remodelled as the Territorial Force. Composed initially of middle-class and often middle-aged gentlemen who elected their own officers and paid for their own uniform and equipment, the Volunteer Force soon became youthful and working-class, with appointed middle-class officers, with a Government subsidy, and a minor military role as an adjunct to the Regular Army.

9781474538329

A GUIDE TO MILITARY ART – CHARLES LYALL'S BRITISH ARMY, 1642 TO 1812

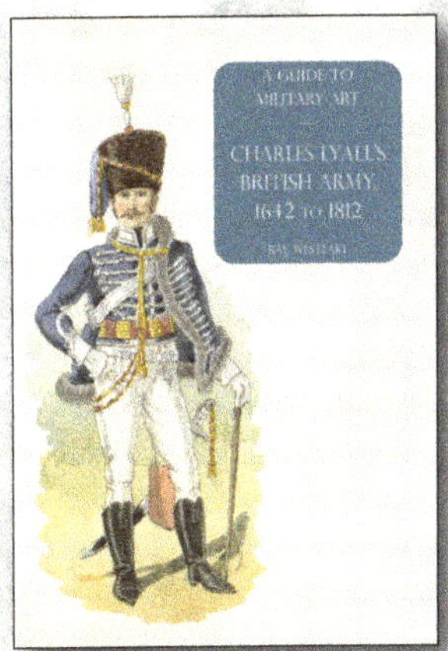

One hundred and twenty military figures are shown, and form part of our developing range of books dedicated to Uniformology.

Drawing on the Anne SK Brown Military Collection, Ray has selected a most useful collection of works by Charles Lyall. Covering a broad span of subjects from the 17th, 18th and early 19th century, this series of illustrations is a good reference work for the military modeller and historian, and inspiration for the wargamer who needs to build his army.

9781474538312

www.ingramcontent.com/pod-product-compliance
Lightning Source LLC
LaVergne TN
LVHW070532110826
845147LV00017BA/974

* 9 7 8 1 4 7 4 5 3 8 3 2 9 *